Convicts and Empire

A

ALAN FROST

Convicts and Empire

A NAVAL QUESTION
1776-1811

I may venture to suppose that the finding a proper place to send our convicts may again become a Naval question . . . having concluded that the [Prime] Minister might imagine it a Naval question . . .

JOHN BLANKETT (AUGUST 1786)

Melbourne
OXFORD UNIVERSITY PRESS
Oxford Wellington New York

Oxford University Press

OXFORD LONDON GLASGOW
NEW YORK TORONTO MELBOURNE WELLINGTON
KUALA LUMPUR SINGAPORE JAKARTA HONG KONG TOKYO
DELHI BOMBAY CALCUTTA MADRAS KARACHI
NAIROBI DAR ES SALAAM CAPE TOWN

First published 1980

NATIONAL LIBRARY OF AUSTRALIA CATALOGUING IN
PUBLICATION DATA

*Frost, Alan John, 1943-
    Convicts and empire.*

*Index
Bibliography*
ISBN 0 19 554255 x

*1. New South Wales — Colonization. 2. Great
Britain — Colonies — Defenses. I. Title.*

325′.341′09944

PRINTED IN AUSTRALIA BY BROWN PRIOR ANDERSON PTY LTD, MELBOURNE
PUBLISHED BY OXFORD UNIVERSITY PRESS, 7 BOWEN CRESCENT, MELBOURNE

Contents

List of maps and portraits

Acknowledgments

I have many people to thank for help in completing this study.

Professors J. A. Salmond, J. S. Gregory, and R. B. Joyce, successively chairmen of the Department of History, La Trobe University, gave generously of their own and of the Department's resources. Mr. D. H. Borchardt, La Trobe University Chief Librarian, and his indefatigable reference staff, Mr. Ray Choate, Miss Margot Hyslop, and Miss Rosemary Griffiths, did likewise. The secretaries of the Department of History typed the versions of the study patiently and cheerfully.

The Australian Research Grants Committee generously supported my research in Great Britain and North America.

The Directors and staffs of the following institutions offered their facilities: the Mitchell and Dixson Libraries, The State Library of New South Wales; the Australian National Library; the La Trobe Library, The State Library of Victoria (where I checked some transcripts of documents in Public Record Office files from Australian Joint Copying Project microfilm); the Sutro Library, San Francisco; the Huntington Library, San Marino; the William L. Clements Library, University of Michigan; the Cleveland Public Library; the Beinecke Library, Yale University; the New Brunswick Museum; the New York Public Library; the New York Historical Society; the Houghton Library, Harvard University; the Perkins Library, Duke University; the British Library; the British Museum (Natural History); the Public Record Office; the India Office Records; the National Maritime Museum; the Royal Society; the Royal Society of Arts; the Royal Botanical Gardens Library; the Royal Commission on Historical Manuscripts; the Corporation of London Records Office; the Guildhall Library; the Bodleian Library, Oxford; the John Rylands Library, Manchester University; the Brotherton Library, University of Leeds; the Suffolk County Record Office; the Essex County Record Office; the National Library of Scotland; the Scottish Record Office.

Where I have cited or quoted from documents in these institutions' collections, I have done so with the generous permission of their Directors and governing bodies. (I have to acknowledge specifically permission to cite and quote from: the Trustees of the National Maritime Museum; the Trustees of the British Library; the Trustees of the British Museum (Natural History); the Trustees of the National Library of Scotland; Mrs. Bence-Jones and the Suffolk Record Office. Unpublished Crown Copyright material in the Public Record Office and India Office Records reproduced in this publication appears by permission of the Controller of Her Majesty's Stationery Office. The Zamboni manuscripts are from the collection of John G. White Department, Cleveland Public Library.)

The following persons helped in my search for information: Mr. J. Bensusan, of the Gibraltar Museum; Miss Helen Sanger, of the Frick Art Reference Library; Miss Dona Atcheson and Miss Marilyn Payne, of the New Brunswick Museum; Miss Eleanor Magee, R. P. Bell Library, Mount Allison University; Miss Catriona Crowe, of the Public Record Office of Ireland; Miss Priscilla Copeman, of the Courtauld Institute of Art; Miss B. R. Masters, Corporation of London Records Office; Mr. G. W. Thompson, Guildhall Library; Mr. Peter Hull, Cornwall County Archives; Mr. M. W. Farr, Warwickshire County Archives; Mr. A. Andrews, City of Birmingham Archives; Mr. B. S. Benedikz, University of Birmingham Library; Mr. A. Jewell, the Museum of English Rural Life, Reading; Mr. I. Baxter, India Office Library; Mr. R. J. Varley, Commonwealth Institute; Mr. D. H. Simpson, the Royal Commonwealth Society; Miss Patricia O'Neill, the Royal United Services Institute; Mrs Arlene Shy and Miss Barbara Mitchell, William L. Clements Library; Sir Evan and Lady Nepean and Mrs. Aylmer Hall.

For help with details of the study, or for comments on the whole, I am grateful to: Dr. Noel McLachlan and Dr. J. B. Hirst, the editors of *Historical Studies*; Dr. William J. Breen; Mr. Roger Benedictus; Mr. David Cunningham; Mr. Frank Eyre; Professor Howard Horsford; Mr. H. B. Carter, who has generously shared his unrivalled knowledge of the Banks papers; Mrs. M. Pain; Mr. John Ehrman; Professor I. R. Christie; Dr. Roger Knight; Professor J. H. Parry; Professor Daniel A. Baugh; Professor Dauril Alden; Professor David Syrett; Professor I. B. Thompson; Professor E. Axelson; Professor G. M. Dening; Mr. A. W. Pearsall.

Professor A. G. L. Shaw and Professor Geoffrey Blainey have given great support and encouragement.

Sir Robin and Lady Mackworth-Young, and the Marquis and Marchioness of Normanby have allowed me access to family items, and been graciously hospitable.

My thanks, too, to Mary Hutchinson, who drew the maps, and Jean Hagger, who compiled the index.

My warmest thanks go too to my friends, who have helped in all necessary ways; and to Melissa and Clea, who have been patient, and loved.

Introduction

Captain James Cook sighted the eastern coast of New Holland on 19 April 1770, in 38°S latitude. For five months, he followed it northwards, charting and naming its features and gathering specimens of its animals and plants. On 22 August, confident that no European before him had 'seen or viseted' this coast, he landed on Possession Island (10°S lat., 219°E long.),

> hoisted English Coulers and in the Name of His Majesty King George the Third took posession of the whole [of it] from the above Latitude down to this place by the name of *New South Wales*, together with all the Bays, Harbours Rivers and Islands situate upon [it].

In August 1786, the Pitt Administration decided to establish a convict colony at Botany Bay, which indents the New South Wales coast in 34°S latitude. Captain Arthur Phillip took the eleven ships of the First Fleet out from Motherbank on 13 May 1787, and these reached their destination in mid-January 1788. In the face of Botany Bay's lack of water and general infertility, Phillip decided rather to settle at Port Jackson, some fifteen kilometres to the north; and he landed at Sydney Cove on 26 January. On 7 February, before the assembled civilians, marines, and convicts, Judge-Advocate Collins proclaimed the colony by reading Phillip's commission and the letters-patent authorizing civil and criminal courts.

Penal exile had been a provision of English law from Tudor times; and across the Eighteenth century successive administrations had developed the policy of paying contractors to ferry those sentenced to transportation beyond the seas to the West Indian and North American colonies, where the merchants sold their charges' labour to planters for the unexpired period of their sentence, and obtained return cargoes. By the early 1770s, the government was sending some 1000 convicts annually across the Atlantic, with the three principal objects of removing these undesirable members from British society, of giving them the benefit of a change in environment, and of providing the colonies with a cheap labour force.

British outlook in the last decades of the Eighteenth century both reflected and supported this practice of using the convicts' labour to national benefit. In 1771, William Eden suggested that the worst offenders amongst the convicts

> might be compelled to dangerous expeditions; or be sent to establish new colonies, factories, or settlements on the coast of Africa, and on small islands for the benefit of navigation.

xi

In 1784, Lord Sydney saw that the crowding of the convicts on the hulks was mostly a consequence of 'the want of a place to convey them where their labour may be of use.' The 1785 House of Commons Committee on Transportation thought that the Government might resume transportation to a new area, if this would contribute, as well as to 'the interior Police of this Kingdom,' to 'the Purposes of future Commerce or of future Hostility in the *South Seas*.' In 1789, W. W. Grenville asked Henry Dundas whether they might use convicts to cut a waterway between Fort William and Fort Augustus in Scotland, so as to make northern navigation easier.

There were, of course, no prior British settlements in New South Wales, with a body of planters to whom contractors might sell convicts' labour, and from whom they might obtain return cargoes. So that, in deciding to settle this region with convicts, the Pitt Administration necessarily broke with past practice and began a new mode of transportation, in which the government made itself responsible both for carrying felons out to the territory designated as their place of transportation, and for maintaining them and employing their labour there.

Why did Pitt and his colleagues do this?

From the early 1800s until the 1950s, historians knew the answer to this question — the politicians had wished to dump the convicts, whom they could no longer transport to a rebellious America, in an out-of-the-way place from which their return would be difficult. This view was already a commonplace in 1819, when Bathurst, the Colonial Secretary, announced that the New South Wales settlements must 'chiefly be considered as receptacles for offenders,' because they had not been established 'with any view to territorial or commercial advantages;' and many writers have repeated it since.

In general, those who held the 'dumping' view have assumed that the Pitt Administration's innovation in the *mode* of transportation also involved a departure from the previous *philosophy* of transportation. They have therefore represented the decision to colonize New South Wales as a gratuitous one, relating only to the nation's loss of her North American colonies as a place of transportation, and to her consequently crowded prisons at home. They have represented this decision as one quite unrelated to the Administration's policies in such other spheres as domestic reform, the re-establishment of colonial administration, or overseas trade.

Underlying this view has been the belief, or assumption, that the loss of the North American colonies caused British administrations of the late Eighteenth and earlier Nineteenth centuries effectively to lose interest in empire. David Mackay developed this perception with particular reference to the Pitt Administration when he said that

> those who put the foundation of the [New South Wales] settlement in the context of a 'swing to the east,' and those who see its establishment as part of some

great commercial endeavour, greatly over-estimate the policy-forming resources and enterprise of the metropolitan government. They assume a capacity for long-term planning which did not exist. They assume the existence of a philosophy of empire without specifying exactly where such a philosophy might reside or how it might be expressed.

Sir John Seeley provided a general rubric when he said that, from reading the historians, we might gather that the British 'conquered and peopled half the world in a fit of absence of mind.'

Both this perception, and the characterization of the New South Wales venture that it gives rise to, are, however, wrong. As recent studies have shown, the case for British disinterest in empire turns on the definition of 'empire'. From V. T. Harlow and John Ehrman's work, especially, we may now see that Pitt and his advisers were capable of formulating thorough-going policies that provided for future developments. And, most to the point, the documentary record shows their colonization of New South Wales to have been one example of this capacity. The historians have been mistaken to see the Pitt Administration's decision to colonize New South Wales as a negative one arising from inertia and incapacity. Rather, it was a positive one, taken in response to the imperatives of Britain's situation in Europe and the East in the mid-1780s.

To say that this situation was parlous is not to exaggerate. Britain had lost the war with her American colonies, and achieved a stand-off only in that with France and Spain. In the process, she had severely strained her economy, and had alienated herself from her European allies and friends—from the Dutch and Prussians, whose support she had previously used to maintain a balance of power; from the Russians, from whom she received the bulk of the naval stores indispensible to her national well-being, and from the Danes and the Swedes, whose cooperation she needed to freight those stores from the Baltic. Shelburne, who negotiated the peace settlement of 1782/3; Pitt, who soon afterwards assumed power; and the advisers to whom these far-sighted men turned for most help, had no illusions about the situation—Britain desperately needed a period of peace, so that she might restore her economy, and strengthen her strategic resources.

The British ministers shared these aims with their French counterparts, and both groups saw that the East would be central to their realization. For Britain, a continued presence there represented the best, and perhaps the only, hope of refurbishing a much-diminished empire. For France, a revitalized presence there might lead to re-emergence as an imperial power. Both groups together conceived that their nations' recovery from ruinous war would largely depend on their maintaining and extending their eastern trade.

As peace returned, France moved to strengthen her position, and to weaken Britain's, especially vis-a-vis India. She did so on three fronts—in Europe; in the Middle East; and in India. And as Britain sought to counter these moves, the two nations entered on an intense diplomatic struggle, in which the stakes were as profound, and the consequences as far-reaching, as if they had warred openly.

France developed a many-pronged endeavour aimed at realizing both economic recovery and the old dreams of empire and hegemony. In September 1784, she concluded an agreement with Sweden giving her the use of the island of Gothenburg, at the entrance to the Baltic Sea, for a naval depot. In 1784/5, her emissaries negotiated an agreement with the rulers of Egypt, for trading rights there, and for the right to send despatches and goods via there to and from India (and the ministers hid ideas of an armed conquest of Egypt behind their overt diplomacy). In April 1785, French merchants reconstituted an official company to conduct eastern trade. Among other help, the Government provided this 'new' East India company with 64-gun ships-of-the-line rendered redundant by the peace. These vessels sailed with their lower gun decks cleared (*armé en flûte*), but they were of course capable of speedy reconversion to their primary purpose.

At the same time, the French moved to confirm the connection with the Dutch which they had built up during the war. Working on Dutch resentment at the terms of peace, they increased their influence with the Patriots, the merchant-based party which had gained control of the States General; and in November 1785, they succeeded in reaching a treaty of defensive alliance with this body. This had the twin effects of opening the Dutch bases in the East to French shipping in the event of war, and of adding the Dutch forces to the French ones.

Informed by their diplomats and spies of these moves, Pitt and his advisers saw well that France's profound purpose was (as a French agent asserted) 'to prepare the way for decisive blows in concert with the United Provinces about the coast of India;' and, progressively more alarmed by the threat, they sought ways of counteracting it. The Board of Trade looked for new sources of naval stores. Pitt extended Government control of the East India Company; and he, Dundas, Mulgrave and Grenville supervised its affairs so that the nation might have more benefit from its considerable resources. They strove repeatedly to draw the Dutch from the French camp. Inevitably without success, they also sought France's agreement that the French and Dutch squadrons in the East should together not exceed the strength Britain and France had agreed to in reaching peace. The commissioners for India established an alternative line of communication with the subcontinent via Egypt, to parallel the French one. As well, they ordered a survey of potential sites for bases in and about the Indian Ocean, and of potential sources of naval materials.

As one of this series of responses to the French threat, Pitt and his advisers decided, quite deliberately, to use the convicts to build a new base that would increase the nation's capacity to protect her Eastern establishment. After considering sites about the southern coasts of Africa, they selected Botany Bay instead. They did so with the particular aims of confirming the nation's claim to New South Wales, and thus precluding settlement of it by the French or the Dutch; and of obtaining a more certain source of naval materials for the fleets in eastern waters. They had the more general aim of creating a port which in wartime would be self-sufficient in food and naval stores, one to which the nation's shipping could retire to refresh and refit, and from which squadrons might sail to attack French, Dutch, and Spanish bases and shipping. To these profound motives, that of the removal of the convicts from the realm was secondary — an accompaniment, but not a cause.

Gaps in the documentary record have been responsible for much of our past misunderstanding of the Pitt Administration's motives for colonizing New South Wales. Until now, this record has been essentially that found by Bonwick and printed in the *Historical Records of New South Wales* in 1892, which offers a great deal of evidence concerning the convict motive, and scattered suggestions only of another. A fresh search has resulted in the recovery of many new documents; and while there are still some gaps, the record is now complete enough to permit a more accurate and extensive analysis of motive than before.

This analysis has of course been my central concern, and has involved relating the decision to the contexts of penal concepts, imperial imperatives, and administrative procedure. In its first aspect I have intended this study to complement the relevant sections of Eris O'Brien and A. G. L. Shaw's accounts of British penal theory and practice, and to support Geoffrey Blainey's view that the obtaining of naval stores was a significant consideration. In its second, it is an attempt at that chapter which Vincent Harlow did not live to draft, concerning New South Wales's place in Britain's 'swing to the East'; and, at the same time, one at a prelude to Gerald Graham's *Great Britain in the Indian Ocean 1810-1850*. Throughout, I have sought to evoke the outlooks and aspirations of the two small groups who set their people towards a migration to the most distant margin of the navigable ocean, which in time gave rise to a new nation.

PART I

*Lord Sydney
and
the convicts, 1776-1786*

Very little is said in the official documents with reference to the commercial or political advantages so forcibly urged by [Matra and Young]; the whole project had apparently dwindled down to a plan for ridding the country of its surplus criminals.

BARTON (1889)

The Government of Pitt chose New South Wales as a prison, commodious, conveniently distant, and, it was hoped, cheap.

HANCOCK (1930)

So the number of convicted persons continued to rise, particularly in the more depressed areas of southern England and Ireland; and the former outlet by way of transportation to the American colonies was closed. When the gaols were crowded, hulks were pressed into service, to become crowded in their turn. This was the situation which pressed Lord Sydney . . . into the action which founded Australia. . . . Necessity and not vision founded Australia.

CRAWFORD (1952)

Domestic needs rather than the implications of Imperial policies were the factors most evident in the determination of the English government to send a number of ships and convicts to the antipodes in 1787. . . . The hard-pressed ministers in Pitt's second administration were little concerned with the importance of the undertaking. They were interested only in finding a solution for pressing political and penal problems in the home country.

CROWLEY (1955)

One factor alone had convinced [Sydney] of the need for a definite decision: the several gaols and places for the confinement of felons were so crowded that the greatest danger was to be apprehended not only from their escape, but from infectious distempers.

CLARK (1962)

CHAPTER 1

Hulks, America and Africa
1776-1785

1 The lapse of transportation to America

English political practice in medieval times encompassed voluntary or involuntary exile, but transportation did not become a sentence in Common Law until the late Tudor period. In 1597, Parliament provided for magistrates to sentence rogues and vagabonds 'dangerous to the inferior Sort of People' to 'be banished out of this Realm and all other the Dominions thereof . . . and conveyed unto such parts beyond the Seas as shall at any time hereafter for that purpose be Assigned by the Privy Council unto Her Majesty, (39 Eliz. I c.4).

During the reign of Charles II, Parliament made transportation to America the sentence for theft and pillage in northern counties (1666: 18 Car.II c.3); and afterwards extended the punishment for the theft of certain articles (e.g., cloth, munitions) to transportation 'to any of his Majesty's Plantations beyond the Seas, there to remain for the Space of seven Years' (1670: 22 Car.II c.5). As well, the Habeas Corpus Act of 1679 (31 Car.II c.2) provided for a person convicted of a felony to be transported on his request.

In the early Eighteenth century, in response to rising urban crime rates, Parliaments fixed transportation as the sentence for robbery, larceny, receiving, burglary, and destruction of property (1717: 4 Geo.I c.11; 1719: 6 Geo.I c.23; 1743: 16 Geo.II c.15). Thereafter Administrations sent felons in increasing numbers to the colonies in the West Indies and North America, where contractors sold ('assigned') their labour for the term of their sentence. By the early 1770s, the British were transporting some 1000 convicts annually across the Atlantic, mostly to Virginia and Maryland.[1]

This practice ceased in 1776, when the American colonies revolted; and the North Administration had to make other arrangements for the transportees. Seeing the need as temporary, they decided to accommodate them on hulks moored in the Thames, and to employ them at public works. North moved to bring the requisite Bill into the House of Commons on 1 April, when one member suggested that they should send the convicts to either the West Indies or the Falkland Islands.

3

Thomas Townshend, Viscount Sydney
By Gilbert Stuart. *Courtesy of the Dixson Galleries, Sydney.*

This suggestion engendered no response. On 9 May, the House went into Committee to consider the 'Felons' Bill.' The Administration's proposals met considerable, if limited, opposition. Thomas Townshend saw that the Bill, if enacted, would cause 'an alteration of the whole system of our criminal law,' and he took the First Minister to task for bringing on such an important measure at the end of the session, when half the House had left town. In Townshend's view, the Bill threatened dangerously to increase the power of the Crown, which was already too extensive; and he asked North to justify it. He also asked that consideration of it be deferred until the next session.

William Eden defended the Bill, repeating views from his *Principles of Penal Justice* (1771). He had helped frame it after consulting judges and other relevant officials, he said; and he argued for sentences to be tailored to the seriousness of the crime:

> Persons convicted of several species of felony, might receive punishments suited to the nature of their crimes. Some might be sent to garrison places situated in unwholesome climates; others might be made to work, and confined in houses of correction; others again [might] be employed in preserving the navigation of rivers; and finally the duration of the punishment might be varied, some for a longer, some for a shorter time, and others during their lives.

Townshend was unimpressed. What he particularly objected to, he replied, was the clause empowering the King to remit punishments. This, if passed, would throw a power into the hands of the crown, which might be the means of perverting justice. The minister might exercise this power as he pleased. He would, besides, be constantly teazed by applications.' He could not, he said, at all approve of a departure from or an alteration in 'that fundamental principle in our criminal law, that the King may pardon crimes, but not alter punishments when once incurred.' He asked that the Bill be published together with that concerning houses of correction, and that the House defer consideration of it until they had the benefit of public opinion. As an alternative, Sir Joseph Mawbey suggested transporting to the Floridas, and the West and East Indies, where the British establishments were 'a continual annual drain of men from this country.'

The Solicitor-General assured these opponents that the Administration intended the proposed measures as an experiment only, 'to answer the spur of the occasion,' and that they would resume the 'usual mode of transportation' when they had restored 'tranquility' in America. The Commons considered the Bill again the next week, and over-rode Townshend's continuing objections. Both Houses then authorized its measures for two years (16 Geo. III c. 43).[2]

These exchanges mark the future Lord Sydney's first discernible involvement with the convicts. Thomas Townshend was born in 1732, into a line of Whig grandees. His grandfather had played a prominent part in Britain's affairs in the first decades of the century, being at different times Ambassador to Holland, Lord President of the Privy Council, and Secretary of State. His father sat in Parliament for fifty-two years. His cousin Charles was a Lord of the Admiralty, President of the Board of Trade, Secretary at War, and Chancellor of the Exchequer.

From these, Townshend inherited an extensive fortune, and an intense political tradition. He graduated M.A. from Clare Hall, Cambridge in 1753, and entered the Commons the next year. He first held a minor appointment in the future George III's household; and the elder Pitt gave him a junior ofice in 1760. He was as well a Lord of the Treasury from 1765 to 1768. He was in opposition throughout Lord North's administration (1770-82), and was thus a potential candidate for office when this Administration fell. In March 1782 Rockingham made him Secretary at War. Four months later, Shelburne appointed him Secretary of State. He left office when Shelburne's ministry fell in February 1783; and in March the King raised him to the peerage. He regained the Secretaryship of State at the end of the year, in the younger Pitt's first administration, to relinquish it finally in June 1789.

In neither personality nor political ability was Townshend distinguished. He was a trifling person, as much interested in his family's social relations as in his nation's affairs. He spoke often, and it seems effectively at times, when in opposition during the American war, but he was then also the easy butt of Lord North's wit. He was not a successful defender of the Shelburne Administration's policies when nominally its leader in the Commons in 1782/3; and he was again quite ineffectual in Pitt's Administration. W. W. Grenville, Pitt's cousin and political confidant, characterized him as 'a Man of upright intentions and honourable character, but proverbially incapable, both as a Minister, and as a Public Speaker.' He was, Grenville considered, 'unequal to the most ordinary business' of his office.[3]

Townshend did not himself possess distinctive views. His response to North and Eden's Felons' Bill, for example, turned on the question of whether their proposals would allow the King to exercise his prerogative in a previously inviolable area of the nation's business, and not on that of the proposals' efficacy. In this response, he both indicated the Whig's traditional concern to limit the King's power, and his own essentially conservative outlook. He guarded long-enunciated principles, but he did so without either imagination or energy.

The hulks first authorized were intended to accommodate about 400 persons, but as magistrates continued to sentence those convicted of felony to transportation at the same rate as before, these were grossly overcrowded by the time the Act was up for renewal. At this time, Townshend again revealed his conservative instincts and his concern for family convenience when he observed that the Act had not the desired effect, for robberies were increased instead of being diminished; that in the course of the winter every day furnished some fresh account of some daring robbery or burglary [, that] scarce a night passed in which there were not robberies committed in Park-lane, and firing of pistols heard.[4]

The Commons appointed a Committee consisting of Lord North, Sir Richard Sutton, Sir Charles Bunbury, and others to investigate the situation. As well as those nominated to the Committee, all other members who attended the hearings might vote. Bunbury reported for the Committee on 15 April, that improvements had been made in the conditions of the hulks; and that it would therefore be proper, 'by a new Bill, to continue the present Mode of punishing Convicts on board the Hulks, by hard Labour, for a certain Time.' This Bill passed both Houses in May (18 Geo.III c.62).[5]

In 1779, when the Hulks Act was again up for renewal, the Committee on Transportation once more investigated the situation. Bunbury was chairman, the named members included Eden, Meredith, and Brett, and, as before, others who attended had voices. The Committee held hearings in February. After gathering details of the overcrowded state of the prisons, the members heard from the Keeper that numbers of transportees remained at Newgate because there was no room for them on the hulks. Duncan Campbell, the contractor, and others reported on further improvements made to the accommodation of the hulks, so that these were not now so crowded as they had been, though there were frequent 'fluxes,' and deaths from 'putrid Fevers.'

After hearing of other ways in which convict labour might be used, the Committee considered larger issues. The members asked Campbell whether transportation to America might be resumed; and the contractor replied that 'He apprehended not in any considerable Number, which was the Reason he declined contracting.' Accordingly, they took up the question of 'how far Transportation might be practicable to other Parts of the World.'

In case it should be thought expedient to establish a Colony of convicted Felons in any distant Part of the Globe, from whence their Escape might be difficult, and where, from the Fertility of the Soil, they might be enabled to maintain themselves, after the First Year, with little or no Aid from the Mother Country,   *emphasis on cost.*

the members heard from Joseph Banks concerning the suitability of Botany Bay for this purpose; and from others concerning that of sites in Gambia and Senegal, and of Gibraltar.

As a consequence of the information they received the Committee members recommended, among other things, that further improvements might be made to the hulks if their use were continued; the building of penitentiary houses on a new plan; that the employment of felons in public works be placed on a more regular footing; that

> the sending atrocious Criminals to unhealthy Places, where their Labour may be used, and their Lives hazarded, in the Place of better Citizens, may in some Cases be advisable;

and that

> the Plan of establishing a Colony or Colonies of young Convicts in some distant Part of the Globe, and in New-discovered Countries, where the Climate is healthy, and the Means of Support attainable, is equally agreeable to the Dictates of Humanity and sound Policy, and might prove in the Result advantageous both to Navigation and Commerce.[6]

The Committee reported on 1 April; and Parliament then extended 16 Geo.III c.43 until 1 July, so as to allow the law officers time to prepare a more comprehensive measure containing the Committee's recommendations. A Bill providing for transportation 'to any Parts beyond the Seas, whether the same is situated in *America*, or elsewhere,' and as well, for the building of 'two plain, strong, and substantial Edifices or Houses,' was accordingly introduced in June and, after some amendment, passed both Houses, with effect until 1 June 1784 (19 Geo.III c.74). Magistrates continued to sentence as the law allowed in the next years, so that the number of transportees continued to increase. By 1782, the metropolitan government was holding some hundreds on the Thames Hulks; more were crowding the county jails; and there was no sign of the Penitentiary houses.[7]

The North Administration did try one expedient. In mid-1781, they approved the raising of two independent companies, consisting mostly of convicts, which they sent together with a small squadron to defend the Africa Company's forts on that continent's equatorial coast.

The venture turned out very badly. The forces reached Cape Coast Castle in February 1782, and, according to John Roberts, the fort's Governor, numbers of the convicts shortly afterwards died 'from the immoderate use of Spirits.' Then, some thirty

> deserted to the principal Dutch Settlement about Nine Miles from Cape Coast Castle, and the major part of those thirty fought against us, at the time we attack'd and destroy'd Fort Vredenburg at Commendar.

As well,

> four or five and twenty of them, who were put on board a Vessel bound to Commenda for the releif of our Fort there, overpower'd the Crew, and run away with the Vessel.

Most of the others soon died, so that not more than thirty of the original two hundred and twelve convicts 'liv'd over a twelvemonth from the day they were landed in Africa.'[8]

Shelburne held the Home Secretaryship in Rockingham's short-lived Administration; and within days of his forming his own in July 1782 he sent his successor a list of matters which required urgent attention. They needed to see to the security of Gibraltar, Shelburne told Townshend; they must plan expeditions to the West Indies and Spanish America; there were important questions concerning India; and, 'Convicts require to be sent to the Coast of Africa.'[9]

In raising the matter of the convicts, Shelburne sketched a tune that Townshend was subsequently to orchestrate. They needed to do something about the rogues immediately, the Minister said, 'for the Judges have repeatedly remonstrated, and the Hulks are in a State, which will excite a Publick Clamor if not attended to.' While Townshend did not respond with any notable vigour, he did organize the despatch, by the end of the year, of an insignificant number of men and women convicts to Goree and Cape Coast Castle.

He considered some other ideas as he did so. In August, he received a suggestion from Dr Wright of the Bow Street Office that they send the transportees into the Royal Navy. By doing so, Wright said, they could at the same time effect the sentence of transportation beyond the seas, and man the fleets. Thomas Robertson raised this idea again three months later, and Townshend asked him to enlarge on it. Some details of the African fiasco had reached London by this time; and when he wrote again, Robertson observed that 'when Exile in Africa was first proposed in Council, it was not considered that it might naturally affect a principal branch of West India Commerce — the Slaving Trade,' but that now they must be mindful of the prospect of convicts seizing ships. The Home Office does not seem to have pursued Wright and Robertson's idea further, however, but the reason for this does not appear.[10] Then, early in 1783, Edward Morse, the sometime Chief Justice of 'Senegambia,' suggested that the Administration establish a convict colony on the Gambia River, where they might obtain many valuable products. The Home Secretary 'approved my Plan, and adopted it,' Morse recorded, but the scheme lapsed when Shelburne's Administration fell in February.[11]

Townshend left office with the problem of the transportees undiminished. Because it had not been his idea, he may not have been very concerned at the failure of the African venture. Had he been more perspicacious, however, he would have understood that the causes of this failure would inevitably attend any placing of convicts in equatorial Africa. And had he understood this, he would not have pursued the Lemane scheme two years later, to his Administration's embarrassment in Parliament, to the cost of whatever confidence Pitt may yet have retained in him.

II   *Lord North at the Home Office, and James Matra*

Putting aside their past differences Lord North and Charles James Fox made a marriage of much political convenience when they combined to bring down the Shelburne ministry in February 1783. Greatly to his distaste, for he abhorred Fox, the King then found himself in the necessity of asking the pair to form an administration; and this they did under the nominal leadership of the Duke of Portland, with Fox taking the Foreign Secretaryship of State, and North the Home one.

North had therefore to deal with the convict problem; and he did so in the same desultory fashion as Townshend, now Lord Sydney, before him. In July, he tried to revive transportation to America, when he arranged for the London merchant George Moore to carry some one hundred and fifty convicts to Virginia and Maryland. This attempt aborted, however, when the convicts ran their vessel ashore, and many escaped into Sussex; and when the Americans, who considered the scheme a 'fraudulent' one, declined to receive the rest.[1]

The next month, North received another proposal which, through no fault of his, was eventually to prove of far greater moment.

On 28 July, James Matra wrote to Sir Joseph Banks:

> Although for many months past, I have been obliged to lead the life of a Solitary fugitive, I have heared a rumour of two plans for a settlement in the South Seas; one of them, for South-Wales, to be immediately under Your direction, and in which Lords Sandwich, Mulgrave, Mr Colman, & several others are to be concerned. The other a distinct plan, in which Sir George Young, & Mr Jackson, formerly of the Admiralty, are the Principals.
>
> I have met these Stories in several romantick Shapes; but secluded as I was from Society, have not been able to get any intelligence to be depended on, except mediately from Sir George Young, who avowed it to an acquaintance of mine, tho' in such cautious, equivocal terms, as barely served to authenticate the fact, without clearing away any of the obscurity it is involved in.
>
> If there be any truth in either of the reports particularly the first, I shall be extremely obliged to You for some information, which I assure You shall never be communicated by me to any one. I have frequently revolved similar plans in my mind & would prefer embarking in such a scheme to anything much better, than what I am likely to get in this Hemisphere.[2]

Very little information about either of these schemes now remains,[3] but Banks clearly discussed his with Matra, for on 23 August the latter sent North a long and detailed proposal for establishing a colony on the coast of New South Wales, and claimed Banks's 'high approbation' of it. Evidently, in this as in so many like instances, Banks was content to retire into the background after raising the idea, for his own project does not appear again in the just-described form.

Matra is an interesting if slight figure, whose family fortunes ran with the age's tides.[4] He was born James, the son of James and Elizabeth *Magra*, in America in or about 1745. His father is reported to have studied medicine at Trinity College, Dublin, and he emigrated to New York before 1740, where he taught prior to being licensed as a doctor. Reputedly of austere manners and original views, Dr Magra built an impressive reputation, and a considerable fortune, in the next thirty years, and died at 'a very advanced age' on 13 April 1774.

Clear-headed the elder Magra may have been, but his sons were inflicted with an over-abundance of quixotry. One, Redmond, was what the age politely termed an 'adventurer', who resigned in disgrace from the Army, and then spent his time in dubious fur-trading ventures which further reduced his credit. Another, Perkins, had a moderate career which included service in the army in North America, as aide-de-camp to Sir George Lennox, and as Consul at Tunis. His surviving letters show him to have been an educated man who enjoyed loyal and affectionate friends, but who habitually miscalculated. One friend said that he was 'utterly unfit' for the world he was so fond of; another remarked that she always suspected him 'of being taken in when money is in question or any new Wild scheme proposed to him.'

James's life ran strangely parallel to Perkins's. After attending school in England (where and when are presently unknown), he entered the Navy in May 1762; and in 1768, he joined the crew of the *Endeavour*, with Cook recording him in the muster book as 'James Maria Magra,' A.B., joining 25 July 1768. The New Yorker seems not to have had the best of voyages with the Yorkshireman, whose displeasure he incurred a number of times. Years later, in the aftermath of Christian's mutiny, Matra claimed to have been at once a ring-leader of, and a deterrent to, similarly-motivated schemes against Cook. How much substance there is to this claim is difficult to assess, for it is not confirmed by any other source. It is clear, however, that Cook held no very high opinion of Matra, describing him as 'one of those gentlemen, frequently found on board Kings Ships, that can very well be spared, or to speake more planer good for nothing.'[5]

Suspicion has persisted that Matra might have been the author of the first extended account of the *Endeavour*'s voyage, *A Journal of a Voyage round the World*, which appeared anonymously in 1771, in contravention of the Admiralty's interdiction on others publishing before the official account. Certainly he possessed the necessary literary abilities to have written the work, which is fluent, if at times highly coloured, and which, as Beaglehole points out, 'is the only document connected with the voyage that seems to show any animus against Cook, or displays him in a disadvantageous light.'[6] In view of Banks's later patronage of him, however, Matra must have kept the secret very well if he were the author of this account, for Banks was insulted by its having been dedicated to him, and was most censorious of others who later broke similar bans.

A year after the *Endeavour*'s return, Matra was appointed Consul at Teneriffe (March 1772); and if he took up his office before Sir George Young had finished his fourth tour of duty on the Africa station, the two may have then met. Matra filled in his time at Teneriffe coping with such things as the Americans using it as a base from which to smuggle tea and wines, the issuing of Mediterranean passes to British ships, the difficulties which the Spanish Governor put in his way, and ship- wrecked British crews being sold into slavery in North Africa. The notes that recur throughout the rest of his life begin in his letters from this time — of his diligent attention to his duties, of the better treatment that should be his as a loyal American-born servant of the King, of his finan- cial difficulties.

This last note intensifies with the death of his father in 1774. On 20 July, Matra wrote to Lord Rochford, the Secretary of State, that his affairs were in 'a very precarious Situation,' and asked for leave to visit New York in order to attend to them. Rochford gave permission for this on 18 November, but there is no indication that Matra then went to America. The next year, he petitioned the King to change his name to James Mario Matra; and George granted his Royal License and Authority for this on 19 February 1776.[7]

In March 1777, with the British again in control of New York, Matra renewed his request for leave to visit there, which Rochford granted on 18 April. He *may* have crossed the Atlantic this time, for his aged mother came over to England towards the end of 1779. The claim for compen- sation which she presented in March 1780 gives some further informa- tion about the family's situation in America, and their losses in the war. Mrs Magra represented that she was

> an inhabitant of New York, and since the commencement of the rebellion in America, she has been deprived of her whole property, and reduced to a dependance on her two sons, who are in His Majesty's service; but they hav- ing also suffered from the same cause, her support is rendered painful and precarious.[8]

Matra next appears as Secretary to the British Embassy at Constan- tinople, a post he evidently obtained with Banks's assistance. He led a varied life in the Sultan's domain, pursuing his interest in local customs and artefacts, sending Banks specimens, and, with an eye to possible financial benefit, trying to re-establish printing there.

He returned to London in mid-1781. How he then spent his time is not entirely clear. He claimed to have offered political advice to the Rus- sians and the Turks, and that Fox promised him an appointment in 1782. In 1783, he may have helped his mother to obtain a pension of £60 a year; and he claimed 'something like a promise from Mr Fox of one of the American Consulages.'[9] With such employment not forthcoming, however, he then worked for periods in the Plantation Department (a small branch of the Home Office created to deal with colonial affairs when Parliament abolished the American Secretaryship of State in 1782), and in the Treasury.

Matra seems to have moved with some freedom in London circles in the mid-1780s. He went to Lord Craven's country seat for the weekend. He dined with Charles Dilly, the bookseller, and with General Paoli. He called on Boswell; he breakfasted with Banks; he was friendly with Evan Nepean, the Under-Secretary of the Home Department.

In mid-1786, Matra was again disappointed in his hope of obtaining a respected and lucrative office, when the Administration declined to appoint him Governor of New South Wales. Banks then had the Home Office give him the Consulship at Tangiers. He took up this post in 1787, and from then until his death in 1806, he worked assiduously for a Government that evidently cared but little for his welfare.

However much the complaints that permeate his letters of the 1790s and 1800s may have been due to his personality and general disillusionment, the Government does seem to have treated him badly as well. The conditions of his service in Morocco were not good. A year after his arrival, he told Nepean how

> we have no Tents here but the half open ones of the Country, nor have I a single conveniency, and I fear that riding all day in heavy African rains, up to my Horse's belly in Mud, and getting into an open wet Tent at night, in a Season when 'tis Cold, will do what little constitution I have, much mischief.

In 1791, he was given the rank of Ambassador in order to negotiate a treaty of friendship and commerce with the new Emperor, only to lose it after the Treaty was signed. And through the long years of war with Revolutionary and Napoleonic France, the Home Office refused his repeated requests for leave to visit England, with the reply that he was needed on the spot, so that after 1786 Matra never again saw his friends or foster homeland. His sight, which had been bad from his youth, had almost totally failed by 1804. He dictated his last despatch on 18 February, and he died on 29 March 1806.

There are good reasons for finding Matra a sad figure. He was forced to live out his adult life in circumstances very different from those of his childhood; and, mixing with great men, constantly he dreamed of being one, though his abilities were never such as to allow him to realize this dream. Altogether, his life very well exemplifies the Loyalists' common fate.

Matra opened his proposal to North by stating that, if followed, it might 'in time, atone for the loss of our American colonies.' He briefly described Cook's exploration of the coast of New South Wales, saying that

> the Climate, & Soil, are so happily adapted to produce every various, & valuable Production of Europe, & of both the Indias, that with good manage-

ment, & a few Settlers, in 20 or 30 Years they might cause a Revolution, in the whole system of European Commerce, & secure to England a monopoly of some part of it, & a very large share in the whole.

New South Wales, he continued, might produce spices, sugar cane, tea, coffee, silk, cotton, indigo, and tobacco. There was the New Zealand flax (*phormium tenax*), the benefits of which might be considerable; and New Zealand timber might be shipped home 'for the use of the Kings Yards.' The country might 'afford an Asylum to those unfortunate American Loyalists, whom Great Britain is bound by every tie of honour and gratitude, to protect & support.' A settlement might lead to the development of the China trade, of the fur trade between north-western America and Asia, and of the British trade in wool, by opening markets in Japan and Korea; and as well, to Britain's exercising the right she had recently obtained, to 'a free Navigation in the Molucca Seas.'

Moreover, Matra represented,

> the place which New South Wales holds on our Globe might give it a very commanding Influence in the policy of Europe. If a Colony from Britain was established in that large Tract of Country, & if we were at War with Holland or Spain, we might very powerfully annoy either State from our new Settlement. We might with a safe, & expeditious Voyage, make Naval Incursions on Java, & the other Dutch Settlements, & we might with equal facility, invade the Coasts of Spanish America, & intercept the Manilla Ships, laden with the Treasures of the West. This check which new South Wales would be in time of War on both those Powers, make it a very important Object when we view it in the Chart of the World, with a Political Eye.

Nor need a colony there require a large body of Britain's populace. Banks thought that 'we may draw any Number of useful Inhabitants from China.' And the scheme was not a frivolous one. Sir Joseph Banks approved of it, and

> some of the most intelligent, & candid Americans, . . . agree that under the patronage & protection of Government, it offers the most favourable Prospects, that have yet occurred to better the Fortunes, & to promote the happiness of their fellow sufferers, & Countrymen.

At the least, 'one Ship of the Peace establishment' could be sent on a preliminary survey. However, if the Government were prepared to entertain a more ambitious project, then

> two Vessels may be sent, with two Companies of Marines, selected from among such of that Corps, as best understand Husbandry, or Manufacturies, & about Twenty Artificers, who are all the Emigration required from the Parent State.

These, 'under a proper Person', might be left at the colony, 'with Materials & Provisions, to prepare for the reception of the intended Settlers, that their wants may be as few as possible on their Arrival.'[11]

We do not know how North received Matra's proposal, but there is no evidence that it interested him. Indeed, there were reasons why it should not have. As it did not yet involve convicts, it did not offer help with the problem they presented. As well, by late 1783 North was a tired man whose political sun had all but set; and he was scarcely likely to be attracted by new schemes of empire when he had so recently presided over the loss of the American colonies. When the King withdrew his commission in December, he was no nearer to solving the problem of how to effect the sentences of the transportees than Sydney had been ten months before.

III   *Lord Sydney and the Transportation Act of 1784*

The situation concerning transportation must have been only too familiar to Sydney when he resumed the Home and Colonial Secretaryship on 23 December. With the Portland Administration having adopted no new scheme, the Thames hulks were still overcrowded. So, too, were the local jails; and county officials were raising their voices louder. John Anderson, the Mayor of Bristol, had complained in November; Northampton officials had complained in December; Lancashire ones complained in January.

Despite the continuing impasse and growing clamour, Sydney seems to have paid little attention to the problem until parliamentary circumstances required him to do so. With the Act for the Temporary Reception of Criminals under Sentence of Transportation (19 Geo.III c.74) coming up for renewal, the Administration found itself under some attack there. The Commons began to consider the question at the beginning of March; and on 11 March, Arden, the Solicitor General, said in reply to criticism of the hulks, that it was impossible to effect sentences of transportation, as 'no place had yet been found to which convicts, under such a sentence, could be sent.' Mr Hussey then observed that 'there was an island where they might be landed, and where they might establish a useful colony'—'New Zealand, lately discovered in the South Seas.' On 17 March, the Commons went into committee in order to amend the Act, so that it should not be lawful 'to transport to *Africa* any Person under Sentence of Transportation to any other Place.' Sir Charles Bunbury reported on 22 March that sites for the proposed penitentiary houses had been investigated, and two recommended, but that there were difficulties in building the houses according to the provisions of the Act. However, he said, work on them would commence in May, and should finish in five years. Parliament then renewed the Act for a further year (24 Geo.III c.12).[1]

Sydney interviewed Matra in the contest of this debate, and asked whether New South Wales might not be 'a very proper Region, for the reception of Criminals condemned to Transportation?' Taking the hint, Matra then added this idea to his scheme. He suggested the Government give convicts 'a few Acres of Ground, as soon as they arrive in New South Wales, in *absolute Property*, with what assistance they may want to till then;' and he pointed out that, since the miscreants could not 'fly from the Country,' and since there was nothing to steal, 'they must work or Starve.' 'By the Plan, which I have now proposed,' he concluded,

> a necessity to continue in the place of his destination, and to be industrious is imposed on the Criminal: — The Expence to the Nation is absolutely imperceptible, comparatively with what Criminals have hitherto cost Government: & thus two Objects of most desirable & beautiful Union will be permanently blended: Economy to the Public, & Humanity to the Individual.[2]

As before, though, Sydney hung fire. Then, rather than pursuing a radically new scheme, he warmed over a familiar one, when he arranged for Moore to transport a load of convicts to Honduras, where an enclave of Britons cut mahogony and cedar. In May, the merchant despatched the *Mercury* with eighty-six convicts, provisions for them for twelve months, and a cargo of goods.

Sydney had hopes for the venture, for he thought that the settlers would welcome the move, and usefully employ the convicts 'either for the cutting of Logwood, or . . . in the Cultivation of their Lands.' Sadly for the Home Secretary, if not for the convicts, who might otherwise have laboured on that malarial coast, the reality was quite otherwise. When the *Mercury* reached Belize in July, the settlers soon took Moore's agent to court, contrived his imprisonment, made free use of his convicts, and made off with his goods.[3]

This venture gives a good insight into the Administration's thinking at this time. They might have lessened their difficulties by removing or restricting the sentence of transportation, but there is no evidence that they considered doing so. Rather than to any alteration in traditional penal provision, they looked to a substantial implementation of it; and for this, of course, they needed an area where British colonists required cheap labour, and did not mind if convicts provided it.

The British presence on the coast of central America was slight and precarious, however, and could not have supported transportation on a North American scale, even if the settlers had received the move well. To resume transportation on the old scale, the Administration needed other areas as well; and in mid-1784, these did not appear. The newly-independent Americans spurned taking British convicts. The Canadian provinces were in a very unsettled state, being crowded with tens of thousands of dispossessed Loyalists. The West Indian planters had their slaves. The voyage to India was long and expensive, and in any case the sub-continent offered an abundance of cheap labour. 'The more I consider the matter, Sydney observed to Governor Clarke, 'the greater difficulty I see in disposing of these people in any other place [than Honduras] in the possession of His Majesty's Subjects.'[4]

A possible solution was to transport to areas not in British hands; and the Administration took account of this contingency when they prepared to resume the practice on a large scale after their return to office in April/May 1784. At the end of July, the Commons considered Bunbury's report again, and resolved to amalgamate the various Statutes dealing with transportation into one. On 11 August, the Administration introduced legislation to provide for the continuance of the hulks, for detention on these as a preliminary to transportation, for the revival of transportation, and for the King in Council to fix the place of transportation.

This last-mentioned provision, allowing as it would for the sending of convicts to places not specifically approved by Parliament, evidently caused some uneasiness. Arden, now the Attorney General, reported that Lord Beauchamp had intended to object 'to the sending Transport Convicts out of the King's Dominions.' Beauchamp had not been present in the Commons when the Bill came on, but in case 'any Peer sho[d] made the same Objection,' Arden gave Sydney a paper showing 'that a Law for this purpose existed in England from 1597 to 1714.'[5]

Despite these murmurings, Parliament seems to have enacted the legislation without giving the Administration many difficulties over it. The Commons considered it on 11 August and agreed to it, with certain amendments, the next day. The Lords agreed to it on 19 August, and the King gave it his assent on the same day. Nepean reported to Arden on 21 August that 'the Bill for the better transportation of Offenders has passed into a Law and I do not understand that any alterations have been made in it since you left Town.'[6]

To this point, Pitt was mostly content to have Sydney deal with the convict question; and it requires little speculation to arrive at his likely reasons for doing so. The convicts were, after all, the responsibility of Sydney's department, and even if the Home Secretary had only mediocre abilities, the problem which the convicts posed was small in comparison to others that then required the young Prime Minister's attention. As well, Sydney's listlessness meant that his Under-Secretary, Evan Nepean, conducted most of the Department's business, and Nepean was a most capable person, habitually drafting those letters concerning the convicts that went out over Sydney's or his own signature.

Nonetheless, 24 Geo.III c. 56 unmistakably bears Pitt's stamp. As Ehrman observes, Pitt had a 'radical intelligence' which 'sought the root of the problem;'[7] and in mid-1784, at the same time as he applied this intelligence to the nation's problems with India, Ireland, and the Northern Powers, he also applied it to that with the convicts.

That Pitt investigated how other nations dealt with their convicts is one sign of this. In May, he asked a French savant how many convicts

c

there were at Nice and Villefranche? Were these paid for public or
private work? What were their rations? Was there a hospital for them?
Did the different types of criminals wear different uniforms? Were they
given shoes? What was the ratio of guards to convicts? Who directed the
convicts? What salary did the guards receive, and what rations? Was
escape punished with death?[8] Another sign is the way in which the
Transportation Act provided so sufficiently for future need as to become
a mainstay of British penal practice until the mid-Nineteenth century,
and a means to empire. In its comprehensiveness and its consequences,
the Act bespeaks the Prime Minister's hand much more than it does the
Home Secretary's.

IV   *The Administration considers suggestions for transportation*

While the Pitt Administration prepared to resume transportation on a
large scale with 24 Geo.III c.56, they could not of course do so without a
suitable overseas region. In the months to the end of the year, they
sought for this will-o-the-wisp in the thicket of proposals that sprang up
with the Act.

Edward Thompson's was one of the first to appear. Thompson had an
eventful life, in which he combined an interest in literature with naval
service. Born about 1738, he went out to the East Indies in 1754, joined
the Royal Navy on his return, and then served in European waters during the Seven Years War. In the early 1770s, he served in the North and
Mediterranean Seas. He early tried his hand at poetry, producing a
number of comic and satiric poems in the 1750s and 1760s. In 1767, he
drew on his voyaging for his *Sailor's Letters.* In the 1770s, he had two plays
performed, and he edited the works of Oldham, Marvell, and
Whitehead.

In May 1778, Thompson took command of the *Hyaena*, and in the
next years made two voyages to the West Indies. In the spring of 1781,
he supervised the occupation of the Dutch colonies of Berbice,
Demerara, and Essequibo. After establishing a fragile government over
these, he escorted a convoy home, where he arrived in January 1782.
With peace, Keppel gave him the command of the *Grampus*, and appointed him Commodore of the West Africa station. He toured this station, and the West Indian one, in the first half of 1784.[1]

Immediately on his return in late July, Thompson sought to tell Pitt
about the island of St Thomas (São Tomé), which lies on the equator a
short distance off the west African coast. The Portuguese had held this
island, but had lost interest in it, Thompson represented, and it was now
inhabited only by some 15,000 Blacks. Once divided into plantations, it
was now 'an Elegant Wilderness,' where sugar cane, cocoa, coffee, corn,
cotton, cinnamon, and tropical fruits grew 'wild, & spontaneously.' A

settlement there would assist the British factories about the equatorial coast, 'serve to refresh the Guinea Ships, & add when cultivated to the general African Commerce.' As well, it would be 'the most profitable, and advantageous Situation [for] the Convicts, who might there be useful as Mechanicks & Husbandmen.' Pitt told Thompson to talk to Sydney, but the Commodore indicated his lack of confidence in this channel, when he tried again to gain Pitt's attention via George Rose, his Treasury Secretary, and Lord Mahon, his cousin. (He was 'at a loss to conceive how to proceed without the countenance of M^r. Pitt,' he told Mahon.)[2]

Presumably as a consequence of his talks with these men, Thompson had changed his proposal somewhat when he approached Sydney the next week. Now, he suggested that the Administration return Negapatam to the Dutch in exchange for Demerara, Berbice, and Essequebo. These colonies, Thompson said, would take British woollen and linen goods and manufactures, and return sugar, coffee, cotton, rum, chocolate, tobacco, and indigo. They would 'nourish, & assist the West India Isles, with Cattle, Corn, Rice, Timber of every quality for ships & Mills;' and a 'great trade' might develop between them & Newfoundland and Nova Scotia. They would be at once 'a most eligible situation, for the unfortunate, American Loyalists — & the properest Asylum for the Convicts.' Thompson enclosed a chart, and told Sydney he was ready to attend an interview.[3]

As Thompson pressed his scheme, so did Matra his. Presumably hoping to have it aired in Parliament, he sent it to Fox on 7 August, enclosing a map of New South Wales, and telling the Opposition leader that he would be happy to provide additional information. Fox does not seem to have obliged the hopeful Loyalist. Matra also wrote to the prominent New Yorker, James de Lancey, to enlist his support in gathering their compatriots for the settlement. This de Lancey offered, but added:

> The Season for a Voyage to that country will soon be elapsed, and unless the Equipment is speedily sett on foot, another year will be lost, and my prospect of procuring Settlers from the Loyalists in Nova Scotia rendered less favorable, for by next year I should suppose, most of them, who have gone there, will have procured some kind of Habitations for themselves, and will not chuse to quit them for an uncertain Settlement in N.S.Wales.[4]

John Call came forward with a proposal. Call was born in 1732, near Tiverton in Devon. The details of his early life are obscured, but in 1749 he sailed to India as secretary to the distinguished mathematician Benjamin Robins, who had been appointed the East India Company's Engineer-General. Call soon followed his mentor in this employment, and ultimately attained the rank of colonel in the Company's military service. He served under Clive in 1752, and along the Coromandel Coast 1752-8. In 1757, he was appointed Chief Military Engineer at

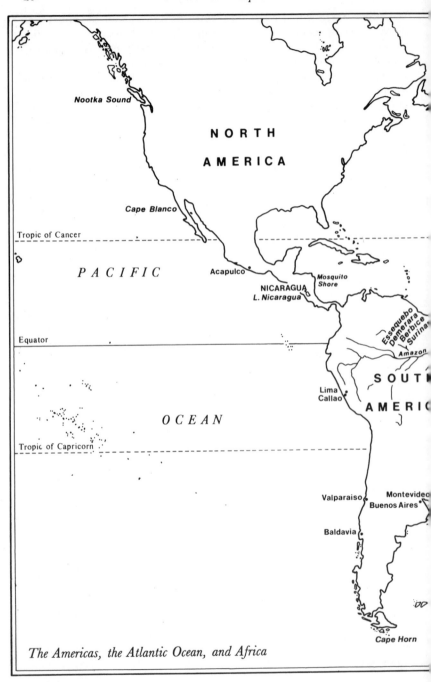

The Americas, the Atlantic Ocean, and Africa

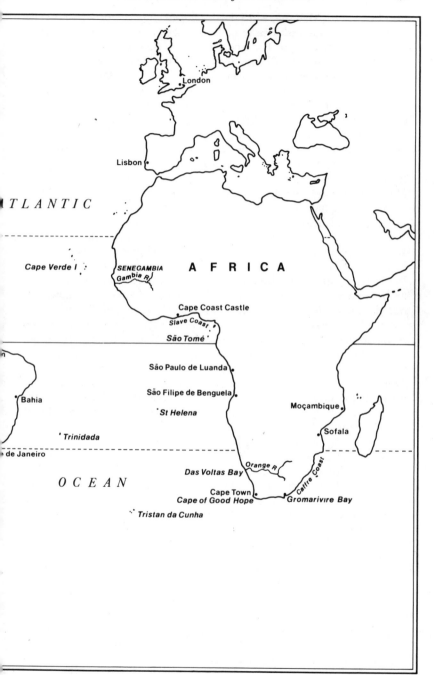

Fort St George (Madras), which he developed and extended. In 1761, he supervised the successful siege of Pondicherry, and became Engineer-General. (From 1764, he had under him Paul Benfield, who was later to become notorious as the Nabob of Arcot's chief creditor.) In 1768 he was one of the field deputies in the first Mysore War, but his career ended with this venture, when he quarrelled with the commanding officers.[5]

Call pursued a commercial career as vigorously as he did his military one. He was appointed a Writer in the Madras establishment of 1752, and he gained a chair on that Council ten years later. By 1768 he held the third chair, and had become Accountant-General to the Presidency. Having incurred the Court of Directors' displeasure, however, he was then twice passed over for the Governorship, first in favour of Warren Hastings, and then of Cartier. Sensible of his loss of favour, he left India early in 1770, taking a fortune with him, to which he soon added by marrying Philadelphia, the daughter of Dr William Battie.

Back in England, Call set about establishing himself as a country gentleman with an interest in politics. He was High Sheriff of Cornwall in 1771-2; and the Royal Society elected him Fellow in November 1775. In 1784, he joined in business with an old friend from Indian days, when he became a partner in John Pybus's merchant banking company. In this year, too, a leader of the 'Arcot' interest whose support Pitt sought or accepted, he was elected member for Callington, in Cornwall.[6] He seems to have been remarkably quiet in the House, but records show that he defended his Indian interest vigorously and successfully behind the scenes. He appeared regularly before the Board of Trade in the 1780s and 1790s, testifying about such matters as the population of, and amount of grain in the kingdom. The King created him Baronet in July 1791, and in 1794 Pitt appointed him to the newly commissioned Board of Agriculture, where he worked hard at his duties, even after becoming blind in 1795. He died on 1 March 1801.

Call seems to have had a mixed character. One of his Indian acquaintances told another concerning the progress of the Mysore War, that he 'is very snug behind the curtain. When any of our actions . . . redound to our credit, he has the power to engross a great share of it: when the contrary, he knows on whose shoulders they will naturally fall.' This writer added two years later,

> our want of success has been in great measure owing to Call; and I will frankly declare . . . that I have seen sufficient of him most heartily to wish that he may never have the administration of affairs lodged in his hands. . . . He has neither steadiness or abilities for such a post; . . . he might make a good Counsellor, but . . . he would be a wretched Governor.[7]

Yet Call also had a profound sense of public service, and was an inveterate proposer of schemes that might benefit the nation. In 1762, in the midst of Clive's campaign on the Coromandel coast, he 'planned &

was to have had a principal part in an Expedition against Mauritius.' In 1770, after the ship on which he was returning to England had unexpectedly stopped at Mauritius, he gave a lengthy description of the island, and two sketches of Port Louis, into the Company, so that it might have information which would be useful in any future expedition. In 1779, he put forward a scheme for invading the Spanish Colonies in South America. He also suggested the creation of a local militia in Cornwall; and when the authorities did not adopt the idea, he formed three companies in his parish, and trained them.[8]

During the war of 1778-83 he suggested giving the Plymouth dockyard a new water supply. Believing that this would reduce the risk of fire, improve public health, and allow fleets to be victualled more quickly, he sent the idea to the Navy, Admiralty, Victualling, and Ordnance Boards in March 1781. According to his later account, these bodies generally agreed about its utility but, in the manner of Government departments, quibbled about which would receive the greatest benefit, and about which, therefore, should pay. In the end, Call offered to meet the cost himself, if in return he were granted a revenue of £2,200 per year for thirty-one years. The Administration did not take up his offer.[9]

In 1784, Call proposed to Benfield in Madras and Hastings in Bengal, that two ships be sent to the north-west coast of North America to establish the fur trade, after the manner described by Cook in the lately-published narrative of the third voyage. He sent a plan for reducing the Company's debts in India to the Court of Directors and the Administration. And he 'suggested to the Ministry the sending of our criminals to an Establishment on New South Wales, or on New Zealand,' with views of making a base from which to trade with the Spanish colonies across the Pacific, and of obtaining naval stores.[10] In June 1785, pursuing the naval stores idea, he and Sir George Young asked the East India Company for permission to colonize Norfolk Island; and in May 1788, the pair renewed the proposal, this time approaching the Government.

In 1788, too, Call again represented, this time to Pitt, his proposal for giving Plymouth a new water supply. As well as the advantages formerly stated, he now suggested that

> possibly the Want of Employment for the Miners in Cornwall, and their Disposition to be riotous at this Juncture, may be obviated by engaging them in some useful Undertaking.

And in January 1800, when the French were occupying Egypt and thus threatening the British position in India, he suggested to Dundas the settling of the 'Island of Socatra and the two Points of Arabia and Africa, as may command the Passage out of and into the Red Sea.'[11]

Whatever the private benefit that might have accrued to Call from the fruition of these schemes, it is clear that this was not his only perspective.

In giving his descriptions of Mauritius to a Court of Directors which had lately effectively dismissed him, he said that he considered it his duty as an Englishman to do so; and it is difficult to see what financial return he might have anticipated from the most sustained task of public utility which he undertook—the survey of the Royal lands and forests.

Call suggested this survey in 1782, when he saw that England's supplies of naval timbers were gravely depleted, and that, unless the situation were changed, 'very serious consequences [were] to be apprehended in diminuition of the Strength and Durability of the Royal Navy.' Shelburne then appointed him and Arthur Holdsworth commissioners for the purpose; and Pitt re-appointed them, together with Sir Charles Middleton, the Navy Comptroller, in 1786.

These men made seventeen reports in all. In their encompassing eleventh one, they asserted that while

> the Estates of Individuals, in every Part of this Kingdom, have been advancing in Improvement, the Property of the Crown in those Forests has been left unprotected, and exposed to unlimited Waste;

and they produced wide-ranging statistics in support of this view. Because they considered it both 'unsafe, and unwise, to suffer this Country to become dependent on Foreign Powers, for what is essential to its own Defence,' they recommended a new system of management for the Royal forests, and the progressive planting with oak of some 70,000 acres. And, they urged the adoption of methods of building and repairing ships, including the use of other timbers, that might lessen the drain on oak.[12]

Call's New South Wales proposal reflects his versatility of outlook and his interest in the nation's welfare. He began it by stating that there was an urgent need to revive and expand the eastern commerce. Only on the foundation of an extended commerce, he said, could 'a formidable Navy be maintained, and thereon depends the Reputation and Security of Great Britain, and all its foreign Possessions.' 'At this juncture,' he pointed out,

> when the Ties of exclusive Commerce with America are dissolved; — When the Trade to the East Indies is in a declining if not in a precarious State; — When Our Trade to the Mediterranean has been long interrupted and almost annihilated, — And when that to Africa and the West Indies does not promise to be what it has been without a Change of Measures; — It will be highly commendable in any Individual to point out a new Source of Trade, or form any probable Scheme for encouraging Attempts to lay the foundations of future Sources.

Stating that he had often considered what advantages Britain might derive from the discoveries of the 'late Circum-Navigators,' Call then gave details of his scheme. While he mentioned many of the same benefits that Matra had argued for, his suggesting the precise mode of settlement that the Administration finally adopted distinguishes his scheme. Drawing on the narratives of Cook's voyages, Call described New South Wales, New Zealand, New Caledonia, and Norfolk Island. He then said:

> according to the Object which may be in view for making an Establishment, either the Coast of New South Wales, or some other part of New Holland, which on a closer Examination may be hereafter discovered, cannot fail to offer a convenient Situation. — But if New Zealand should be deemed a more promising Island either for Ports or Fertility, there cannot be a Doubt but Situations may be found attended with every Convenience that Nature furnishes, and perfectly adapted to receive the Improvements of Art. — Let the Choice therefore fall on either, or both, for principal Establishments, it is obvious that New Caledonia and Norfolk Island will afford useful Auxiliaries.

The purpose of making secondary settlements on either New Caledonia or Norfolk Island would be to obtain naval materials, with Norfolk Island having the advantage 'not common to the Others by not being Inhabited;' and where as well

> the Climate, Soil, and Sea promise every thing that can be expected from them. — The Timber, Shrubs, Vegetables & Fish already found there, need no Embellishment to pronounce them excellent Samples, but the most invaluable of all, is, the Flax Plant, which grows more luxuriant than in New Zealand.

Call countered possible objections in detail. The comparative sparsity of population in these areas made settlement of them preferable to that of the Friendly and Society Islands; and since the augmenting of trade and empire was necessary to Britain's welfare, she should not be discouraged from doing so by her late and bitter experience with her American colonies. Indeed, the progress of these colonies showed what might come from unpromising beginnings. Since emigration from Britain was inevitable, it was better that those who left should go to territories from which the mother country might receive some benefit. The Loyalists might make new homes in New South Wales free of the 'Taxes or Burthens' they faced in Britain. And the convicts could be transported there — a move which would be of more help to them in their attempts at regeneration than the present one of confining them to the hulks.

Call ended with a plea that his proposal be well considered.

> Should other Inducements be wanting to give a serious Consideration to some Enterprise of the Kind pointed out and to derive some immediate or lay the foundation for some future Advantages to be drawn from the Discoveries of Captain Cook, and other Circum-Navigators, many Objects not undeserving Notice might be enumerated. But surely enough has been said to merit a discussion.

'If the whole Sea Coast and Interior Part of New Holland,' he concluded, were peopled in any comparative Degree with Europe, Asia, or America, it would receive and return Objects of Commerce equal to any Quarter of the Globe.[13]

Sir George Young added his voice. Young was born in 1732, and entered the Royal Navy in 1746. In 1747, he sailed to the East Indies in Boscawen's command, and then joined the East India Company Marine in 1749. He left this service at the end of 1756, to rejoin the Royal Navy, enlisting on the *York*, Captain Pigot. A year later, he sailed with Pigot to North America, taking part in the siege and capture of Louisberg in June and July 1758, which turned the war decisively in Britain's favour. He returned to England towards the end of that year; and then in 1759 transferred with Pigot to the *Royal William*, and took part in the siege of Quebec. He returned home after the fall of this fortress, then served in the West Indies in 1762. He went back to England again with peace, and married Elizabeth Bradshaw; and the pair had four children in the following years. In these years, too, he made four tours of the Africa station, in 1767, 1768, 1771, and 1772, and may have met Matra on the last.

In 1776, following duty in home waters, Young received the command of the *Cormorant*, a small vessel of 14 guns, and went out to the East Indies in Vernon's squadron. He took part in the siege of Pondicherry between August and October 1778, and then sailed home with despatches, to find on his arrival the next March that his wife had just died. He married again before the end of the year, to Anne, the eldest daughter of Dr. William Battie, who had provided well for her, and thus become Call's brother-in-law.

Young found a patron in the Prince of Wales, and received the command of the Royal yacht *William and Mary* in August 1781, and a knighthood. The command of another yacht, the *Katherine*, followed a few years later. In the 1780s, he was one of those who supervised the Thames navigation. But though he applied repeatedly for it, he did not see active service again. He was promoted to Admiral in October 1794, and died in 1810.[14]

Like many of his time, Young had an amateur's interest in natural philosophy. In 1772, he took off from Teneriffe a dried body he found in a case on the Peak, and presented it to Lord Sandwich on his return home. He was elected Fellow of the Royal Society on 15 February 1781, with his nominees describing him as 'A Gentleman well versed in several Branches of natural Knowledge.'[15] And he shared with Sandwich a love of concerts.

About 1783, Young proposed the settlement of Madagascar as a help to strategy and trade, but while Sandwich 'very much approved' the idea, the East India company's monopoly in the area from the Cape of Good Hope to Cape Horn mitigated against an administration's adopting it.[16]

Though disappointed over Madagascar, Young tried again the next year, this time for New South Wales. He told Pitt that a settlement at Botany Bay would allow the British to open a trade in manufactures with South America; and that, in the event of another war with Spain, 'Here is a Port of Shelter & refreshment for our Ships should it be necessary to send any into the South Seas.' Settlers might cultivate exotic plants and spices there to commercial advantage. There was the New Zealand flax, the uses of which 'are more extensive than any Vegetable hitherto known,' and the products of which would be cheaper than those of the Russian fibre plants; and he pointed out how Russia 'may, perhaps, at some future period, think it Her interest to prohibit our Trade with Her for such Articles.' The British might establish an entrepôt there, the Loyalists would find a home there; and it would be a suitable place to send the convicts.[17]

Matra and Young joined forces to press their proposal. In November, Matra told Nepean that Young had spoken to Captains of East Indiamen about the prospect of sailing to China via New South Wales, and had had favourable responses — which removed the only difficulty he could see in the way of the scheme. And he asked whether the ministers 'have come to a decided Resolution to reject the Plan; or if there be any chance, of its being entered on, in the Spring season?[18]

Young added to his first sketch. 'Had I the Command of this Expedition,' he now said,

> I should require a Ship of War; say the *Old Rainbow*, now at Woolwich, formerly a Ship of 40 Guns, as the best Constructed for that purpose of any in the Navy; with only half her lower Deck Guns, and 250 Men, One hundred of which should be Marines, a Store Ship likewise of about 600 Tons Burthen with 40 Seamen and 10 Marines, and a small Vessel of about 100 Tons, of the Brig or Schooner kind with 20 Men, both fitted as Ships of War, and Commanded by *Proper Officers*.

The settlers might import 'Inhabitants and usefull Plants' from the Friendly Islands. As well,

> The China Ships belonging to the India Company, after leaving the Cape of Good Hope, and keeping more to the Southerd than usual, may land the Felons on the Coast; and then proceed to the Northerd round new Ireland, &c. or through Saint George's Channel, and so on to the Island *Formosa* for Canton. — With a little Geographical investigation, this Passage will be found more Short, Easy, and a safer Navigation, than the general Route of the China Ships, from Madrass through the Streights of Malacca.[19]

Now, too, drawing on his experience of taking Portuguese criminals to Brazil, Captain Arthur Phillip suggested that the Administration might send British convicts there.[20]

These proposals had much in common, for Thompson, Matra, Call, and Young each linked the use of the convicts' labour with the obtaining of strategic and commercial benefit and each suggested a new area in which to realize this aim. (Phillip may also have done so, but we presently know too little about his proposal to decide.) Together, they developed a new rationale for transportation, and offered the Administration practical means of implementing the provisions of 24 Geo.III c.56. And the Administration did consider them seriously. Arden talked to Thompson on 10 August; Sydney interviewed him on 29 September; he saw Nepean on 1 October. Nepean put Phillip's suggestion to C. R. Freire, the Portuguese Ambassador in London, who relayed it to his Court. Arden interviewed Young. Pitt and Sydney asked Howe's opinion of Matra's scheme.[21]

For various reasons, some of them now unclear, the politicans did not decide in favour of any of these schemes. They certainly were interested in the possibility of gaining Guiana in exchange for Negapatam, but evidently did not see it as a region for the Loyalists and convicts. The Portuguese Queen found the idea of having British rogues in her dominions 'inconvenient.' Howe thought that 'the length of the Navigation, subject to all the retardments of an India Voyage,' mitigated against 'a return of the many advantages, in commerce or War, which Mr. M. Matra has in contemplation.' Arden, on the other hand, saw Young's scheme as 'the most likely method of effectually disposing of convicts, the number of which requires the immediate interference of government.' He also said, though, that he was 'totally ignorant of the probability of the Success of such a Scheme.'[22]

The Administration may have found the decision to establish a new mode of transportation daunting in itself; they may have been uncertain about the prospects of success of any of these particular schemes; they may have looked askance at their likely cost. These are all likely reasons for their not adopting them, but we need more information before we may know if they were actual ones. What we can be surer of is that in late 1784 the primary responsibility for deciding how to dispose of the convicts still rested with Lord Sydney, and that his Lordship's thoughts had turned to Africa again.

V   Sydney's decision for Africa

Just as the Administration's legislating 24 Geo.III c.56 encouraged Thompson, Matra, Call, Young, and Phillip to anticipate the resumption of transportation, so, too, did it encourage county officials to look towards some relief for their overcrowded jails, and to press the louder for it. Fraser, the Foreign Under-Secretary, added to the clamour when he wrote to Nepean about the risk of some of the five hundred convicts then held in the Thames hulks escaping. Sydney took an incidental action in November, when he appointed Duncan Campbell Overseer for the custody of felons sentenced to transportation, and thereby activated the provision that these might be held on the hulks prior to the effecting of their sentences. This move, however, really only legalized the status quo, which Sydney described when he told Lord Robert Spencer,

> It would make me very happy to have it in my power to give effectual releif* to the Goal* of Oxford, but the great difficulty which has for some Years past existed of carrying the Sentence of Transportation into Execution, has, I am sorry to say, been a means of crowding all the Goals and Places of Confinement in and near this Metropolis as well as the Hulks in the River Thames.[1]

In these circumstances, Sydney chose a familiar path, and asked the Africa Company to take convicts into their forts again. His idea was that the slavers should take some two hundred felons annually, and set them to cultivating cotton and vegetables. The merchants 'sharply objected' to this idea, however, on the grounds that such a large number of rogues would be dangerous to their settlements. When Sydney pressed his request, they most unwillingly agreed to take some twenty out to Cape Coast Castle. Sydney then contracted with Anthony Calvert to transport these, and the Treasury approved the arrangement.[2]

Though the merchants scarcely co-operated with Sydney in his scheme, they did suggest an alternative one, which the Home Secretary seems to have received gratefully. Reviving the idea which John Roberts had offered to the Commons Committee on Transportation in 1779, John Barnes, the Africa Company's Governor, suggested that the Administration send the convicts to the island of Lemane (Le Main), some seven hundred kilometres up the Gambia River; and he then developed his idea in conversations with Sydney and Nepean.[3] While it does not appear explicitly, we do not need to look far for the merchants' motive — transportation to Africa would have given them a most suitable outward cargo for their ships, and, hence, a greater return from each voyage.

With the general features of the probable scheme fixed, Nepean sought further advice from a Mr Bradley, who in turn consulted his brother Richard, who had been to the area, and saw the possibility of gainful employment. Richard Bradley, his brother told the Under-Secretary, could secure permission to land the convicts on Lemane,

> and by paying an annual custom he is certain they will be allowed to remain there while they conduct themselves properly, but he has very great doubts of their being able to procure a subsistence in that Country after the Provisions proposed to be delivered to them by Government are expended.

The Administration then adopted the scheme; and they must have done this before the end of the year, for Nepean wrote privately to John

---

* These forms indicate that the letter was drafted by Evan Nepean, Sydney's Under-Secretary, who habitually used them.

Nichol, the Mayor of Plymouth, on 29 December, 'It is at last determined that [the convicts on board the *Dunkirk*] shall forthwith be removed, with some others who are now in the Goals in and about London, to the Coast of Africa.'[4]

The new year opened with Nepean working assiduously to further the scheme. He met Barnes on 1 January, and told him of Richard Bradley's opinion and offer. Barnes was disturbed, for he doubted Bradley's qualifications 'to treat with effect for a Cession of the Island of Lemain and to reconcile the Natives to a Settlement upon it of the Convicts.' He then investigated, and told Nepean two days later,

> I was the more confirmed in this Opinion upon my return to the City where I found that Mr Bradley has never been but once, and then a short time in the Gambia, and that he has never been near the Country and consequently could not have any knowledge of or Acquaintance with the People with whom he is to treat upon this Occasion. In short that he can not be better qualified for this service than any other Gentleman of equal Abilities who has never been in the Gambia; I can not help therefore repeating to you, that I shall have very little hopes of the Success of this Plan if it is not conducted in Africa by a Person who has a perfect knowledge of, and powerful Interest with the Princes of the Country.

He recommended instead a Mr Heatley, as 'the only Man by whose means the Scheme is most Likely to Succeed.'[5]

At least in part, Nepean accepted Barnes's opinion, for he asked for references for Heatley. Barnes forwarded one on 13 January, from Mr Stater, the President of the Liverpool Chamber of Commerce, who stressed the importance of the Africa trade to his city, and said that Heatley

> has a perfect Knowledge of the Natives, is well acquainted with the Interests of that River, and is Seasoned to the Climate; [and that] he has been entrusted with the management of very large Concerns and has conducted them much to the Satisfaction of his Employers.

The Home Office then divided the responsibility, giving Bradley the task of obtaining the island, and Heatley the charge of the colonization. Bradley sailed by the middle of the month.[6]

When the Home Office sought Treasury approval for the scheme on 9 February, they sent a description of Lemane 'collected from the Information of Gentlemen who have been Members of the African Committee.' These gentlemen, (who seem to have been principally Barnes and Heatley) represented that the island

> abounds with plenty of Timber for Building, and the Land [is] extremely fertile, a great part of which has already been cleared. The Country adjacent is plentifully stored with Black Cattle, Goats and Sheep, and the Natives are hospitable & inoffensive.

A curious feature is the idea that the convicts should not be directly supervised, but should rather

> . . . be left entirely to themselves, and before they leave the River, be directed to elect a Chief and at least four more, as a Council, out of their own Body, and to invest such Chief with powers to appoint any subordinate Officers that might be necessary for the regulation of their Affairs, and to have charge of the Provisions and Property provided for their Use, and also to try and punish any of them for Crimes.

The writers recognized that 'upon the first Settlement a great many of the Convicts would die from the Change of Climate;' on the other hand, the survivors could not escape through the country, and a guard ship would prevent their doing so down the river. And they foresaw that 'a regular Succession of Convicts might be sent out annually.' Their experience as slavers informed their views throughout — as when they observed, for example, that

> the second Cargo would hardly be in want of Provisions, for those of the first would in one year secure, with tolerable Industry, a sufficient Quantity for at least five times their Number, and in a very few years they would become Planters, and take those who might be sent out hereafter into their Service — as they grow rich they naturally grow honest, and from the Commodities which might be collected from the Natives, it is more than probable that it would in a short Series of years be of considerable advantage to this Country.

If things proceeded in this way, they thought, Lemane might in time accommodate some 4000 people.[7] As a blue print for the redemption of society's flawed members, the scheme was of course fantastic, but it reflected prevailing assumptions. Even the usually hard-headed Banks put forward a similar idea; so, too, did John Call.

The Home Office accompanied this description with Anthony Calvert's terms for transporting one hundred and fifty convicts to Lemane, Heatley's for serving as Governor, and Barnes's for supplying a guardship. In his covering letter, Sydney struck a favorite note when he said by way of introduction that

> the several Goals & Places for the Confinement of Felons in this Kingdom are so crowded that the greatest danger is to be apprehended, not only from their Escape, but from infectious Distempers which may hourly be expected to break out amongst them.

Accordingly, the King had already sent Bradley to negotiate the purchase of Lemane; he, Sydney, would shortly send a list of articles that would be needed; and would Treasury consider Calvert, Heatley, and Barnes's terms in the meantime, for if the convicts were to arrive at a good season they must soon sail. On 12 February, Sydney wrote to the Treasury again, seeking approval for two hundred convicts to be sent, since it was now 'indispensably necessary' to send this larger number 'in order to give effectual Relief to the Goals.'[8]

The Treasury asked the Navy Board's opinion of the merchants' terms on 23 February. Five days later, the Commissioners replied that 'Mr Calvert's terms for carrying out the Convicts appear high, but taking into consideration the Nature & danger of the Service We see no objection to closing with him for his Ship of 250 Tons;' but that Barnes's were 'very extravagant,' and a suitable ship could be obtained 'on more reasonable terms.'[9] Cabinet then adopted the scheme, and asked Arden to draft Orders in Council, in the terms of the Transportation Act of 1784, fixing Africa as a place to transportation. They promulgated these on 11 March, but kept them secret.

By the time the Administration had concluded these arrangements the proper seasons for sailing was past, and the Home Office put off the scheme. On 4 March, Nepean asked Duncan Campbell if he could accommodate the convicts destined for Lemane until September. Campbell replied that he could, since he would shortly have another hulk. Sydney then wrote to the Treasury, announcing the delay, and seeking approval for them to be sent to Campbell.[10]

As the Administration hung fire on the scheme, Richard Bradley pursued his charge in Africa. Arriving in February, he opened negotiations with the local chief for Lemane, and after some difficulty obtained it in return for a payment equal to about £7.10.0 a year. He also obtained a promise that the convicts would not 'meet with the least molestation.' He then sought, and obtained, the approval of European planters in Gambia, who said that they hoped the Government would not drop 'so prudent a plan,' and who advised that December would be the best month for the convicts to arrive.[11]

Bradley told Sydney of these arrangements on his return when he gave his claim for expenses. He said in explanation of it that

> in conducting this Business I experienced Difficulties which I had no Idea of when I engaged with Your Lordship to undertake it. The Principal Men of the Country disputed the Right of the Chief to dispose of the Island, and to obtain their Consent the expence of the Purchase was increased in the Manner set forth in the Account.

Nepean wrote to Rose, the Treasury Secretary, on 3 February 1786, recommending that Bradley be paid £375 for goods given to the natives, and fifty guineas 'in consideration of his Trouble.' The Treasury Lords approved these payments on 18 August, as Nepean prepared to announce to them the scheme which had superseded the Lemane one.[12]

CHAPTER 2

Towards a new policy
1785-1786

I   The Lemane embroglio

The Administration evidently adopted the Lemane scheme with some trepidation, for in announcing it to Nichol, Nepean cautioned,

> You are certainly the best Judge, whether any Person brought before You for a Petit Larceny should suffer so severe a Sentence as that [of transportation to Africa], which You know in the routine of Punishment is considered as next in degree to that of Death. . . . If you follow my advice You will Sentence the Convicts generally to 'Transportation beyond the Seas,' for should the Present Plan, from obstacles that may hereafter appear, be laid aside, some other must shortly be adopted, and upon that general Sentence You can have no further trouble.[1]

Obstacles were not long in appearing. Five days after Nepean wrote to Nichol, Sydney discussed the scheme with Edward Thompson, and received a most unfavorable response. Thompson recorded that

> I had a long conference with Lord *Sidney* about the state of the public jayls — & the disposal of the convicts. He informed me — by the recommendation of some African Captains, particularly M.ʳ *Bradley* that they had agreed to send 150 people — 500 miles up Gambia River, to the Isle *Le Main* — with implements & six months provisions — & the Negroes were to receive a Stipend to retain them there.

Thompson responded that

> there was an inhuman appearance in the style of the business, & it would never be received by the people of England — it was in one word an African grave, & they went there devoted to Death. M.ʳ *Pit* came in, & they stared, surprised at the boldness of my assertion — & concluded — it was immediately necessary to clear the prisons. I proposed to investigate *Sierra Leona* — & I did hope it was a better place — & that a Colony might be cherished there.[2]

A more positive result of this conference, however, was that Thompson added the idea of convicts to an earlier one of settling the Das Voltas Bay region of southwest Africa. A year and a half before, he had suggested to Lord Keppel that he explore this coast between 20° and 30°S,

'where there was a fertile Country defended North from the Portuguese
& South from the Dutch by high, barren, inaccessible mountains—&
between these extremes there were fine Harbours.' Cape Das Voltas
would 'answer in point of Harbour, climate, & fertile Country,' he had
said, and he proposed settling there 'for our Indiamen to call at & refit &
come up with [the] SE trade in war to avoid the Enemy—without returning the beaten road from the Cape, & the necessity of puting into the
Rio de Janario.' Keppel and Portland, Thompson recorded, 'minutely attended' to his proposal, but they thought 'in so infant a peace it would be
dangerous to alarm our new Friends by exploring. & they therefore proposed to postpone it until the succeeding year—when vessels should sail
under my directions.'[3]

Now, shifting his focus from South America back to Africa, Thompson put this idea forward again, first in conversations with Charles
Jenkinson on eastern strategy, then to the Lord Mayor and Judges of
London, then to Sydney. On 25 February, he told Jenkinson that the
Ministry should investigate the Andaman Islands, 'as a protection for
our fleets to secure & defend *Coromandel* & *Bengal*. after which I repeated
to him the advantage of De Voltas in South Africa for our India men.'
He then wrote up a proposal to settle the area with Loyalists and convicts, which he gave to Sydney on 21 March.[4]

Thompson's hostility to the Lemane scheme was the first discernible
ripple of what shortly became a very strong surf. On 3 February, in the
second week of the new session, a Commons member asked for information about the steps that the Administration were taking to implement
the Transportation Act;[5] and on 16 March Burke denounced transportation to Africa in the strongest terms. 'Every principle of justice and
humanity,' he said, required

> that punishment should not be inflicted beyond those prescribed and defined
> to particular kinds of delinquency. . . . There was, in the mode of punishing
> by transportation, no distinction made between trivial crimes, and those of
> greater enormity, all indiscriminately suffered the same miserable fate,
> however unequal their transgressions, or different their circumstances. [As
> well] . . . some regard should, in these times of difficulty and distress, be paid
> to frugality and economy; [and transportation] was . . . attended with a very
> considerable expense.

He then said that

> he wished to know what was to be done with these unhappy wretches; and to
> what part of the world it was intended, by the minister, they should be sent.
> He hoped it was not to Gambia, which though represented as a wholesome
> place, was the capital seat of plague, pestilence, and famine. The gates of Hell
> were there open night and day to receive the victims of the law; but not those
> victims which either the letter, or the spirit of the law, had doomed to a
> punishment, attended with certain death.

He proposed that the House should be told of the state of the prisons; and he ended by asking 'whether any contract had yet been entered into for sending these convicts to the coast of Africa,' for Pitt to answer, 'No.'[6]

Burke's enquiry came after the Administration had decided to postpone the scheme until September — which was undoubtedly as fortunate for the Minister as it was for the convicts who would have been sent. With the postponement, the Administration could effectively deny that they had finally adopted the scheme when their critics again took the matter up the next month. On 11 April, Lord Beauchamp, who had voiced some opposition the previous year, pointed out that the Commons had yet to receive details of how the Administration intended 'to dispose of felons under sentence of transportation.' Pitt pleaded the excuse of 'a very great hurry of public business,' but said he would speed the report. He then tried to learn Beauchamp's likely grounds of objection, by asking 'the nature of the motion that he intended to propose on a future day,' but Beauchamp would not be drawn.

Burke then joined in, saying that

> he could not reconcile it with justice, that persons whom the rigour of the law had spared from death, should, after a mock display of mercy, be compelled to undergo it, by being sent to a country where they could not live, and where the manner of the death might be singularly horrid; so that the apparent mercy of transporting those wretched people to Africa, might with justice be called cruelty: the merciful gallows of England would rid them of their lives in a far less dreadful manner, than the climate or the savages of Africa would take them.

Pitt interrupted that Burke was 'assuming facts, without any better authority than report.' Burke replied that 'he understood that 75 of them were now on board a ship, which might sail before morning, and the wind would soon carry them out of the reach of the interposition of parliament;' and he cuttingly compared the full state of the prisons with the empty state of the House.[7]

The result of these interchanges was first, that the Government presented the Orders in Council of 11 March to Parliament on 12 April; and next, that on 20 April the Commons reconvened the Committee on Transportation, under Beauchamp's chairmanship,

> to enquire what Proceedings have been had in the Execution of an Act, passed in the Twenty-fourth Year of the Reign of His present Majesty, intituled, 'An Act for the effectual Transportation of Felons and other Offenders'.[8]

The Committee had a heterogeneous composition. In addition to Beauchamp, Fox, Burke, Fergusson, Burgoyne, Eden, Maitland, Mulgrave, and Palmerston were named to it; and as well, 'all Knights for Shires, Gentlemen of the Long Robe, and Merchants, in the House.'[9] Altogether, some 46 members attended at least once the hearings that the Committee held between late April and late May. Prominent among those who came with some regularity were the Chairman (all the eleven sessions for which minutes have survived), Burke (6), Philips (7), Strachey (6), Eden (3), and John Call (8). Call was thus after Beauchamp the most frequent attender—a point of considerable significance.[10]

Call was not present when the Committee was formally convened on 26 April, and Thomas Bailey, a magistrate, told of the recent difficulties in effecting sentences of transportation. He was there the next day, however, when Nepean testified about the Administration's intentions. Nepean did not have an easy task. He explained that the Africa Company had refused to take any more convicts at its settlements, and that therefore 'a Plan has been suggested, for the Transportation of Convicts to the Island of *Lemane*, about 400 Miles up the River Gambia'. He said that this site had been chosen partly in the absence of suggestions of others. In reply to the question of 'whether the Plan respecting the Island of *Lemane* is finally determined on', the Under-Secretary said 'that it is under the Contemplation of Government, and preferred to every other Plan, though not finally resolved on;' and he added, that it would have been put into effect were the season for sailing not so far advanced. He then gave details of the scheme.[11]

John Boon, a surgeon who had lived in Sengal for three years, followed Nepean, to tell of 'Putrid Fevers' and 'Fluxes' being prevalent among Europeans in the area, and that a Field Labourer 'could not live a Month, unless he had an able Surgeon with him.' Moreover, he said 'that no Reliance could be placed on the Faith of the Natives—That they would rob any Settlers that might be sent there of their Tools, and of every Thing they could lay their Hands upon, particularly Iron.'[12]

The Committee then heard from John Barnes, who announced that the Lemane idea was originally his, and that he and Sydney had worked out its details in conversation. Barnes testified to the healthiness and fertility of the area; that the natives were friendly; to the efficacy of the scheme proposed; and that Britain was likely to receive benefits from it.[13]

Call and the Recorder of London testified on 28 April. Call said that he had visited both Senegal and Gambia in 1750, that '*Europeans* almost generally laboured under Fluxes or Fevers,' that convicts were likely to arrive debilitated and unfit for work, that conflicts with the natives would inevitably follow, and that the inescapable mortality amongst the crew would reduce the guardship's effectiveness. The Recorder described the working of the new Act, with its provisions for the fixing of the place of transportation by Order in Council.[14]

Sir George Young, Sturt, Edward Thompson, Henry Smeathman, and Barnes appeared on 2 May. Young cited his four tours of duty on the Africa station, and said that it would be impossible to restrain 'a Colony of Convicts, without Order or Government,' that 'if the Convicts

were armed they would probably kill and rob the Natives, or if un-
armed, the Natives would rob and kill them;' that the natives of Gambia
were 'very peaceable, if well treated, but very revengeful, if insulted;'
and that 'Death would be the Consequence of [European labourers] continuing an Hour exposed to the Sun.'[15]

Sturt, who had accompanied the convicts to Cape Coast Castle in
1782, gave details of their bad behaviour and desertion. Thompson said
that the area was generally unhealthy, and that the natives were likely to
kill the convicts—and that, if they didn't, fevers and the climate would.
Moreover, he said, a convict settlement needed more control than a
guardship stationed downstream would provide. Smeathman, who had
lived in Sierra Leone for four years, said that the natives were 'exceedingly vindictive.' Barnes offered what opposing testimony he
could.[16]

The next day, Nevan and Nesbitt added to the testimony concerning
the unhealthiness of the area, and the treachery of the natives; and
Richard Akerman gave details of Newgate's crowded state.[17]

The Committee then ended the first stage of their hearings, by preparing an interim report in which they reproduced this testimony, and
which they presented to the House on 9 May. Pitt could scarcely have
been happy with the results. He had been embarrassed, first by Thompson's private attack on Barnes and Sydney's scheme, then by Beauchamp
and Burke's public ones. Then, under Beauchamp's guidance, the Committee had heard a stream of witnesses, Administration supporters
among them, who had tellingly exposed the scheme's inadequacies, and
castigated it for its callousness. The scheme of course thoroughly deserved the censure it received—one of simple 'dumping', it was ill-
conceived and grossly expedient; and the adverse opinions which the
Committee gathered made it impossible for the Administration to
persevere with it.

Why they adopted it in the first place is a matter for speculation. The
most likely explanation is that the other Cabinet ministers simply accepted it at Sydney's suggestion, without examining it closely. The
Committee's interim report also helped to end this situation, for, from
this point onwards, Pitt saw to it that his Majesty's Principle Secretary of
State for Home and Colonial affairs had a nominal hand only in the real
business of his office.

II   *Botany Bay or Das Voltas Bay?*

The Administration acted decisively in the second stage of the
Beauchamp Committee's hearings to turn affairs in their favour; and
their manoeuvrings give a fascinating insight into the political process of

the time. They had friendly Committee members ask their questions;
they fed the Committee information; they intervened to relieve
Beauchamp of the responsibility for the Committee's final recommendations, and thus ensure that these endorsed their new scheme for the convicts. Evan Nepean and John Call took the leading parts in this play; we
may therefore know that Pitt quietly directed it.

Having determined that Gambia was not a suitable region to which to
transport convicts, the Committee now looked for one that was; and
almost all the testimony which they gathered concerned New South
Wales. James Matra spoke to this point three times. The Committee's
minutes for the first of these occasions, 6 May, have not survived, but
those of the second show that Matra first presented the proposal he had
earlier made to the Government. On 9 May, when Matra again appeared (and with Call among the members present), the Committee
opened their questioning with:

> Supposing Colonization to be out of the Question & that the only Object was
> the Inquiry of this Committee Viz. to send Criminals out of the Kingdom,
> that a Guard Ship and some Marines being sent to controul them 3 or 400
> might not be sent in proper Transports and established in a Situation where
> by hard Labour if furnished with proper Tools and Seeds they might be able to
> provide convenient Residence and future Subsistence for themselves and
> those appointed to govern and direct them.

Matra thought that 500 might be safely sent, if the guard ship remained.

Interestingly, the members showed that they did nor rule out a free
colonization of New South Wales. Could both sorts of settlements exist
at a distance from each other, so that there might be no intercourse between them, they asked? Matra was certain that both could. He thought
that an expedition should sail from England not later than the beginning
of August, and that, given necessary stops for provisions and materials
at the Cape and other places, the voyage would take a minimum of
about six months. He told how on Cook's first voyage they had been on
the coast of New South Wales between April and July, and had found
the climate 'perfectly agreeable to European Constitution;' that the inhabitants of New Caledonia and Tahiti were 'of a quiet Nature;' and as
happy 'as human Nature generally are;' that since the Tahitian women
preferred European men, they could be brought to the new settlement
'in any Number.'

The Committee then raised a point that was later to be of considerable
significance. 'Do you think,' they asked, 'Government would run any
risk in attempting this plan without further examination than you or any
body you know would give them of that Country?' 'I think they would
not,' Matra replied. He added that rather than see the idea dropped he
would, if the Administration wished, 'undertake it not on the footing of a
Contractor but as an Officer under the Governm.ᵗ to be the Conductor &

Governor.' On being asked whether he meant 'as a sober regular Colony or as a Colony of Convicts,' he replied, 'Both or either.'

If the scheme were for a colony of 500 convicts, Matra continued, he would need a force of 200 Marines and a guardship (a 40-gun ship 'of the Old Build' would be most suitable). The colony would need to be under military law, and ministers of religion should be sent. He concluded by saying that he had not calculated the likely costs of transporting convicts to New South Wales; and that the seeds and livestock needed to begin agriculture in the new settlement might be purchased at the Cape of Good Hope, Madagascar, or the Moluccas.[1]

Sir Joseph Banks appeared before the Committee the next day (10 May). The members told him that in view of their charge, they would be glad to know

> whe.r in your Voyage with Captain Cook it occurred to you that there were any places in the new discovered Islands to which persons of such Description might be sent in a Situation where they might be able by Labour to support themselves?

Banks replied that he had

> no doubt that the Soil of many Parts of the Eastern Coast of New South Wales between the Latitudes of 30 & 40 is sufficiently fertile to support a Considerable Number of Europeans who would cultivate it in the Ordinary Modes used in England;

and that Botany Bay was 'in every respect adapted to the purpose.' He confessed himself ignorant of the Aborigines' language and form of government, so he could not advise about negotiating the cession of an area, but he said that fish were plentiful on the coast, and there were no wild beasts. The timber appeared 'fit for all the purposes of House Building and Ship Building,' European cattle should thrive there, as should corn and pulse. Women for the 500 convicts might be brought from the Pacific Islands. Banks concluded by saying that 'from the Fertility of the Soil the timid Disposition of the Inhabitants and the Climate being so analogous to that of Europe I give this place the preference to all that I have seen.'

The Home Office now prepared a list of questions for a friendly member to ask Duncan Campbell,[2] whom the Committee interviewed together with Charles Coggan, the Clerk of the East India Company's shipping committee, on 12 May. The members heard Coggan first, obviously so as to have some idea of how much it might cost to send a convict to Botany Bay, a subject on which Matra had not offered advice. This is one of those moves which show both that the Committee took the idea of colonizing New South Wales seriously, and that they examined it with some care, for the Company's cost in sending men to their establishments in India was at the time the only likely guide to that of

sending convicts a further distance to the East. Coggan supplied figures
that showed this to be on average about £25 per man, but he pointed out
that this sum did not include the cost of a surgeon's services on the
voyage, of food or accommodation, and of some other minor expenditures.

Campbell followed Coggan. The old contractor briefly described his
transportation and trading activities to America, saying that, on
average, he had received £13 for the sale of each convict's labour, and
that he had also had the advantage of a homeward trade in tobacco. He
thought that he should have required a minimum of £12 per man 'for
Convicts to be debarred from any Export Trade & to be obliged to come
back in Ballast.' Then came the questions to which the Home Office
wanted answers.

> If you were to carry Convicts a Voyage of probably six Months to a place
> where no kind of Trade is carried on how much per man would you contract
> for? — I think the Ship ought not to be of less Tonnage than 700 or 800 for this
> purpose it ought to carry out 300 Convicts exclusive of Crew — then if she goes
> alone I apprehend 70 or 80 Men wo.^{d} be enough to man her — I must reckon
> on a 15 Months Voyage — provisions for the Ships Company for that
> time — for Convicts for the Outward Voyage, for 7 Months — I think it could
> not be contracted for less then £30 a Man. — If the Ship carried only 200 what
> could it be done for then? — about £40 a Man.

Did these figures include the costs of a Surgeon and medicine? — yes, 'all
Expenses and a profit to the Undertaker of the plan.'

A letter from Campbell, 'relative to the Expence of transporting Convicts into the Southern Ocean beyond the Cape of Good Hope' was read
when the Committee next met, on 23 May. Then, the members had
some more questions for Matra, concerning how a colony in New South
Wales might obtain supplies. Could 'Cattle Sheep Poultry Hogs and
other Live Stock' be obtained 'more easily and expeditiously both for
Consumption as well as propagation from Countries much nearer to
New South Wales than the Cape of Good Hope,' they asked? Matra
thought so — variously from the Molucca, and the Society and Friendly
Islands. Could grain and vegetables be similarly obtained — Yes. Matra
also thought that the difficulty Campbell raised about a ship not being
able to carry 300 convicts and sufficient stores to feed them and the crew
would be removed if the ship were of 800 tons, or if a frigate and a store
ship accompanied her. He told the members that so far as he knew,
Cook was the only European to have claimed possession of the country;
and he concluded by saying that he foresaw no difficulty in negotiating
with the Dutch agent at Savu in the Moluccas, for food and livestock.

Anyone attending the Committee's deliberations to this point would
have been in no doubt that they would recommend transportation to
New South Wales. All the testimony they had heard at this second sitting

had related to this region, and offered materials from which to build a well-found and comprehensive scheme.

Despite their obvious interest in this prospect, however, the Administration decided again for Africa, even before the Committee completed its hearings. Nepean indicated this change in a tantalizingly incomplete memorandum, when he observed that

> as so much noise has been made and so many objections started to the sending the Convicts to the Island of Lemain, on Account of its very unhealthy situation, it may be adviseable to change the place of their Destination; The Southern Coast of Africa at or near Angra de Voltas between the Latitudes . . . is not subject to the same objections the Climate being nearly the same as that of Lisbon, and although the interior part is very little known or indeed even the Coast, it has been ascertained by Ships that have touched at places upon that Coast that the Natives are not inclined to Act with Hostility, and that they are amply. . . .[3]

While Nepean does not state the reasons for going to Das Voltas Bay, as he is obviously paraphrasing Thompson we may know these were commercial and strategic. Though incomplete, then, his memorandum is of great importance in our understanding of the Administration's motives henceforth for a convict colonization, for it is the earliest indication we have of what (for the reasons given in Part II) we may know to have been Pitt's acceptance of the view that they needed profoundly to increase their naval resources in the East. It also shows that Nepean had a central hand in this acceptance.

Signs of the Administration's new determination soon appeared. On 13 May, they issued another Order-in-Council fixing Africa as the place of transportation for a number of convicts. Then, when the Beauchamp Committee met on 25 May, John Call brought 'a paper containing Information with regard to the Western part of the Southern Coast of Africa accompanied with some Observations of his own.' This paper can have been no other than that which Thompson gave to Sydney on 21 March; and Call presumably had it from Nepean. Thompson's diary entries, and the Committee's final report, allow us to know its substance. Call's proposal for New South Wales tells us the substance of his 'Observations.'

The Committee now instructed Beauchamp to examine *Voyages* and *Travels* for information about, and to ask the Administration for any papers they might have relating to south-west Africa; and to form 'such a Report as he conceives they may be warranted to make relative to the Coast of New South Wales or the West Coast of Africa between the Latitude of 20° and 30° South.'

No minutes of any further discussions the Committee may have had are to be found, but their instructions to Beauchamp indicate the limits of their subsequent attention. Beauchamp evidently felt some chagrin at these limits, for he shortly afterwards said rather darkly,

The fact was, he, as chairman of the committee, should have stated some place; but a particular circumstance occurred during the sitting of the committee, that rendered it improper for him to mention it at the time.[4]

The Committee had their final report ready by 21 June,[5] and there are some very curious aspects to it. First, though they had requested Beauchamp to draw it up, it contains phrases, sentences, and indeed whole paragraphs, from Call's 1784 proposal for a settlement in the south Pacific. If Call did not in fact draft it, then Beauchamp accepted Call's perspectives and reproduced them. Second, despite all the Committee's attention in their hearings to New South Wales, and despite their charge to Beauchamp, it does not mention this region.

The Committee began by deploring the situation obtaining in the prisons and hulks. They asserted that 'these Mischiefs are in great Measure to be attributed to the Want of a proper Place for the Transportation of Criminals;' and they praised the former transportation to America.[6] They had not at all entertained the idea of sending convicts to labour under other European powers, they continued, and they then set forth the criteria they considered necessary for a new place of transportation:

> the Climate and Situation ought to be healthy; as, although many of [the convicts] have forfeited their Lives by their original Sentences, it is implied, by His Majesty's conditional Pardon, that their Transportation shall not expose them to any imminent Danger of their Lives—That unless they are removed to a considerable Distance, from whence the Means of returning may be rendered difficult, the End of their Transportation will be defeated—That, subject to this Caution, a Coast Situation is preferable to an Inland one, for the Convenience of supplying the Settlers until they are able to provide for their own Subsistence, as likewise to furnish them an Asylum, if any Natives should be disposed to annoy them.

The Committee were strongly opposed to one premise of Banks's 1779 suggestion, Call's New South Wales proposal, and Barnes's Gambia scheme. 'It was their decided Opinion,' they said,

> that the Idea of composing an entire Colony of Male and Female Convicts, without any other Government or Controul but what they may from Necessity be led to establish for themselves, can answer no good or rational Purpose—That such an Experiment has never been made in the History of Mankind—That the Outcasts of an old Society will not serve as the sole Foundation of a new one, which cannot exist without Justice, without Order, and without Subordination, to which the Objects in Question must of Necessity be Strangers—That Confusion and Bloodshed would probably soon take place among them; and that no Spot, however distant, can be pointed out by the Committee, in which the Mischiefs of realizing so dangerous a Project might not be felt on the Trade and Navigation of these Kingdoms.

They hen enunciated the principles that they had followed in their deliberations—that the nation should employ the convicts 'to the most useful Purposes,' namely, the enlarging of its commerce; and that places of transportation should, 'by the Commercial and Political Advantages . . . derived from them, indemnify the Public for the original Charge.' Accordingly, they said, they had considered

First, those parts of *Africa* which already belong to the Crown of *Great Britain*, or which may probably be acquired for the Purpose in Question. — Secondly, the Provinces as well as Islands which are subject to His Majesty in *America*. — And, lastly, such other Parts of the Globe as have been already, or which may be, taken Possession of for the Object under Consideration (if Policy warrants the Measure) without violating the Territorial Rights of any *European* Potentate or State.

They gave details only of their findings on Africa. They thought that grave disadvantages would attend transportation to either Gambia or Guinea, but that the area about the Das Voltas River was promising. No other Europeans had settled or claimed this region, the native inhabitants were peaceable, and it was highly probable that these would, 'without Resistance, acquiesce in Ceding as much Land as may be necessary, for a stipulated Rent.' It was coastal, it was fertile and had abundant water, there were great herds of horses, cattle, and sheep, and the climate was healthy. There was copper in the mountains,* and a 'fine Bay and Harbour for the Shelter of Shipping' at Angra Das Voltas. A settlement here might become a useful port of supply for ships returning from the East, and might also 'promote the Purposes of future Commerce or of future Hostility in the *South Seas*.'

The Committee thought that region would be a suitable one for the Loyalists as well as the convicts, but they said that if the Administration established a convict colony here, they should police it with marines, and place a wise and prudent officer in charge, giving him 'the most absolute Controul over the Settlers;' and they recommended Thompson as 'the

---

* Copper had become of considerable strategic importance during the war of 1776-83, as the following statement by Middleton indicates:

It was at this time that I recommended to Lord Sandwich the coppering of our line of battle ships, as the only means of augmenting our force. His lordship liked the measure, but thought it too bold to be adopted without his Majesty's concurrence. For this purpose I accompanied him to Buckingham House, when his Majesty, on being informed of the means used to prevent injury to the iron work, immediately saw the propriety of the measure and approved of it. Having, in consequence of this approbation, secured all the copper at the different mines, at the then market price, we went immediately to work, and in a few months produced upwards of thirty sail of the line, and more frigates, swimming on copper; and by the end of two years more, the whole fleet was coppered. The measure may have been said to have increased the services of the fleet [by] one third, and was the means of preventing more than one of our line of battle ships (the Ardent) from being captured during the whole of the war, notwithstanding we had more than two ships to one opposed to us — French, Spanish and Dutch.

(Barham, III, 16)

fittest Person for the Service.' They also said that they recommended the idea

> so far only as the Commercial and Political Benefits of a Settlement on the South West Coast of *Africa* may be deemed of sufficient Consequence to warrant the Expence inseparable from such an undertaking.

Yet at the same time they mitigated the effect of this caution by appealing to the nation's imperial inclination. In Call's voice, they pointed out that

> all the Discoveries as well as great Commercial Establishments now existing in distant Parts of the Globe, have been owing to the Enterprize and persevering Exertions of Individuals, who, at great personal Risks, frequent Losses, and in some cases total Ruin, have opened the Way to the greatest National Advantages—That the First Settlements in *North America* were undertaken under every Circumstance of an inhospitable Climate and an ungrateful Soil, as well as the fiercest Attacks from the Natives; yet, in the Space of 200 Years, a new World has sprung up, under many untoward Circumstances to which the Undertaking in Question does not appear to be exposed.

In recommending Das Voltas Bay, then, the Beauchamp Committee gave both Thompson and the Administration what they wanted; and the Administration moved quickly to implement the recommendation. On 22 August, Sydney formally asked the Admiralty to have Thompson survey the region, 'in order to fix upon a proper Spot for making a Settlement upon that Coast, if such a Measure should hereafter be judged expedient.' Thompson had been preparing for such service for some time. Late the previous year, he had begun to gather officers skilled in survey, and had asked Howe for a suitable ship, so that he might be able to 'produce an accurate Chart of Africa—from Blanco to S! Thomas.' Howe had approved the idea, and added the *Nautilus* to Thompson's command; and the Navy Board had begun to fit the squadron out. On Sydney's request, the Board completed this task quickly, and Thompson sailed at the end of September.[7]

### III	*After the decision for Das Voltas Bay*

Pitt and Thompson may have had what they wanted from the Beauchamp Committee hearings, but others were disappointed. In September 1785, Sydney arranged for Moore to ship some thirty transportees to Honduras, 'a part of them to be employed in cutting Logwood, on his own account, and the others to be disposed of as Opportunities may offer.' In October, after consulting Howe, he turned down the Dutch Ambassador's proposal to send transportees into his country's merchant marine. Between September and December, following a suggestion from Rose, the Home Office arranged for some three hundred convicts to be put on hulks at Langston Harbour, to be employed on public works at Portsmouth and Plymouth 'until such Time as their Sentences can be conveniently carried into execution.' These were measures unambitious, and while their implementation gave Nepean the opportunity to repeat the office formula about crowded prisons and imminent epidemics, they were very much stop-gap ones.[1]

By 1786, Sydney was taking very little hand in Colonial, and even in Home affairs. Pitt was deciding matters, and Nepean was implementing his decisions. William Smith described the prevailing situation pointedly when, piqued with Sydney's dilation in confirming his appointment as Chief Justice of Quebec, he observed: 'Poor Nepean! He knows not what to say & is willing to conceal Mr. Pitt's Contempt of the Secretary of State.'[2] After disagreeing with Pitt over the slave trade in mid-1789, Sydney resigned from the Ministry, to receive the Chief-Justiceship of the Eyre of Forests north of the Trent, a sinecure worth £2,500 a year. Then, as now, political mediocrity might have its rewards.

Little now remains to mark Sydney's tenure of great office, more than that during it Britain colonized New South Wales, and the first governor of this colonization gave his name to what has become one of the world's great cities. Because the convicts were the Home Office's responsibility, historians have considered Sydney as the principal in this move; and generations of Australians have known him as the person who defined the circumstances of their nation's beginning when he announced the decision to colonize with the preamble,

> The several Goals and Places for the Confinement of Felons in this Kingdom being in so crouded a State that the greatest danger is to be apprehended not only from their Escape but from Infectious Distempers which may hourly be expected to break out amongst them; His Majesty desirous of preventing by every possible means the ill consequences which might happen from either of these causes, has been pleased to signify to me His Royal Commands that Measures should immediately be pursued for sending out of this Kingdom such of the Convicts as are under Sentence or Order of Transportation.

It is ironic, and yet indicative of Sydney's true role, that he was primarily responsible for neither decision nor definition, nor, indeed, even for the letter which conveyed these.

The wheel of Call and Young's fortunes also turned unfavourably. There are some very curious, and still obscure, aspects to the brothers-in-law's activities at this time. On the one hand, in testifying against the Lemane scheme, they assisted in what was evidently a well-concerted attempt to embarrass the Administration and prevent their pursuing it. On the other hand, Call then helped the Administration, by bringing Thompson's Das Voltas Bay scheme to the Committee's attention, and, seemingly, by writing the final report recommending it. Then, on the day on which this report was ready, the pair asked for a grant of Norfolk Island. They must have done so knowing that the Committee's recommendation was for Das Voltas Bay; and we may therefore wonder further about their motives, for with the Administration's attention turned to Africa in preference to New South Wales, they might have seen the way open for private interests to exploit the Pacific's resources.

On 21 June, Call and Young told the East India Company that they and others had

> it in the Contemplation to form a Settlement in the Pacific Ocean, in the lat.^{de} 29° South, and Longitude 168°16 East, and other small Islands adjacent; for the pursuit of further Discoveries — for the Cultivation of the Flax plant — & Manufacture of that valuable Material into Cordage — and for the supplying Masts from thence for Shipping with which it abounds.
>
> The Memorialists conceive before they enter upon the pursuit of this Enterprise or make Application for a Grant of Norfolk Island, or any other Territory in the Southern Ocean between the Cape of Good Hope and the Streights of Magellan, it would be proper to obtain the Sanction of the East India Company to this Undertaking lest it might be construed into an Infraction of their chartered rights.
>
> Your Memorialists therefore humbly sollicit Your Concurrence & Support in forwarding this Enterprise which, if carried into effect, they are persuaded will prove of great Utility, by furnishing a Supply of those valuable Articles of Cordage and Masts for Your Shipping in India, which are now obtain'd at a most enormous Expence; and from their Scarcity have often reduced the maritime Force employed in the East Indies, to great Inconvenience and even Distress.[3]

The Court of Directors considered the request the next day, and referred it to the Committee of Correspondence.[4] This committee then sought Alexander Dalrymple's opinion of the scheme.

The hydrographer gave this in on 13 July. He began by asserting that Norfolk Island was 'unequivocally' within the limits of the Company's charter. He thought the resources of this small island would scarcely be able to provide a regular supply of naval materials; that it would be 'madness' to leave the East India squadron dependant on such a remote place; and that in any case supplies might be had from India, and places much nearer to it. 'This Project of a Settlement in that quarter has appeared in many Proteus-like forms,' he continued,

> sometimes as a half-way house to China, again as a check upon the Spaniards at Manila; and their Accapulco Trade; sometimes as a receptacle for transported Convicts; then as a Place of Asylum, for American Refugees; and sometimes as an Emporium, for supplying our Marine Yards with Hemp or Cordage: or for carrying on the Fur-Trade to the NW Coast of America; just as the Temper of Ministers was supposed to be inclined to receive a favourable impression.

He disparaged the reasons that had been variously advanced in justification of the idea. The bulk of the hemp, and the distance, meant that the idea of shipping it to India (or anywhere else) was not a feasible one. The colony in the south Pacific was hardly likely to bother the Spaniards. This route to China was not shorter or easier than the usual one. Such a settlement was not likely to further the fur trade. Any colony in New Holland would soon become independent, with inconvenience both to the Company and the nation.

Dalrymple was firmly convinced that these were specious reasons; and that the true purpose underlying the proposal was the engaging in illicit trade, which would undermine the Company's position. 'When I first heard of the Project,' he said,

> I was clearly convinced, that the greater part, at least, of these pretentions, were only the ostensible reasons, urged to cover other designs, of great and important consequence to the Welfare of this Country and of The Company, which, so far as concerns the exclusive Charter, is indivisible.

At one time, he asserted, the project was 'to have been protected by Imperial Colours, as well as English' and that 'the true prospects of the Undertakers' were to conduct 'an illicit Trade, under pretext of a Colony.' He urged the Company to reject it.[5]

It is now difficult to know how much substance there is to Dalrymple's claims, some of which do not appear elsewhere. He was not a disinterested commentator where the Company was concerned, he was prone to letting his obsessions run rampant. On the other hand, since he had some acquaintance with Banks, and since he was one of those who had proposed Young for election to the Royal Society, he may have had private information.

There are some aspects to Call and Young's activities which suggest that Dalrymple's claims may have been valid. There is the question of whom the pair's partners were, for the Administration was under some pressure at this time from independent merchants to remove the Company's monopoly of eastern trade; and when Call described his New South Wales proposal to Hastings, he mentioned the attractions of South American trade and north-west Pacific fur trade, but not that of south Pacific naval stores.[6] Dalrymple's reference to a former prospect of 'Imperial' protection suggests that the pair may have had some link with William Bolts, who pursued ambitious trading schemes in the East on behalf of the Austrians and the French in the 1780s.

Again, Call and Young were not on good terms with the Company. The Court of Directors had censured Call in the late 1760s; and in 1784, against the Court's wishes, he had persuaded Pitt and Dundas to recognize the validity of all the private claims against the Nabob of Arcot. Young was at this time engaged in a law suit against one of the

Company's agents, by which he sought to obtain prize money he thought due to him from 1778.

In any event, the Company quickly dismissed the pair's request, with the Committee of Correspondence recommending against it, and the Court accepting this recommendation, on 13 July, and the Court informing the petitioners of this a week later.[7]

What other steps Young and Call may then have taken to realize their scheme for a south Pacific colonization are also obscure. Young later remarked that it 'seem'd to fall asleep for two Years, and as M.[r] Matra was about to leave England, I put the plan into the hands of some merchants, when it was immediately adopted.'[8] Thomas Rowcroft later said that Young had enlisted the help of his relative, Thomas Hubbert, a shipbroker and sailcloth manufacturer; and that these men had decided that he, who was then only eighteen, should be the '*first Settler*, to populate that *almost* continent [New Holland].' 'A principle Object at the Moment,' Rowcroft explained, 'was the cultivation of the New Zealand Flax plant for the purposes of Hemp & Flax to place the British Navy out of the dependance on Russia.' The proposers made some progress towards mounting the scheme, 'with an adventure of the sum of £20,000 towards prosecuting the object . . ., on the condition, or implied dependance, on the approbation of *some protection* from the Government.' Then 'M.[r] Pitt very unexpectedly turned all he had heard & considered on this Spot to the redemption of a pledge he had made in Parliament or else where, to find some plan of relieving the over-crowded jails of the Kingdoms.'[9]

Rowcroft said that Young then abandoned 'his plans and views,' but this was clearly not so. In May 1788, Young and Call once more applied, this time directly to the Government, for a grant of Norfolk Island 'to them and their heirs for ever,' so that they might 'promote the Cultivation of the New Zeland Flax Plant, and the Growth of Pine Timber for Masts . . . for his Majestie's Ships of War in India.' The pair did not succeed with this application either, and they thereafter seem to have given the idea up.[10]

Matra, too, gave up his plans and views after the Beauchamp Committee hearings. He wrote rather melodramatically to Nepean on 18 May,

> it may be some satisfaction to you, that from the present nature and situation of things, I foresee my correspondence with you draws near a conclusion. I have indeed, a kind of presentiment, that even this, is the last letter you will have the trouble of receiving from me.

He said that he had now 'entirely relinquished all thoughts of another avocation, which was at one period of my life the ultimate object of my ambition'—which is presumably a reference to his repeatedly expressed desire to become the Governor of a minor colony. Accordingly, he asked

Nepean to renew his application for a grant in recognition of past service, so that he could liquidate his debts, and buy into a profession.[11]

There is no record of any Administration response to this plea; and Matra seems to have taken no further part in the colonization of New South Wales. In mid-1786, no doubt knowing that the Administration would not choose the unhappy Loyalist to head a colony, Banks had the Home Office give him the Consulship at Tangiers. Matra wrote to his mentor in May 1787: 'the Country you so kindly helped to place me in received me yesterday, and in high health and spirits.' It would have been good if his circumstances had more often allowed him to write in this vein.[12]

The Beauchamp Committee hearings constitute a great turning point in Britain's practice of transportation. On the one hand, they marked the end of hopes that the nation might simply and quickly resume the old mode, where contractors shipped the convicts to areas already settled by British nationals, and sold their labour to individuals. And they killed the prospects of alternative schemes built on the sands of expediency and private interest. On the other hand, they marked the development of what would soon become the new mode, where the Government itself would use the convicts to colonize a region not previously settled by British or other Europeans, in order to increase the nation's empire, and add to her capacity to defend her commerce.

PART II

*William Pitt
and naval strategy about
India, 1778-1811*

There ought to be no object more impressive on the feelings of the House, than to endeavour to preserve from further dismemberment and diminution, to unite and to connect what yet remained of our reduced and shattered empire.

PITT (1785)

[Britain and Holland] have each one original great object in view, . . . which do not clash in the smallest degree; That of Great-Britain is to maintain and preserve the Empire which she has acquired, in comparison of which even trade is a subordinate or collateral consideration.

DUNDAS (1787)

That the Power possessing the Cape of Good Hope has the key to and from the East Indies, appears to us self-evident and unquestionable. Indeed we must consider the Cape of Good Hope as the Gibraltar of India. . . . No fleet can possibly sail to or return from India without touching at some proper place for refreshment, and, in time of war, it must be equally necessary for protection.

CHAIRMEN, EAST INDIA COMPANY (1781)

I have desired Devaynes also to send you some papers relative to a scheme of a settlement on the Caffre coast, to answer in some respects the purposes of the Cape, and to serve also as a receptacle for convicts.

PITT (OCTOBER 1785)

It seemed to me to be Mr. Pitt's intention at all events that if Cape Voltas was not found to correspond with our expectations for the Settlement of the Convicts that some other Spot should be fixed upon to the Southward of the Line, and as that is his determination. . . .

NEPEAN (JUNE 1786)

I may venture to suppose that the finding a proper place to send our Convicts may again become a Naval question . . . having concluded that the [Prime] Minister might imagine it a Naval question. . . .

BLANKETT (AUGUST 1786)

I shall not, I hope, leave the Colony till it is in such a State as to repay Government the Annual Expence, as well as to be of the greatest consequence to this Country.

PHILLIP (OCTOBER 1786)

CHAPTER 3

War, 1778-1783

I *European seaborne empires*

There were great advances in naval technology in Europe in the fifteenth century, as shipwrights altered the build and rigging of vessels, astronomers and mathematicians evolved new navigational techniques, and engineers improved weapons. With the means of crossing oceans, of carrying exotic products home cheaply, and of defending their commerce and territory effectively, the European nations then entered on an extraordinary expansion. From the turn of the century, the Portuguese and Spanish explored and colonized the far-flung reaches of the world, and gained greatly in wealth, luxury, and political power. Desirous of similar good fortune, the Dutch, British, and French followed these southern neighbours into the New World and the East.[1]

The Dutch reached the East Indies in the 1590s, and in the next years established factories in Bantam, Acheen, Amboina and other places, and in Japan. Within thirty years, they had made Batavia (Jakarta) their headquarters, had commenced an administrative system to regulate spice production and centralize trade in the archipelago, and had all but expelled the British from it. By mid-century, they had greatly diminished the Portuguese presence there and in Ceylon. By its end, they had acquired a territorial empire with which to underwrite their trading one. As they established themselves in the East Indies, they also set up factories about the coasts of India. After capturing Negapatam on the south-east coast from the Portuguese in 1658, they made this their principal base there. While they were unable to gain the ascendency in India, they remained masters of the archipelago until towards the mid-1790s, and were the major suppliers of the spices which Europe so much desired.

The English moved into the East at the same time as the Dutch. Elizabeth granted the Governor and Company of Merchants of London trading into the East Indies their Royal charter on 31 December 1600, and after the Dutch had forced them from the archipelago, they concentrated their ventures on India, where they developed a profitable trade in indigo, cotton goods, saltpetre, pepper, cinnamon, sugar, calicoes, and coffee across the Seventeenth century. By the century's end, they had opened a trade with China. This Company was reorganized at the beginning of the Eighteenth century, and the merchants thereafter steadily consolidated their position. By 1750, they had divided their now substantial Indian establishment into three presidencies centred on Bombay, Fort St. George (Madras), and Fort William (Calcutta) in Bengal; and they maintained satellite factories at surrounding points.

The French became interested in eastern trade at the beginning of the Seventeenth century, but they did nothing substantial about this interest until 1664, when the King granted the Compagnie des Indes Orientales its letters-patent. This established factories at various points in India, but did not prosper much in fifty years, and was incorporated into the Compagnie des Indes in 1719, when the Government amalgamated the various companies trading overseas. This combine soon went bankrupt, however, when the East India branch was again reorganized, and thereafter had better success. By the mid-Eighteenth century, the French had developed a considerable centre at Pondicherry, and lesser ones at Mahé, Calicut, Surat, Masulipatam, and Chandernagore.

To lesser extents, other Europeans also adventured to the East. The Danes set up a company in 1616, which established factories about India, most notably at Tranquebar on the Coromandel Coast. This struggled until the 1730s, when it built up a successful trade in tea. The Austrian Emperor Charles VI licenced the Ostend Company in 1722. This quickly became a cover for independent merchants wishing to compete against the established companies, and, under pressure from other governments, Charles abolished it in 1731. The Swedes set up an India Company in 1731, which accommodated some of those merchants dispossessed of Ostend protection. In the mid-1770s, imbued with imperial aspirations, the Empress Maria Theresa chartered the Imperial Asiatic Company of Trieste, and engaged the Dutch-born adventurer William Bolts to further its fortunes. In the next years, Bolts set up factories at Delagoa in east Africa, and on the Malabar and Coromandel coasts.

Inevitably, this maritime expansion gave powerful images to national iconographies as it gave wealth to exchequers. The sturdy oak repelled waves and formed walls that kept the enemy at bay. Masts and spars were 'Jewells that so highly concern the safety and service of the State.' Cordage made 'the very sinews and muscles of a Ship.' Sails unfurling transformed a wintered forest to one suffused with spring. Ships in motion seemed like swans athwart the tide. Navigators probed the dark recesses of the world. Missionaries and settlers set torches of true religion and civilization burning there. Merchants freighted argosies home.

Striking as this imagery was (and is), the technology which gave rise to it had inherent limitations. The Europeans needed constant supplies of naval timber, masts, spars, and hemp and flax to build and maintain their marines. Curvature, magnetic variation, ocean currents, and the absence of accurate timepieces made it impossible for navigators to calculate longitude accurately. Scurvy and other diseases wrecked havoc amongst the crews.

Until they developed theoretical bases which allowed them to find fundamental solutions, the Europeans coped with these difficulties by sailing with winds and currents, and by establishing places of supply along their routes. A typical sailing pattern for India ships involved leaving the home port in winter or spring, proceeding beyond the European and north-west African coasts, refreshing if necessary at the Azores or Cape Verde Islands, then heading towards and along the coast of Brazil, perhaps refreshing at Rio de Janeiro. They would then catch the westerlies, and pass below Africa into the Indian Ocean. Reaching this ocean in summer, they were then able to run up to their destinations with, first the south-east trades, and, when above the equator, the south-west monsoons.

Because the winds were less certain, ships generally made a longer voyage home. They would sail from India in winter, cross the top of the Indian Ocean, edge southwards along the east coast either of Madagascar or Africa (the 'outer' and 'inner' passages), refresh at the Cape of Good Hope, and then proceed to Europe, refreshing again if necessary at the Cape Verde Islands.

The Europeans established a network of bases to service their ships plying these routes. In South America, amongst others, the Portuguese possessed the great port of Rio, with its fine harbour and abundant hinterlands. They had São Paulo de Luanda and São Filipe de Benguela on the west coast of Africa, and Sofala and Moçambique on the east. They had Diu and Goa with its good harbour and dockyards in India, Timor in the East Indies, and Macau on the edge of China.

The Dutch had the incomparable Cape of Good Hope, which formed a fulcrum of the southern oceans' wind and current systems. This colony's two bays together provided anchorage for most of the year, and while the docks at Simon's Bay were not extensive enough to permit either careening or rebuilding, they were adequate to the making of other repairs. Its fortifications were sound, its climate healthy, and its agriculture abundant. On the south-east coast of India, the Dutch had Negapatam, which gave reasonable anchorage for half a year and some food; and on the north-east coast of Ceylon, Trincomalee, the only port in European possession to face the Bay of Bengal and offer safe anchorage year round. Trincomalee had one of the finest of natural harbours, but its hinterland was unproductive jungle, and in the eighteenth century the Dutch had not developed its naval potential much, nor fortified it extensively. In the East Indies, they had a network of minor bases, and major ones at Malacca and Batavia. Batavia was notoriously unhealthy, but it stood at the junction of great sea routes, and offered sheltered anchorage, efficient dockyards, and abundant food and naval supplies, and was accordingly of considerable strategic importance.

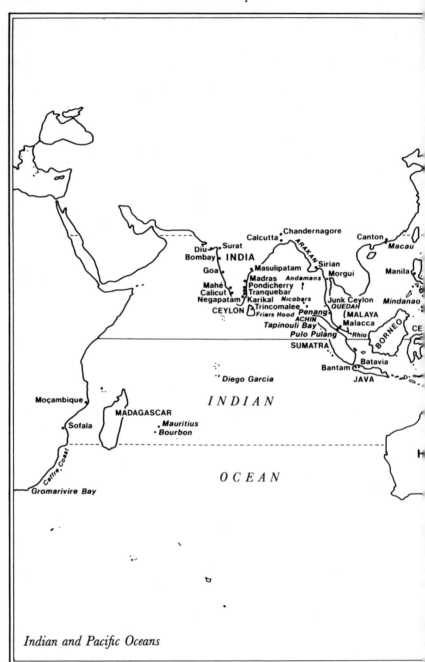

Indian and Pacific Oceans

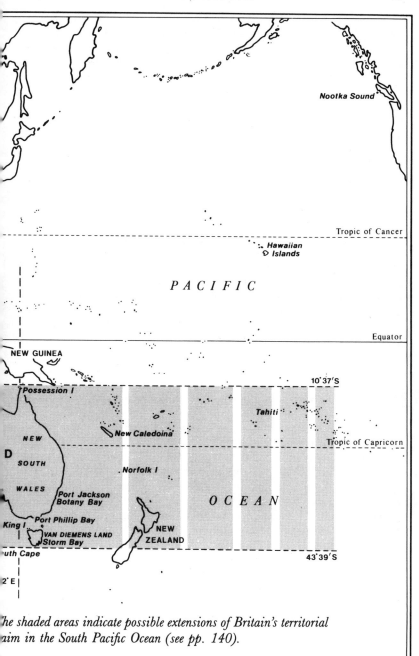

Nootka Sound

Tropic of Cancer

:. Hawaiian
Ꝺ Islands

P A C I F I C

Equator

NEW GUINEA

10°37'S

Possession I

Tahiti

NEW

New Caledoina

Tropic of Capricorn

D

SOUTH

WALES

Norfolk I

O C E A N

Port Jackson
Botany Bay

King I

Port Phillip Bay

VAN DIEMENS LAND
Storm Bay

NEW
ZEALAND

uth Cape

43°39'S

2° E

*he shaded areas indicate possible extensions of Britain's territorial
aim in the South Pacific Ocean (see pp. 140).*

France possessed a major base at Mauritius, and a lesser one at Bourbon (Réunion). Mauritius was not self-sufficient in food, and the authorities had to import from the Cape and Java (and in a minor way from Madagascar). As well, the climate was unhealthy, the weather was unpredictable, and reefs and prevailing winds made the approach to the island hazardous. However, it had a good harbour, where the French built adequate dockyards which they kept well-supplied. Bourbon was of limited use, for it too had the disadvantages of inadequate agriculture, hazardous approaches, and unhealthy climate; and it lacked a good harbour as well. Both bases lay adjacent to the outward as well as homeward routes, however, and while their distance from India detracted a little from their usefulness, together they constituted a satisfactory springboard for war or trade. This was as well for the French, for they had only minor anchorages about the coasts of India (at Mahé, Pondicherry, and Karikal, among other places).

The Danes kept a supply of stores at Tranquebar; and on the Austrians' behalf, Bolts settled Car-Nicobar as a place of refreshment and refit, and investigated Tristan da Cunha.

Between Europe and India, the British possessed only St. Helena to assist their ships. This small island had no harbour, only an open roadstead. It was not self-sufficient in food, and authorities had to import supplies from the Cape. As the winds prevailed from the south-east, it was not easily approached from Europe; and conversely, shipping in its road was very vulnerable to attack by cruisers sailing out of Mauritius or the Cape. In India, Bombay served them better for it had good harbour and dockyard facilities, and a large hinterland with food supplies. They were less well-placed on the eastern coasts, however, for though Madras and Calcutta were also foci of extensive hinterlands, these places offered only inadequate shelter to large ships during the north-east monsoon, and poor dockyard facilities.

The Europeans equipped their naval arsenals at these bases in a combination of ways. Brazil offered good ship timber, and the Portuguese, less prejudiced than others in favour of things European, built small warships and merchantmen in their yards at Bahia, Rio de Janeiro, and Belém do Pará. They also built ships of local timber in their Goa yard, but found Asian cordage and canvas inferior to European varieties, which they brought out. The Cape of Good Hope was very deficient in timber, and the Dutch sent building and naval varieties there from Europe, as well as other stores. They made more use of local materials at Batavia, but also brought out European ones. The French supplied their dockyards at Mauritius almost entirely from Europe, sending out timber, masts and spars, cables and cordage, and canvas. So, too, did the British at Bombay, despite the fact that the Indian artificers they employed otherwise used teak and other local materials. The Dutch, French, Portuguese and the British all obtained saltpetre in India.

As a consequence of this general habit of the Europeans drawing their stores from Europe, these yards were often severely limited in their ability to meet the calls on them. A yard's having supplies depended first on the general availability in Europe, then on home officials obtaining adequate quantities of these, then on their despatching them with foresight. It depended, too, on store ships surviving tempests and shoals, and reaching their destination. Moreover, the safe arrival of a cargo did not in itself guarantee that stores would be available. Sails mildewed and rotted on the voyage out, cables deteriorated in the tropical heat, masts and spars rotted in the warm ponds, a cyclone might see a carefully-compiled supply reduced at once, with no prospect of its being rapidly replaced. In peace, the Europeans countered these vicissitudes by drawing on each others' resources; in war, these vicissitudes often had a marked effect.

II   *British schemes to attack their neighbours' colonies*

Nowhere do we see this effect better than in the war of 1778-83. Britain and France opened hostilities in the spring of 1778, and while Mauritius and Bombay were too well fortified for either nation seriously to contemplate their capture, they were soon probing other bases for their weaknesses, and in the process realizing those of their own. Hastings and Vernon invested Pondicherry as soon as they received news of war, and Vernon engaged the French squadron there on 10 August. He had the best of the battle, but he could not pursue the retreating French because his artificers lacked materials to replace damaged masts, cordage, and sails. Sir George Young, whom Vernon then sent home to report on the state of the squadron, referred to this situation when he later wrote that scarcity of masts and cordage 'often reduced the Maritime Force, employ'd in the East Indies to great inconvenience and even distress:' and the Admiralty took account of it when they sent Hughes out to replace Vernon late in the year, loading the *York* with the stores Hughes would need to keep his ships at sea.[1]

Spain's entry into the war on the side of France in mid-1779 caused the British to consider at length how they might best employ their naval capacity in the East. John Call, that indefatigable proposer of schemes, suggested to North that the Administration mount

> an Expedition to the South Seas, to give countenance and Support to the In-
> habitants of Chili and Peru, by Assistance of Arms, ammunition, and Troops
> from India, that these Provinces or Kingdoms might be enabled to fulfil their
> disposition and throw off the Spanish yoke.[2]

The Administration then received another such proposal. Believing that the nation would be undone if it acted only in the defensive, Sir

John Dalrymple, one of the Barons of the Scottish Exchequer, suggested to Lord Germain, the Secretary of State for America, that a privateering expedition, sailing either from Britain by way of the Cape of Good Hope and New Zealand, or from India 'by the Phillipines to hold north, or by New Holland to hold south,' should raid the Spanish settlements on the west coast of South America. The adventurers might take initial goods and prizes to China and India, realize their value, re-equip their ships, and make another sally. As he waited for Germain to reply, Dalrymple acted on his belief that private persons should make 'public exertions,' and interested some Glasgow merchant friends in the venture.[3]

At first, the Secretary said that he approved of the idea, but that the nation lacked the naval resources to support it. He soon afterwards wrote more optimistically, however, and Dalrymple and his friends set to refining their proposal. In September, they said that they would take three ships via the Cape and New Zealand, though they were willing to enact a grander scheme if the Administration would help with a 40-gun ship and some frigates. Germain had Lord Sandwich appraise the proposal, and he continued to discuss it with the merchants, but then, at the turn of the year the Administration preferred 'another, to take the same route by the Cape of Good Hope, but to be conducted by the public.'[4]

The new version came from a William Fullarton and friends, who proposed a privateering voyage to the South Seas, which they would mostly finance, to sail in the spring, and to consist of two regiments and five warships, including one of 64 guns. At the same time, though, the Administration continued interested in another which Dalrymple was urging. This one, which originated with his brother, Major William Dalrymple, then serving in the West Indies, involved attacking the Spanish on the eastern coast of Central America, with 'the view . . . of obtaining possession of the River St. John and Lake Niccaragua and opening through them a communication with the South Sea.'[5]

Fullarton gave Germain a detailed proposal on 22 January 1780, and the Cabinet must then have formally approved both projects, for the Administration proceeded with preparations for them. On the one hand, they hastened their despatch to the West Indies of a squadron under Commodore Walsingham and an army under General Garth, who were to carry out the Nicaragua scheme if the Governor of Jamaica had not been able to. On the other, they commissioned Fullarton and Humberston as Lieutenant-Colonels, authorizing them to raise regiments of five hundred men, ordered artillery for these, and set about gathering another squadron.[6]

Both gods and men now made difficulties. Adverse winds kept Walsingham's squadron in port until the end of May, and the Opposition attacked the commissioning of Fullarton and Humberston. These circumstances effectively aborted both expeditions. By the time Walsingham and Garth reached the West Indies so too had the combined

Spanish-French fleet of some nineteen battleships and one hundred and fifty transports, with twenty-five thousand men — which meant that the British forces could not afford to leave the islands to help those which Dalling had sent to Nicaragua and which were floundering in the swamps. The Parliamentary attacks dissipated the Administration's enthusiasm for Fullarton and Humberston's scheme, and they effectively let it lapse.[7]

Fullarton, who was nothing if not persistent, and who besides saw the prospect of South American treasure diminishing, now seems to have sought the advice of Lord Mulgrave, Banks's friend and Sandwich's protege at the Admiralty, as a prelude to a renewed application. In a detailed memorandum seemingly written in May, Mulgrave weighed carefully the idea of complementary expeditions to the west and east coasts of Spanish America. If the Administration were to send orders early in June, he thought, these could arrive at Madras by mid-October, so that a force could leave from there in November. This could rendezvous with that from England at Trincomalee, and, if they were to attack Manila, they might pass below Java, proceed northwards through the Bali-Lombok passage, and reach their object in January. From Manila, they could shortly afterwards sail for Cape Blanco, refreshing at the (newly-discovered) Sandwich Islands on the way, so that they should arrive off the American coast in April. If the capture of Manila were not an object, the forces could either sail directly to the Sandwich Islands from their rendezvous, to arrive in March or April, or, they 'might proceed directly South touching at New Holland or New Zealand for refreshments & cross the Pacific Ocean in South Latitudes,' again to arrive at the coast of South America about mid-March at the earliest.

Concerning the 'Application of the Force in the Idea of Cooperation on the Eastern Side of Spanish America,' he observed that

> all Operations on that Side about St Johns River & Nicaragua should be compleated by the beginning of April, as the Rains set in in that Month which render the Climate fatal to Europeans.

If an expedition were to sail from England in late September or October, it might arrive at its destination in December or January, which was the earliest time it ought to be there.[8]

Mulgrave's raising the possibility of attacking Manila directly rather altered the scope of the proposed expedition, and, attending to the omen, Fullarton followed this revision when he again approached the Administration on 3 June.[9] While the need to quell the Gordon Riots delayed the Ministers' deciding on the merits of the new version immediately, North clearly obtained some provisional approval from his colleagues, for the next month he asked the Chairmen of the East India Company if they favoured it, and, if so, what help the Company could provide from India.

Either in preparation for the interview they had with the Minister and Fullarton on 18 July, or as a consequence of it, Devaynes and Sulivan produced a 'Sketch of an Expedition to the South Seas,' in which they agreed to provide transport for some one thousand, one hundred soldiers to Madras, and one 20- and two 40-gun ships there. They suggested that the expedition establish bases on Mindanao and Celebes, as spring-boards for the venture to the South Seas. While they saw that it might damage Spain's commerce and recover the sum she had agreed to pay the Company at the end of the last war, they doubted that it would be able to hold any settlement in Chile, Peru, or Mexico permanently. (Rather than because of any prospects it offered of enlarging British trade with South America, the Chairmen were interested in it because it offered the Company an opportunity to establish itself in the spice-producing islands of the East Indies.) North gave Fullarton and the Chairmen's proposals to Cabinet on 5 August, and the Ministers decided to send one 64-gun and one 32-gun ship and two thousand troops to join those the Company would supply in India.[10]

In consultation with North and Amherst, Sandwich then oversaw the planning of the expedition. Altering their ground somewhat, the Chairmen said on 9 August that they would furnish transport to Madras for 800 troops, and, in India, two 20-gun ships, and 2000 sepoys. They now doubted that the expedition could do much materially to injure Spain in America, however, and thought that it would be better employed in gaining an ascendency in the Eastern archipelago. They passed on Carteret's descriptions of sailing routes in this area the next day; and on 19 August, they said that they wished to occupy Celebes so as to 'secure them a share in the most valuable of all Commercial Branches, the Spices.'[11]

Cabinet approved these alterations, and the Administration reached a formal agreement with the Company a month later. Two thousand Royal troops would sail from England, and the Company would supply two thousand sepoys. The force would establish a naval base on Mindanao, and a commercial one on Celebes. They would them move against the Spanish settlements about the Pacific. The British section of the expedition would sail in December, to arrive at Madras the following April. The court notified the Indian Presidencies of the scheme in despatches of 2 October.[12]

Preparations for the expedition then went forward. The naval command was given to Commodore George Johnstone, an unsavoury character who had once been Governor of West Florida, and had failed as a negotiator in America, but who was of the King's party. The military command went to Colonel William Medows; and levies were raised. The Administration continued unsettled in their view of the expedition's purpose, however, for in October and November they added the idea of an attack on Buenos Aires.[13]

In order the better to realize this third objective Sandwich sought the help of Captain Arthur Phillip, who had served in the Portuguese Navy from late 1774 to the outbreak of war with France in 1778. Phillip obliged his Lordship by supplying charts of the South American coast, with places where a squadron might shelter and refresh indicated, descriptions of the Spanish colony's situation, and details of the distances between its principal settlements. He would leave copies of these charts in the care of a merchant friend, he said, in case he should be at sea when Sandwich required them, but he assured the First Lord that his friend would 'be an intire stranger to any thing more, than that they are Charts, which the [Admiralty] may wish to have.' (He also asked that he 'reap the Credit & advantage, that will naturally arise' from the use of his charts.)[14]

Britain's declaration of war on the United Provinces (hereafter Holland) in December 1780 gave a decision direction to the project, however, for with the Cape of Good Hope, Mauritius, Trincomalee, Negapatam, and Batavia now controlled by her enemies, Britain's lines of communication with India were most fragile, and it was of primary importance to secure them. The East India Company declared that in the new circumstances they could not risk their ships in the proposed attack on Buenos Aires; and on 29 December Cabinet agreed that the whole force then being organized should be 'employed in an attack upon the Cape of Good Hope;' that, if this failed, 'the two thousand Men originally intended for the East Indies [should] pursue their voyage thither, and the additional thousand with the Artillery Stores &c. originally allotted to them [should] go to the West Indies;' and that Johnstone might then still move against Buenos Aires.[15]

The expedition sailed on 12 March (1781), but through general ineptitude and Johnstone's lack of commitment, the attack on the Cape did not materialize. In August, the forces split up, with the ships sent to reinforce Hughes' squadron proceeding to India with Medows and his troops, and the others turning west. In order not to lose his reputation entirely, Johnstone looked about for a secondary goal. He sent two of his ships to patrol off the River Plate, in the hope of capturing some prizes; and he occupied the island of Trinidada, which lies some eight hundred miles east of Rio, in the hope that it might become a place of refreshment on the way to India, and thus 'an invaluable Jewell in His Majesty's Crown.' No doubt to the Commodore's further chagrin, a committee of Admiralty and East India Company officials concluded that they were not 'competent at present to decide' whether Trinidada might be such a jewel. In December 1782, Captain Burney took off the small party that Johnstone had left there, and the idea ended.[16]

The addition of the Dutch to the ranks of Britain's enemies alerted the Directors of the East India Company both to the intrinsic benefits of possessing the Cape, and to the vulnerability of their establishments in the East; and they remained profoundly conscious of these points thereafter. In September 1781, they told Hillsborough that if Johnstone's expedition against the Cape succeeded, they would strengthen the garrison he was to leave there; and they urged that a squadron be stationed there, since this would then be able to give speedy assistance to India as need arose.[17]

The failure of Johnstone's expedition increased both the Director's anxiety and desire. On 18 October the Secret Court took into 'their most serious consideration the late advices received from St. Helena, and the state of that Island, . . . and the practicability . . . of obtaining possession of the Cape of Good Hope'. The Chairmen pointed to the great vulnerability of St. Helena if the French ruled the Cape, both to direct attack, and because it was not itself 'capable of affording supplies of provision to the Company's homeward bound Ships, much less to His Majesty's Fleets'. While they thought one solution to this latter problem might lie in making a settlement on Madagascar, they saw that the best one lay in the taking of the Cape. They therefore urged this upon Hillsborough, suggesting that the six ships of the line and 5,000 troops then taken up for India should accomplish the task en route. 'The obvious consequences must be', they concluded,

> the cutting off from the French and Dutch those resources of supply, without which they must be reduced to the utmost distress for the means of support to their Islands, and for the maintenance of their Fleets in India; and the certain acquisition to Britain, and consequently to the East-India-Company, of every requisite furnished at present from the Cape of Good Hope to our enemies.[18]

Hillsborough asked when the Company's troops and ships might be ready to sail, and how the Company proposed to defend the garrison that they would establish at the Cape, were the attempt successful, from attacks from Mauritius or Batavia once the main force had proceeded to India. The Chairmen responded that the ships would be ready to sail at the end of November. A garrison of 3,000 men, as previously suggested, should be sufficient, but if not, it could be reinforced with 'any number of disciplined Sepoys from India.' The Cape could become the general rendezvous of the British fleets in Indian waters, from which they could conveniently watch and attack the enemy. The capture of the Cape, they repeated, would preserve St. Helena, and ensure that the King and Company's homeward bound ships continued to receive refreshment and supply.

The Chairmen concluded with an assessment of Britain's general strategic situation in the East, in which they enunciated the broad concern that, a few years later, underlay the Pitt Administration's colonization of New South Wales. 'That the Power possessing the Cape of Good Hope has the key to and from the East Indies, appears to us self-evident and unquestionable', they began, and continued:

Indeed we must consider the Cape of Good Hope as the Gibraltar of India. This circumstance, my Lord, has not been felt during the long peace subsisting between Great Britain and the States General; but the present rupture with the Dutch has totally changed the scene, and rendered the possession of the Cape of the last importance. No fleet can possibly sail to or return from India without touching at some proper place for refreshment, and, in time of war, it must be equally necessary for protection. The places about the midway are the Cape of Good Hope, Madagascar and St. Helena. Refreshment at Madagascar is uncertain and dangerous from storms, climate and the disposition of the natives. The French obtain from thence with the greatest difficulty very scanty supplies although the situation of their own islands is near and consequently favourable for their purpose. They have made several unsuccessful attempts to settle at Madagascar, but the climate and treachery of the inhabitants have rendered their utmost endeavours abortive; and Madagascar, on that account, has proved the grave of thousands. The Island of St. Helena, even in time of peace, has scarcely been able to accommodate the Company's ships. During times of war with France that island has been constantly assisted from the Cape. This resource being utterly cut off, the future consequences must be so serious that we crave leave to offer it as our clear opinion, that not only the Company's possessions in India, but also the immense trade between Britain and that part of the world will be hazarded and in extreme danger, if the Dutch and French are permitted to hold possession of the Cape of Good Hope.[19]

A few days later the Chairmen received news that the Comte de Bussy was about to sail for India with large reinforcements, and they reiterated their arguments. As a consequence, Hillsborough saw them on 2 November, but delayed a decision by asking questions to which their previous correspondence would have given answers. The Chairmen once again repeated their points and arguments in considerable detail.[20]

The Chairmen's addresses did not succeed, however, for on 8 November the Cabinet decided that in the circumstances then obtaining, 'it would not be expedient to withdraw any part of the Force that was intended for India'—i.e., that the reinforcements should proceed directly there as originally planned. The Ministers' reasoning was evidently that the forces presently ready would need to be augmented for an attack on the Cape and that this would make for too long a delay in the expedition's sailing. The Chairmen wrote to Hillsborough again on 15 November, expressing their 'infinite concern' that the Administration had not adopted their proposal.[21]

Obtaining no satisfaction, the Directors then suggested instead that the nation should attack the French in the Seychelles, and make a substantial settlement at Acheen, with smaller supporting ones in the Nicobar and Andaman groups, 'where Ship Timber, of which Acheen is deficient, is procureable in great abundance.' While Hillsborough responded unenthusiastically to this new scheme, he did ask for further details; and the Chairmen accordingly sent a draft of proposed instructions. Hillsborough then gave his approval, and the Court asked the Bengal Government to pursue it. Because of their hard-pressed circumstances, however, Hastings and Hughes could not do so.[22]

III   *The naval war about India*

As the Administration considered special projects to obtain strategic advantage throughout the southern oceans, Admiral Hughes sought this in the ordinary course of his duties in Indian waters. He met a number of grave impediments—his French opponent, Admiral de Suffren, possessed great energy and tactical skill; the Madras Council consistently declined to work in concert with him; he was unable to obtain stores to refit his ships quickly or adequately. All these factors, but the last especially, operated to hinder his using his squadron efficiently, and conspired to nullify his initial gains.

Hughes succeeded to the command of the India squadron in July 1778, and sailed from England towards the end of the year, with the expectation that the *York* storeship would follow with the materials he would need to refit his ships. He began to patrol the Bay of Bengal in early 1780, and his ships soon showed the effects, both of this service, and of the long voyage out. He wrote to Stephens, the Admiralty Secretary, in April that he needed to refit at Bombay, and that, should the *York* not have arrived, 'we must be very much distressed by the want of Canvas, running Rigging, Cables, Sticks for Topmasts and Spars of all sorts, as there is not one to be got in Bengal, or on either of the coasts.'[1]

The *York* did arrive in mid-1780, Hughes took the squadron to Bombay in October, and the artificers completed their work at the end of April 1781. Hughes reported to Stephens that without the *York*'s cargo,

> it would have been impossible to have refitted the Squadron for Sea, as there was not any where in India, so much as a Spar fit to make a Jibb Boom for a 64 Gun Ship, nor any Timber to be had of a size to make an Anchor Stock for a Line of Battle Ship.

He added that they now needed another cargo of stores, and complained that sails 'never arrive in Condition for Service, always rotten, and not answering the proper Dimensions.'[2]

That Hughes should not have been able to keep his squadron at sea without the *York*'s arrival is one indication of the fragility and inadequacy of the resources of the only substantial British dockyard east of the Cape of Good Hope. Another is how quickly, even after their refit, the ships' equipment wore out.

On learning that Britain had declared war on Holland, Hughes sailed to capture Negapatam, so as to deny the French and Dutch squadrons the use of its resources. He arrived off this port in early July 1782, and it surrendered on 12 November. The ships' equipment deteriorated steadily during this unexceptional service. On 31 July, Captain Reddall reported 'a small bower Cable so much rubbed and worn as to be deemed unserviceable' on board the *Eagle*. Hughes ordered a careful survey of it. On 4 August, he ordered a survey of canvas stocks on the *Exeter*, *Worcester*, and *Burford*, following captains' reports. On 6 August, Captain Rainier of the *Burford* reported a worn cable; and on 15 August, that he had on board twelve coils of local rope which were unfit for use. On 7 September, Captain Parr of the *Chaser* reported 'three Bower Cables, The Main Stay, The Topgallant Rigging, the Foretopmast Backstays, and sundry Running Rigging, unfit for use;' and in addition, 'a Foretopmast, a Jibb Boom, & Maintopmast Studding Sail Boom, very much sprung, and sundry small Sparrs rotten and unfit for use.' On 17 September, Captain Stevens of Hughes's flagship, *Superb*, reported numerous cables and cordage 'much rubbed and worn, and unfit for their proper Uses.' The same day, Captain Talbot of the *Worcester* similarly reported various spars unfit for use. On 9 October, Captain Gell of the *Monarca* reported 'one Maintopmast Stay Sail, Two Topgallantsails, one Main, one Fore, One Foretopmast Staysail & Two Maintopmast Studding Sails, that are much worn and unfit for their proper uses.' In all these and other instances, conscious of the need to husband resources, Hughes ordered 'strict and careful' surveys. Some of this wear would have occurred in any circumstances, of course, but it would not have been so severe if the materials had been sound at first.[3]

Despite this, however, Hughes had gained a distinct advantage over de Suffren by early 1782, more especially as the latter, who had also been patrolling for some time, was likewise feeling the need of cordage and men. A convoy from Mauritius brought him stores and sailors at the end of March, and, with his ships refurbished, he engaged Hughes on 12 April. The battle was inconclusive, and de Suffren did not press it partly because he had no means or repairing damaged rigging, and needed twelve spare topmasts. These deficiencies made his position serious, for he was faced with having either to seek supplies at Malacca, or to return to Mauritius.[4]

Hughes, too, was glad of a respite, as his ships had also suffered damage that he could not easily repair. The next day, Captain Alms reported that the *Monmouth*, for example, was 'rendered unfit for any further Service from the loss she has sustained in her Main & Mizen Masts, from the number of Shot Holes, and the great loss of men.' On 22 April, seeking means of making temporary repairs, Hughes requested from all captains an account

of the number & Dimension of every rough Mast and Sparr, now on board His Majesty's Ship under your Command, and at the same time specify what part of them are absolutely wanted to compleat the said Ship but you are not to convert any of them without my Order first had for that purpose.[5]

De Suffren found an unexpected solution to his difficulties when he captured a British storeship, and Hughes obtained what new supplies he could. They met again on 6 July, and damaged each other as before. De Suffren found after the battle that he needed nineteen topmasts, as well as lower masts, rigging, sails, and anchors. He retired to Cuddalore, towing the dismasted *Brilliant*. Storeships from Mauritius with artificers, and supplies of spars and cordage joined him there, and, in a convenient anchorage, he was able quickly to refit and refresh his ships. He sailed for Batticaloa in Ceylon on 1 August, where provisions were waiting for him. Reinforcements joined him there on 16 and 21 August. He then sailed for Trincomalee, which he took a week later.[6]

After the battle of 6 July, Hughes found that he needed to repair or replace 'sixteen lower masts, seventeen topmasts, eighteen lower and topsail yards and four bowsprits,' as well as rigging and sails; and that many of 'his spare spars on the booms had been shot to pieces.' With the majority of his ships 'greatly disabled and in general ungovernable,' he retired to Negapatam roadstead, where he made makeshift adjustments by again redistributing spares from ship to ship. Then, finding Negapatam's resources quite inadequate, he sailed for Madras, in the hope of better effecting repairs there, with spars 'only secured sufficient to prevent them falling in the short passage.' On arrival, he ordered a detailed survey of the damage to the ships, underlining the seriousness of the situation by having the carpenters report, not on their own, but on each other's ships. At the same time, he directed these to seek a six-months' re-supply of masts, spars, and stores from the Madras yard. Despite these efforts, though, Hughes had to report that 'our distress for Anchors Cables, Cordage and Spars of all Sizes, is still very great, no Naval Stores having been imported at this Place since the arrival of the York Storeship in July 1780.' Because of this lack of spares and stores, and because of that of a secure anchorage and extensive dockyards in which to effect repairs, Hughes was not able to get to sea again quickly enough to prevent de Suffren from capturing Trincomalee.[7]

The squadrons next engaged off Trincomalee in September, and both again sustained much damage. Two of the French Ships were dismasted, and de Suffren towed them back to harbour. When the 74-gun *Orient* ran aground there, the French used her equipment to repair the other ships. At the same time, de Suffren sent to an Indian ally for spars. After makeshift repairs, he carried reinforcements to Cuddalore at the end of September. He then went to Acheen to winter. Arriving at the beginning of November, he despatched frigates to Batavia for stores and food, and set about repairing his ships more fully.[8]

The British ships were severely damaged aloft. Hughes despatched the squadron storekeeper to the Danish factory at Tranquebar, to see what materials might be had there, with orders to rejoin the squadron at Madras. The reports which he received from his captains when they reached that port tell a sorry story. The *Magnamine* needed new bower cables, the *Monarou* a bower cable and running rigging, the *Sceptre* a bower cable. Other ships were badly in need of spars. Finding again that Madras's resources would not allow him to make adequate repairs, with the onset of the monsoon imminent, and without a Trincomalee or Acheen to winter in, Hughes was forced to abandon his eastern position, and retire to Bombay. He later wrote of how he limped into that harbour in December, with 'the Nine Sail of His Majesty's Line of Battle Ships . . . [with] not a serviceable Lower Mast on board any of them, nor a Fish for a Mast, or a Spar for a Topmast to be found but at Bombay.'[9]

Because of the war, service in these years was obviously abnormal; but neither did the situation improve greatly with peace. Hughes told to Stephens on 10 September 1784 that the

> Line of Battle Ships in these Seas are in the greatest want of Cables, no Supply of that Article or any Naval stores having been sent to India for these Eighteen Months past, & what Cables are brought out for Sale on the Company's Ships are few & too small for 64 Gun Ships and unless a Supply of Cables arrives at Bombay before March next, the Line of Battle Ships must be reduced to the use of Coir Cables.[10]

Just as he continued to attend to the particular needs of the squadron after the war, so too did Hughes consider its general situation, and that of the British establishment in the East. 'The safety of Bombay,' he told the India Company, was

> of the utmost importance to the safety of the whole, for at no other Port or Place in our possession could the Ships of the Squadron be even properly re-fitted, much less repaired; — At Bombay, as the only place of refit, are deposited all the Masts and other Stores for the Ships, and it not only furnishes a great number of expert Native Artificers, but its Docks are of the unmost consequence; in short, without Bombay or some other as convenient Harbour in our possession, no Squadron of Force could be kept up in this Country.[11]

IV *The peace settlement*

Objects to hold for war, these bases were inevitably also counters to bargain for peace. The British and French began to sound each other out on possible terms in the spring of 1782, with both governments profoundly aware of how ruinous another campaign would be to their exchequers. The French insisted that any peace must be a total one — that is, that the British must reach terms simultaneously with the Americans, the Spanish, the Dutch, and themselves; but they also dominated their

European allies, and increasingly as negotiations proceeded, they insisted on these agreeing to the terms which they could accept. Essentially, the French directed the negotiations on their neighbours' behalf. Vergennes, the Foreign Minister, and his lieutenant, Rayneval, were their principal negotiators. Shelburne, the Prime Minister, Grantham, the Foreign Minister, and Fitzherbert, the plenipotentiary to France, principally put the British position.[1]

It was clear by the middle of the year that a comprehensive settlement would require agreement over five geographical fronts — North America (including Newfoundland, off which the French had traditional fishing interests); the West Indies and central America (where the British had captured some Spanish territory); the Mediterranean (where Spain was much aggrieved at Britain's continued possession of Gibraltar); Africa (where Britain and France competed for slaves); and India and the East Indies. The British and French knew that they might soon adjust their claims in North America and Africa to reach a compromise. However, the Spanish obsession with Gibraltar rendered much more complex the issue of West Indian and Central American possessions, and, of course, of Mediterranean ones. The rival aspirations which the French, Dutch, and British had for themselves in the East conflicted greatly.

As they prepared for detailed discussions, the Shelburne Administration considered ways of ensuring that the Spanish and Dutch claims would not stand as insuperable obstacles to their reaching agreement with the French; and as most of the issues involved present or former possessions, the politicians called for proposals for adding to those which they might bargain. Edward Thompson gave in a scheme for a squadron and 2,500 troops to capture the Dutch colonies of Surinam, Berbice, Demerara, and Essequibo in equatorial South America. If properly equipped, he said decisively, he would answer for the venture's success with his life. John Blankett, Shelburne's private agent, presented a scheme for the capture of the Cape of Good Hope. Without this base, Blankett said, the Dutch would be unable to maintain their settlements further east; without the use of it, the French would not be able to supply their fleets. With it, the British would have a flourishing colony, an *entrepôt* between East and West, and the means to be 'Masters of the whole trade of Africa.' 'In every Point of Consideration,' he asserted, its capture was 'of the utmost consequence.' Blankett also drew up a scheme for an expedition to sail against Montevideo and Callao, and then either patrol in the Pacific Ocean, or reinforce the India squadron.[2]

Vergennes sent Rayneval secretly to London early in September, to open talks with Shelburne. In the negotiations which followed, the British Prime Minister's over-riding concern was to retain the nation's commercial and territorial dominance in the Caribbean and India, and, if possible, to strengthen the lines of communication with the establishments in these regions, so that they might have the means of recovering their prosperity. It was enough to have lost one world, he told Rayneval, without losing a second.

On the other hand, the French were equally determined to regain their old position in India, and to extend it. They asked for the return of the territories which they had held in 1754, when Dupleix had been at the height of his power and influence, and which they had then lost in battle, and in the peace negotiations of 1763. This claim involved territories on the coasts of Orissa, Malabar, and the Carnatic; trading rights there and in Bengal; and the fortification of settlements, including Chandernagore in Bengal. The French asked, too, that they receive more territory about their old centres of Pondicherry, Karikal, and Masulipatam; and that the British recognise their claim to the Northern Circars. At the same time, they pointed out that while they wanted the use of territories in order to support and extend their trade, they did not desire the costly sovereignty of dominions in the manner of the British in Bengal.

The recognition of these claims would have led to a fundamental diminuition of British power in India, as Shelburne knew, and as the Directors of the East India Company were quick to point out when the Administration consulted them. Accordingly, the British told the French that they could by no means entertain such a settlement. They might be willing, they said, to restore certain territories and trading rights, on the basis of the French position prior to 1749, but the French should not expect more. A return to the positions of 1754 would mean a resurgence of their old rivalry, and competition for influence with the Indian princes. This would hinder trade, which was their true object in India.

Negotiations over India continued through October and November, with neither side willing to make concessions before receiving fresh information about their relative positions there. On the one hand, the French had despatched a considerable expedition under Bussy between November 1781 and April 1782, who was to join with well-disposed Princes, and drive the British out; and as yet they had received no news of decisive victories. On the other hand, the British had the comfort of Hasting's dogged defense of territories, and of Hughes's capture of the Dutch bases of Negapatam and Trincomalee.[3]

As, in view of the empty treasury, it became increasingly urgent to conclude a peace, the French were forced to give most way, and accept a settlement based on commercial rather than territorial or political considerations, for, as Rayneval pointed out repeatedly to Vergennes, they had little by way of territories or influence to bargain with. In the end, the two nations agreed that to France should be restored Pondicherry and Karikal, with their territories augmented by some 161 villages; the *comptoirs* (i.e., commercial houses) at Mahé and Surat, at Chandernagore in Bengal, and at Masulipatam and Balassore on the Orissa Coast; Pondicherry and Karikal might be fortified, but not

Masulipatam or Chandernagore; and the French were to enjoy a 'free, certain, and independent commerce' about these coasts and settlements. Britain and France signed the Preliminary Articles of Peace on 20 January 1783, and exchanged ratifications on 3 February. They signed the Definitive Treaty on 3 September 1783, at Versailles.

As these negotiations progressed, the Spanish continued to demand Gibraltar, and to offer little that was satisfactory in return. In the face of this intransigence, the British continued with their plan to capture or destroy some of Spain's South American possessions. In September, ostensibly on leave from his command 'to settle his private affairs,' Arthur Phillip developed Blankett's plan. At the end of the month Keppel, the First Lord of the Admiralty, cautioned Townshend that, should it take place, it 'should come from You as the Kings Commands, for the Admiralty to collect & order to fitt for Secret service.' He added, 'If you have nothing further for Captain Phillip we shall send him to his ship.'[4]

At year's-end, after briefly deciding to cede Gibraltar and then recanting in the face of public clamour, the Administration proceeded to equip three ships-of-the-line and a frigate for this 'Southern Expedition'. They gave Phillip the command of one of the battle ships; and the squadron sailed on 16 January 1783, just two days before the Spanish gave way, and signed Preliminaries on France and Britain's terms. A fierce storm ravaged the ships in the Bay of Biscay, and effectively aborted the expedition.[5]

While it lay outside the scope of the formal agreement, the satisfactory resolution of the question of which nations would control the Dutch bases at the Cape of Good Hope, Negapatam, and Trincomalee, was central to Britain and France's reaching terms about India. Shelburne made it clear to Reyneval at their first meetings that the retention of Trincomalee was what the British cared most about, and that, conversely, they expected that the French would not occupy the Cape. Indeed, he said, they would prefer to see the Cape recognized as neutral territory open to all nations trading to the East, with ownership resting with the colonists. For their part, the French were determined that Trincomalee should be returned to the Dutch, because possession of it would make Britain 'the arbiter of all India'.

When Britain and Holland opened negotiations, the Dutch asked for the restitution in full of all captured territories, for compensation for losses, and for the recognition of the principle of the Armed Neutrality — i.e., 'free ships, free goods'. In return, Britain proposed three principles:

(1) A Renewal of the Treaties subsisting with the Republick at the time of the Rupture.
(2) A Restitution of all Places taken from them in the War, except Trincomalé.
(3) A Refusal to allow the Demand of Indemnification claimed by them.

The British did not expect the Dutch to accept the first, for they knew that the prevailing political temper of the Republic precluded it. However, they considered that the Dutch had 'no Pretence to expect a compleat Restitution of what the Fate of War has deprived them'; and since Britain's situation in India made Trincomalee 'not only desirable but almost necessary', the Dutch could not expect that it, especially, would be returned. In addition, the British requested the 'Liberty' to sail amongst the East Indies. Finally, they said that they would not entertain extraordinary claims for compensation; the Dutch might pursue ordinary ones in the normal way (i.e., through the Admiralty Courts).[6]

Inevitably, the French supported the Dutch demand for the return of Trincomalee, and they and the British pressed their respective points of view on this question to the last possible moment. On 3 January 1783, Vergennes repeated to Rayneval that they simply could not accept a settlement where the British, already masters of the base points of the 'Grand Triangle' (Bombay and the Ganges delta), should also gain possession of the apex (Trincomalee), for these would then be able to close the coasts of India. He felt encouraged to hold his view, he added, by the fact of several other of the 'Powers of Europe' which trade to the East asking him to have regard of the general interest.[7] The British ministers likewise continued to hold out for their object. Shelburne told Fitzherbert in a letter of 9 January 1783 that he had made concessions in North America and the West Indies

> with a view to obtaining Trincomalé, . . . which from the very first conversation I have ever had with Monsieur de Rayneval to this very last, I have always insisted upon as a point which we had most at heart.[8]

At the same time as they argued about this possession of the Dutch base, however, the British and French indicated that they did not wish to delay the peace so necessary to them both over one or two points, no matter how important those points might in themselves be. Grantham instructed Fitzherbert, also on 9 January, that if

> you shall be perfectly convinced that Trincomalé cannot be obtained, You have His Majesty's permission to desist from that Claim . . . Therefore on finding Yourself obliged to desist from the Demand of Trincomalé, You will insist as strenuously for keeping Negapatnam, & procuring Demerary & Esequibo. If, upon the same Resistance on the Part of the Dutch Plenipotentiaries or France, those cannot be obtained, Negapatnam alone must be insisted upon.

However, Grantham cautioned,

> the Importance . . . of Trincomalé is so great, & the Expectation of keeping it is so high that nothing I am persuaded will be left undone by You, to obtain so capital a Point.[9]

When Vergennes learned that the British were at last willing to relinquish Trincomalee, he accepted that they should retain Negapatam. He then forced the unwilling Dutch plenipotentiaries to agree to this, as well as to Britain's having the right of navigating amongst the Indonesian Archipelago.

The fact that Britain and France had reached agreement on India did not, however, mean that the issues disappeared. The British and Dutch had still to sign Preliminaries, and both nations continued very conscious of what was in their respective interests. The Secret Committee of the Court of Directors wrote to Grantham on 12 February 1783,

> your Lordship will at once see the propriety of procuring from the Dutch an unequivocal declaration of the Company's right to a free navigation to the Eastern Seas, and to an uncontrouled Trade to any of the Islands situated in those Seas, not possessed by the Dutch.

They wrote again on 8 March, to stress the importance of retaining Negapatam.[10] When the North-Fox coalition took office, the Administration attempted to obtain Trincomalee again, with Cabinet asking the King 'to direct Mr. Fox to insist upon the Restitution of [it] to Your Majesty'.[11] For their part, the Dutch cavilled at allowing Britain to navigate in the East Indies.

In the end, both sides had to give up these attempts at altering the basis upon which a comprehensive peace had earlier been achieved; and Britain and Holland signed Preliminary Articles of Peace on 2 September 1783. On 18 September, the British Cabinet asked the King

> to direct Mr. Fox to authorize the Duke of Manchester to agree to the Mode of receiving Trincomalé proposed in Msr. de Vergennes's letter . . . provided the Cape of Good Hope be restored to the States General at the same Time.

On 9 October Manchester, who had signed the Preliminary Articles for Britain, advised that the right of free navigation in Eastern seas comprehended that of touching at 'any Place or Island not possess'd by the Dutch.' On 15 October, Fox informed the Court of Directors that 'it had been settled with France the English were to give up Trincomalee and the French were to restore the Cape.'[12]

The British found themselves at the close of the war, then, with only the minor base of Negapatam as consolation for the knowledge that they depended 'in a very great degree if not entirely . . . on the superiority or exertions' of the India squadron for the defence of their Eastern establishments, and that these establishments could not support the squadron adequately.[13] From the war they knew clearly that their situation would be desperate if the French and the Dutch should again combine against them, unless they should find other, more secure, bases, and more reliable sources for the supply of naval stores to these bases. This task fell to the younger Pitt.

CHAPTER 4

Rival aspirations for India
1784-1785

I William Pitt and his colleagues

Some men are born great, Shakespeare said, some achieve greatness, and some have greatness thrust upon them. Each of these rubrics is appropriate to the younger William Pitt, who became First Minister of Britain at twenty-four, and made a career such as none of his predecessors had had, and as none of his successors has since had.

Pitt was the second son of William Pitt, Earl of Chatham, and Hester Grenville. His father steered the nation through the darkness of the Seven Years War to massive victories over France in North America and India, and over all European rivals on the seas. His mother's family was greatly involved in politics. From his parents, Pitt had variously an intense political consciousness, a steadfastness of purpose, and a sense of destiny.[1]

His father raised him well to realize this destiny. Educated first at home, he became very proficient in Latin and Greek, attending to the classical authors' modulations of style as well as to their political and social philosophies. It is said that his father would set him upon a block in the garden, prescribe a subject, and have him address the trees as though they were the members of Commons. Pitt continued his education at Cambridge, enlarging it to include modern authors, from his fourteenth to his twentieth year, when he came down to London to make his way in law as a prelude to doing so in politics.

Pitt entered the House of Commons in January 1781, and quickly distinguished himself by his carriage, eloquence, and command of subject. His voice, the *Parliamentary Register*'s reporter said after his first speech, was 'rich and striking, full of melody and force;' his manner, 'easy and elegant;' his language, 'beautiful and luxuriant.'[2] He dissected opponents' arguments to expose their weaknesses, he marshalled the details of his own so as to convey their force. As he did so, he showed himself to be of a serious and independent outlook, and already, despite his youth, a mature speaker and politician.

He found a number of occasions appropriate to these gifts in his first sessions. He had been present in the House of Lords in April 1778,

William Pitt, First Lord of the Treasury
By Gainsborough. *Courtesy of The honourable Society of Lincoln's Inn*

when his father had spoken against the North Administration's American policies and then collapsed, not to recover; and across 1781 into 1782, as the Americans succeeded in the war, and Holland joined with France and Spain to assail Britain in Europe, in the West Indies, and in the East, he too reprobated the Administration's conduct of the nation's affairs. The American war, he said on one occasion, had led

> to the most calamitous and disgraceful situation that ever a once flourishing and glorious empire could possibly be driven to! A situation that threatened the final dissolution of the empire, if not prevented by timely, wise, and vigorous efforts.[3]

'We hear every day the most pathetic accounts of the present State of the Kingdoms,' he said on another—

> The dominion of the Sea apparently lost, The Navy of England flying before an Enemy—Our Docks and Harbors left almost at their Mercy,—America separated from Us for ever,—Our other Possessions scarcely defensible,—and our own Island trembling at the Idea of an Invasion, with a People sinking under a load of taxes, and a growing debt adding every hour to the Burden.'[4]

Shelburne, who had been Secretary of State under his father in 1766, gave Pitt the Chancellorship of the Exchequer in July 1782. This was a Cabinet office, and the young man accordingly was privy to the peace negotiations across the rest of the year. What he then learned of the nation's situation at home and abroad, added to what he already knew, shaped his perception of the general task before him when he in turn became Prime Minister in December 1783—the 'uniting and connecting' of a 'shattered' empire.[5]

The events of the war, and the terms of peace, made this task daunting in the extreme. Britain had lost the struggle with her American colonies, and attained an uneasy peace only with France, Spain, and Holland. She had emptied her exchequer and lost her friends. Her commercial system had broken down. She had barely salvaged the war in the East, and her India Company was in severe difficulties.

Pitt applied himself to the task of national revival from the mid-1780s into the 1790s. In his radical intelligence, in his command of detail, and in his extraordinary energy and application, he was well-suited indeed to it. In the personality of his first Cabinet, he was peculiarly ill-suited.

The natural reluctance of politicians to commit themselves to a minority administration evidently destined for early failure, family connections, and the indiscretion of his cousin Lord Temple, combined to give Pitt a narrow field from which to take his ministers. Lord Sydney and Lord Carmarthen, his Secretaries of State for Home and Foreign affairs, 'were unequal to the most ordinary business of their own Offices.' Howe, the First Lord of the Admiralty, was perhaps the finest fighting officer of the day, but his character was otherwise 'cold & repulsive,' and his thinking in civil matters 'clouded & confused;' and he took litle part either in the 'councils of the Government' or 'the general business of the Country.' The social Gower, the Lord President, 'lent his prestige rather than his efforts.' Camden, who took the Lord Presidency in 1784 when Gower replaced Rutland as Lord Privy Seal, was 'experienced and shrewd, but indecisive and rather tired.' Richmond, the Master-General of the Ordnance, had considerable intellectual ability, but was 'capricious in his disposition,' 'uncertain' in his opinions, and 'visionary' in his plans. Thurlow, the Lord Chancellor, was a notable lawyer, but an 'irresolute and timid' statesman, one

> fearful of responsibility, fertile in the suggestion of doubts, and powerful in objecting to the opinions of others, but ever wavering in His own judgment; unwearied in discussion, which He loved as He excelled in it, but embarassed with the contrariety of His own suggestions, and shunning with studied ingenuity the labour and hazard of decision.

As well, Thurlow was of 'the most impracticable disposition and the utmost unhappiness of temper. Morose and sullen, captious and unaccommodating, He vented on all who approached Him the uneasiness of a mind perpetually at variance with itself.' He disliked Pitt, Pitt disliked and distrusted him, and he soon began to work against, rather than for, the young Minister.[6]

Pitt was to drop these unhelpful ministers when political circumstances permitted it, but the first did not go until mid-1788, so that in the early years he was forced into another strategy for coping with their deficiencies. This was to acquiesce in their dealing with the ceremonial and mundane business of their offices, but to direct or bypass them in matters greatly affecting the nation. As First Lord of the Treasury and Chancellor of the Exchequer, he watched over the nation's financial affairs. He supervised its foreign affairs from the first, especially those which involved Holland and France, frequently drafting despatches for Carmarthen to sign, sometimes even having the Under-Secretary send these out without Carmarthen's having seen them. From mid-1785, with Nepean's help, he also did much of its colonial business.

If Pitt became 'essentially the Government in all its Departments,'[7] he did not determine policies alone. Rather, he sought solutions to the nation's difficulties in concert with a small group of men who were masters of their business, and in whom he had confidence — Henry Dundas, W. W. Grenville, and Lord Mulgrave, especially, and Charles Jenkinson to a lesser extent. He discussed matters privately with these men, and he put them on the Boards he set up to develop policies in detail. On particulars he also sought the advice of the trusted and efficient Department heads via whom he implemented policies — George Rose and Thomas Steele (Treasury), Evan Nepean (Home Office), William Fraser

(Foreign Office), Philip Stephens (Admiralty), Sir Charles Middleton (Navy Board).

Making things difficult for historians, Pitt conducted much of his business with these men, and those whom they consulted, in conversation. In reply to a would-be biographer's request for papers, Dundas said,

> I don't recollect amidst the many years in which we lived almost unremittingly together that I ever had a walk or a ride with [Pitt] that a very considerable part of the time was not occupied in discussions of a public concern, and for the same reason it is that most of the useful knowledge I possess of his sentiments either as to men or measures does not exist in any written documents, but rests upon my memory and recollection, and must die with myself.

Pitt and Dundas consulted Sir Joseph Banks at length on arrangements for Lord Macartney's embassy to China, and Banks later annotated his file: 'as most of the business of arranging this Embassy was done in Conversation, the Parties being all in London, little Curious matter can be expected among these Papers.' In 1795, the Chairman of the East India Company drafted orders for the importation of rice as a consequence of 'a verbal Message from W. Pitt through the medium of W. Scott.' Indeed, so constant was this habit that, at times, the reports or actions of the men to whom Pitt talked provide the only evidence of his intentions.[8]

The way in which Pitt dealt with Colonel Cathcart's negotiations with the French shows his general procedure well. Cathcart reached England in mid-August 1786, and gave the Secret Court of Directors details of the convention which he and the Marquis de Souillac had reached at Mauritius in March. The Directors sent Cathcart's information to the India Board, and Pitt, Dundas, and Mulgrave read the various papers formally on 26 August. They then gathered privately at Dundas's Wimbledon house to consider the convention, and found it unsatisfactory because it did not have the premise which they had earlier had Carmarthen draw to the attention of Hailes and Eden in Paris, of basing commercial rights in India on territorial possession.[9]

Pitt accordingly told Carmarthen that

> it is the opinion of the India Board, in which I fully concur, that no time should be lost in sending an intimation to the French Court that we do not mean to hold that treaty as binding in all its details.

[margin handwritten note: didn't want to keep original treaty]

He suggested that they announce this in such a way as to prepare the French 'for a temperate and friendly discussion of the points in question;' and he enclosed some 'heads of a dispatch' which he and the others had prepared, for Carmarthen to send if he 'concurred.' He added that he had sent Fraser 'a letter to Eden to accompany this dispatch if you send it.' Two days later, Carmarthen asked him whether he should also send Eden a copy of the convention. Pitt replied that it would be better to leave discussion of the details of this until Britain and France had concluded a general commercial treaty. Carmarthen sent Pitt's drafts.[10]

Pitt, Dundas, and Mulgrave next met as the India Board to make their response official, and drafted a despatch to the Bengal government in which they disavowed the Convention in its details and said that they did not at all approve of the Company's servants treating with foreign powers, as this was the responsibility and prerogative of the home government alone.[11]

They then moved to obtain a convention which did relate commercial privileges to territorial possession. After consulting Hawkesbury, Dundas drew up a draft, and sent it to Eden at the end of September. He and the others framed Eden's instructions the next month, and sent copies to India as well, so that the Company's servants there would know within what limits they might operate. Eden began negotiations early the next year. In April, Pitt went through the resulting draft 'article by article;' and he, Dundas, and Eden put the final touches to the British version in July. The two nations signed their new convention the next month.[12]

II   *Pitt's outlook and policies*

Pitt found that the task of national revival required much effort on many fronts. The national debt, for example, had almost doubled between 1774 and 1784, from some £128 millions to £243 millions; and the interest on this had risen to about £8 millions. As well, at the end of the war there were also some £14 millions in Navy bills and Ordnance debentures outstanding for short-term redemption. At the same time, the government's annual income amounted only to some £12-£13 millions, so that a good deal more than half of it went towards servicing or redeeming debt.

Pitt sought a fundamental improvement. He reduced duties on tea and alcohol, so as to make the massive smuggling of these items unprofitable, and to obtain a secure income from a larger licit consumption. He taxed a wide range of luxury goods and services (including windows and servants). He established a sinking fund to purchase Government stock, and thus reduce the national debt. He rationalized the maze of customs and excise duties, so as to allow more satisfactory accounting and planning. He reined in Government spending; and he began to overhaul the government's cumbersome and inefficient systems of administration.[1]

The nation's defences were similarly at a low ebb. Britain had built up a great fleet during the Seven Years War, which had made her mistress of the seas, but this had decayed through the 1770s. By the beginning of the war, only forty-three of the navy's eighty-six ships of the line were serviceable, and some twenty-six of these had 'undergone considerable repair.'[2] As well, centuries of short-sighted exploitation of the native forests, and the careless use of good timber in minor repairs, lack of attention to the purchasing of foreign supplies, and shortages of those supplies anyway, meant that the Navy Board was unable to refit ships properly during the war. By its end, those who cared to look might see that belief in British naval superiority was 'visionary and baseless.'[3]

Sandwich had made a start at improving the situation, by ordering new constructions, and the re-stocking of the yards; and Shelburne had then contributed in another way, by appointing Call and Holdsworth commissioners to enquire into the state of the forests. Pitt, who had a considerable interest in naval affairs, and who habitually joined the nation's imperial welfare to the state of its navy, continued the process when he came to power.[4]

With advice from Mulgrave, Pitt began a far-reaching enquiry into the navy, which led him into sustained contact with Sir Charles Middleton, its Comptroller. Middleton sent the Minister voluminous papers, in which he emphasized the dangerous dependence on Russia for stores. Pitt accordingly added Middleton to the commission enquiring into the forests; he raised the service's peacetime complement from 15,000 to 20,000 men; and he provided funds for the construction of more that thirty ships of the line across the 1780s. Always, he took a close interest. 'It was no uncommon thing,' one who knew wrote later,

> for Mr. Pitt to visit the Navy Office to discuss naval matters with the Comptroller, and to see the returns made from the yards of the progress in building and repairing the ships of the line; he also desired to have a periodical statement from the Comptroller of the state of the fleet, wisely holding that officer responsible personally to him, without any regard to the Board.[5]

Pitt's examination of England's relations with Ireland shows the manner in which he habitually linked economic and naval circumstances. During the war years, the English Parliament had granted the Irish one some independence, and had freed Irish trade of many old restrictions; but these relaxations had inevitably raised questions about mutual obligation and ultimate authority. Pitt moved to resolve these questions by what he hoped would be a 'permanent and tranquil system,' in which Ireland would have a still freer trade, but would also contribute significantly to the cost of imperial defence. He wished, he said,

> to give Ireland an almost unlimited communication of commercial advantages, if we can receive in return some security that her strength and riches will be our benefit, and that she will contribute from time to time in their increasing proportions to the common exigencies of the empire.

These 'common exigencies' were explicitly naval ones—'naval strength,' he told Orde, was of the 'utmost importance' in any Irish settlement.[6]

Pitt's examination of commercial relations with Ireland was part of a larger one into the nation's trade generally. In March 1784, so as to have machinery with which to investigate commercial questions, and to formulate future policy, he revived the Privy Council's Committee of Trade. With Jenkinson leading, and with Dundas, Grenville, and Mulgrave among its members, he had this Committee first consider prospective relations with the newly-independent United States, and the Canadian and West Indian colonies. Then, he had it consider relations with Ireland, Bermuda and French, Spain and Russia, the opening of the Nootka Sound fur trade, the Newfoundland and Southern Whale Fishers' circumstances, and the application of the Navigation Acts. When the consequences of this Committee's limited commission appeared, Pitt reconstituted it to give it permanent machinery, raised Jenkinson to the peerage (Lord Hawkesbury), and appointed him its formal head.

As he attended to its economic circumstances, so too did Pitt move to improve the nation's diplomatic ones. He discussed European politics with Carmarthen in detail in May 1784. The Foreign Secretary then drew up a series of memoranda on Britain's needs and options, and with the Minister's cautious approval, he took up the task of restoring links with the 'Northern Powers.'[7] In October, Pitt had Carmarthen discuss with Russia the question of France's recent treaty with Sweden. Late in the year, he sent Sir James Harris as Ambassador to the Hague, to see what might be salvaged with the Dutch. In September 1785, he sent Cornwallis to discuss the European situation with Frederick the Great of Prussia.

Britain's needs and problems came together over India, which required the closest attention. By the early 1780s, the East India Company's fortunes had declined from their high point under Clive, for as it had acquired extensive territories it had gathered great expenses, and allowed the intricacies of Indian politics to distract it from trade. Graft and corruption were widespread amongst its servants. It had become chronically short of funds, and had had to appeal repeatedly to the government for help, yet it had continued to pay shareholders substantial dividends. W. W. Grenville described the situation eloquently. When Parliament met towards the close of 1783, he said,

> the most gloomy apprehensions on this subject were universally entertained. The extent and disasters of the Indian War, aggravated by the general difficulties of the Empire, had absorbed the resources and nearly destroyed the credit of the Company. . . . our fortunes in the East seemed hastening to irrecoverable ruin, the consequence of the same inherent Vices which had before subverted both the Portuguese and Dutch Dominion.[8]

Pitt was only too well aware of the problems which India presented, but he also thought that, with 'proper management,' the sub-continent might be made 'the source of infinite benefit to the empire at large.' For these reasons, and because he had come to power in the aftermath of the Lords' rejection of North and Fox's India Bill, he made the framing of 'a system for the government of India' his great and immediate object.[9] In January 1784, he presented a Bill based largely on Dundas's proposals of two years before, to have it rejected by the hostile House. After the general election had given him a majority, he brought forward a revised version, which both Houses accepted.

Pitt framed his India Act (24 Geo III c.25) with the general aim of taking 'from the Company the entire management of the territorial possessions, and the political government of [India].'[10] It provided for a Board of Commissioners to supervise and control the Company's activities; and when constituted on 31 August, this Board consisted of Lord Sydney (as Secretary of State for Home and Colonial affairs, formally the Chairman), Pitt (as Chancellor of the Exchequer, formally the Deputy-Chairman), Henry Dundas, W. W. Grenville, Lord Walsingham, and Lord Mulgrave.

These men soon took up distinct, if informally defined, roles, as they acted to obtain more benefit for the nation from the Company's great resources, and less trouble from its servants. Sydney played little part in proceedings, soon telling Pitt that he was 'ready to abandon it to the ambition of those who like the department.' 'Lord Sydney never attends, nor reads or signs a paper,' Dundas told Cornwallis in July 1787.[11] Walsingham attended the Board's meetings frequently in the first eighteen months, but does not seem to have contributed significantly to the policies which it developed, and in 1786 he resigned to go as Ambassador to Spain. Grenville busied himself with financial questions for some eighteen months, but he, too, then effectively withdrew from Indian deliberations in favour of Board of Trade ones.

Pitt supervised the India Board's activities generally, but was for some time content to do so from a distance, attending only one of its meetings in 1784, and only eight out of fifty-seven in 1785. From the beginning of 1786, however, in Sydney, Walsingham, and Grenville's absence, he came frequently. 'Mr. Pitt is a real active member,' Dundas told Cornwallis, 'and makes himself thoroughly master of the business.' To Dundas fell the responsibility for the Board's day-to-day working. He was from the first its effective Chairmen, and he did not overstate the situation when he told Cornwallis privately in mid-1786 that Pitt intended to reconstitute the Board so as

> to supersede the necessity of either the Secretary of State or Chancellor of the Exchequer being of it, in which case I suppose your humble servant, not only in reality but declaredly, will be understood as the Cabinet Minister for India.[12]

Pitt and Dundas together concerned themselves particularly with questions of administration and finance. Lord Mulgrave, the Arctic explorer and Sir Joseph Bank's friend, who is said to have had the finest naval library in England, took primary responsibility for strategic matters.

From September 1784, Pitt, Dundas, Grenville, and Mulgrave attended closely to the nation's interests in India. They reformed the Company's administrative procedures. They investigated its troubled finances. They constrained its servants from involving themselves in Indian or European politics. In the spring of 1786, they amended the India Act, so that the Governor-General of Bengal should have supreme civil as well as military control, and be able to act independently of his Council, and they persuaded Cornwallis, who was untainted by corruption, to accept the appointment. In May, 'much against [his] will and with grief at heart' the trusted soldier sailed for India to further their reforms.

At the same time these men knew that reform of the Company's procedures, and renewal of its trading role, were only half their task, for any gains they might obtain from directing the Company, they might quickly lose if Britain lost her position in the East. Accordingly, they looked for ways to strengthen the nation's strategic position there.

Pitt and his colleagues knew that they needed time to bring these policies to fruition. Reviewing circumstances in mid-1784, Carmarthen said that Britain needed a period of peace, 'so as to be able by a prudent line of conduct in her domestic Government to recruit her strength almost exhausted by the late long & expensive war.' Pitt agreed wholeheartedly. 'Let peace continue for five years,' he told Rutland in August 1785, 'and we shall again look any Power in Europe in the face.' They had this wish in the end, but not before time and the enemy's chariots had threatened to swoop and deprive them of India, the fulcrum of their plans.[13]

III   *French outlook and policies*

The British found themselves threatened with war and loss in the mid-1780s because their old enemy the French also had aspirations which turned on India. After decades of effort, Dupleix's gains in the later 1740s and 1750s had promised them their long-looked-for hegemony and empire in the East; but Clive's subsequent victories there, and the general British ones in North America and on the seas, had reduced the promise. The French had guarded their aspirations, however, and when war broke out again in 1778, they saw another opportunity to realize them.

By mid-1781, in the face of slow gains in other theatres, the French Ministers had come to the Comte de Bussy's view that it was India, rather than the Americas or Europe, where they might shatter their enemy and gain ascendency. Bussy had been Dupleix's lieutenent, and spoke with great authority on Indian matters. The most powerful of the Indian princes, he said,

> offer to join us against the common enemy as soon as they see us appear in force; and, if the revolution were such as one could expect were suitable measures adopted, it would, by depriving the British of a part of those establishments from which they derive their chief resources, certainly compel the Court of London to ask for peace.

He suggested that a force of ten ships of the line with support vessels, and some 19,000 men should proceed against the British at Bombay, Surat, and Madras, when 'the English establishments would automatically collapse and fall into your Majesty's hand.'[1]

The French had then organized this expedition, giving Bussy the command, and it sailed between November 1781 and April 1782. Later in 1782, they had considered a proposal from Joseph II that would have brought them Egypt in return for success in an action with the Austrians and Russians against the Turks. They saw that possession of Egypt would give them the means of reaching India without having to pass the Cape of Good Hope, but they took no action.[2] Bussy's expedition brought no decisive gains, either. He was unable to leave Mauritius until the very end of 1782, and he had achieved little by the time news of peace reached India in June 1783.

The French Minister pursued contradictory policies in the opening years of the peace. On the one hand, they moved to restore the nation's economy. Among other measures, Vergennes pressed Britain to conclude a commercial treaty; and Calonne (Comptroller General) re-established an East India Company, and sought the English one's help. On the other hand, they moved to give themselves the advantage in any sudden renewal of war, with de Castries, the Minister of Marine, obtaining new supplies of naval stores and ordering the construction of warships, and with the ministers generally seeking a dominant voice in Dutch politics.

J. H. Rose thought that this schizophrenia probably arose from conscious and profound duplicity—that in seeking economic co-operation with Britain Vergennes and Calonne were swayed by

> the desire to keep England quiet and friendly while they laid their schemes with a view to the ascendancy of France in the Dutch affairs, . . . and thereafter to the combination of their efforts for the overthrow of British power in the East.

This explanation does not really correspond with the character and outlook of Vergennes, however, and a better one is that the contradictory policies arose from powerful ministers pursuing divergent aims.

Vergennes knew that the nation could not afford another war, and he opposed de Castries, who dreamed of decisive victories and extensive empire. 'I believe there is no Minister in the [French] Cabinet that looks with so jealous an Eye on our Superiority in India as the Maréchal,' Hailes reported, who 'would go farther to raise the French Interest [there] from the state of Subjection in which it languishes at present.'[3]

It was this interest in India which led the French into the forest of Dutch politics. Like the British, they too had seen from the events of the late war that the possession or use of the Dutch bases in the East was central to the gaining of ascendency there. Accordingly, between 1783 and 1787, they strove mightily to confirm their wartime alliance with their northern friends, so as to gain control of these bases. Whatever the immediate benefits the French might have received in Europe from these efforts, their profound intention with them was, as one agent put it, to prepare the way for decisive blows in concert with the Dutch against the British about the coasts of India at the opening of any future conflict.[4]

The French sought control of Dutch affairs by intriguing for the merchant-based Patriot party to gain power at the expense of the Stadtholder's aristocratic followers, and by then concluding a treaty of defensive alliance with these, which had the effect of adding the Dutch forces to theirs, and giving them the use of the Dutch bases in the event of war. So as to minimize alarm, in Holland as well as in England, the French took pains to stress that this treaty was *defensive* only; but such assertions could but ill-mask its offensive potential.

Indeed, even as they concluded it, the French prepared for the realization of its offensive potential by asking the Dutch to give a French officer the general supervision of their colonies in the East, and the supreme command of their armed forces there.[5] They recommended the Marquis de Bouillé, who had distinguished Indian service, but to their considerable chagrin, they found that this idea conflicted with one that the Rhingrave de Salm was simultaneously pursuing with the same view of checking the 'insatiable Ambition and destroying the power' of the British in India.

The Rhingrave's plan had many facets. Holland would conclude treaties for the mutual defense of eastern possessions with France and Spain, and perhaps Portugal. Holland and France would augment their military and naval establishments in the East, with the Rhingrave taking supreme command of the Dutch East India Company's forces. France would send an emissary to India, to negotiate or re-activate treaties with favourably-disposed Indian princes. These princes would then make war on the British all about the sub-continent, to the ruin of the English Company, and the distraction of the nation. In these circumstances, Holland and France would offer Britain the unenviable choice of renouncing pretensions to control of Indian politics and commerce, or of losing her position entirely in decisive war.

The French doubted the Rhingrave's qualifications for the grand task he set out for himself, but found that his influence with the Patriots made it expedient to accept his scheme in preference to their own. The Rhingrave accordingly proceeded with it, seeking a favourable decision from the Dutch Company, and planning secretly to increase to ten thousand the number of its troops in the East. At the same time, the French sought a pretext for beginning war again.

These plans came to nothing when the balance of Dutch politics altered dramatically in the autumn of 1787, and France formally terminated her interest in them. Before this sudden turn-around, however, Pitt and his colleagues became alarmed to the last degree by the prospect of renewed war in the East. Knowing that control of India turned about the naval question of who commanded the eastern seas, they claimed territories and established strategic outliers to increase their capacity to defend their possessions. In the process they found a use for the convicts.

CHAPTER 5

Auguries of war
1784-1785

I *Naval questions and diplomatic negotiations*

The belligerent nations left a number of matters for future resolution when they signed the Preliminaries and Treaties in 1783. Britain agreed to restore and return Pondicherry to France, and Trincomalee to Holland, within six months. Britain and Holland agreed to Britain's retaining Negapatam until Holland could offer a satisfactory substitute. France agreed to withdraw her forces from the Cape of Good Hope. Britain and France agreed to settle in further discussions the size of the squadrons they would henceforth maintain in the East.

The North-Fox coalition gave the East India Company the responsibility of restoring and returning Pondicherry and Trincomalee, and the Directors sent appropriate instructions to Madras on 24 September 1783. The Madras Government then opened negotiations with Bussy; and the two parties reached an agreement on a procedure according to the terms of the Definitive Treaty, whereby the French and the Dutch troops would withdraw from Trincomalee, the British occupy it, restore it, and hand it over to the Dutch. No sooner had they done so, however, than Bussy received orders from de Castries that, pursuant to 'a particular Agreement' between Britain and France, the French troops should not evacuate the base until the British had restored the fortifications — in effect, the French should hand it over directly to the Dutch.[1]

On this, the Madras Government refused to proceed without fresh instructions. Bussy magnanimously suggested that they send a representative home on the frigate he was then despatching, so that there might be no avoidable delay in resolving the dispute; and the Madras officials gratefully accepted the offer. Nonetheless, all this meant that they could not meet the European agreement to restore and return within six months.

This contretemps raised tensions as well as delaying restitution. Admiral Hughes wrote that the French were so anxious to keep possession of Trincomalee, and to see that the British did not regain it, that they had moored four battleships 'in the entrance of the Harbour, with Springs on their Cables to bring their Guns to bear should His Majesty's

Squadron attempt it.' Because of the conflicting instructions, he observed, 'no cession or Restoration of any place has hitherto been made in
this Country except that the French have found means to creep by
Degrees into Pondicherry.'[2]

When the Court of Directors received the Madras government's
report of the dispute, they immediately sought clarification from Carmarthen, with the Chairmen observing acidly that while the Company
had 'never been favored with a Copy of the particular Agreement between the two Courts,' de Castries was not justified,

> even by his own statement thereof, nor by the Definitive Treaty, in insisting,
> that the French Troops were to deliver over the Harbor and Forts of Trin-
> comallee to the Dutch Troops alone.

Dundas looked into things, and found to the Administration's chagrin
that the French were 'in the right,' and that neither Fox nor North had
informed either the Directors at home or Lord Macartney at Madras of
the 'particular Agreement.' ('It is not possible to conceive a grosser Piece
of official Negligence,' he commented.) The Directors re-instructed the
Madras officials, who handed Trincomalee over on 23 April 1785.[3]

The nations kept their agreement on Negapatam uneasily too.
Holland had accepted Britain's retaining this port and having a free
navigation in the East Indies only at France's insistence. The Dutch
resented the duress, and regretted the concessions from the first, for they
suspected and feared that the British would try to usurp their monopoly
of the spice trade.

For their part, the British were always dissatisfied with Negapatam,
considering it a very poor substitute for Trincomalee, and they soon
looked about for a more acceptable one. In mid-1783, Edward Thompson told Fox that they should trade it for Demerara and Essequibo. Fox
listened, but instead pursued a short-lived attempt to recover the eastern
base. When Thompson returned from his tour of the Africa and West
India stations in mid-1784, he offered his advice again. Failing at first to
gain Pitt's attention, he told Mahon and Rose that if they might effect
the trade, they 'would not feel a loss in *Georgia, Carolina,* Virginia, &
Maryland,' and that the Dutch colonies would be a suitable region for
the Loyalists and convicts. He told Sydney this too, and the Administration became interested. Pitt discussed the idea with him in November;
so, too, did Sir James Harris, newly-appointed Minister to the Hague.
The next month, William Fawkener, the Clerk of the Privy Council, told
him that the King had instructed Harris to negotiate the exchange.[4]

Difficulties also arose over the size of the naval forces that the nations
would keep up in the East. At the end of 1783 the Foreign Office received reports that the French had sent warships 'under the usual
disguise of being *Armés en flûtes*' (i.e., with guns removed from the lower
decks and then converted to carry cargo) to Africa and the West and

East Indies. The British were suspicious, for they knew (as the Bengal government later advised) that 'every Precaution should be taken that no large French Ships *armé en flûte* should visit [the Indian] Seas, for they may soon be fitted out at Mauritius as Ships of the Line.'[5]

On 1 January 1784 Carmarthen asked Stone in Paris

> to obtain any Information, when by any Means you can acquire of a Nature to be depended upon, as to the Ships of Force which may have sailed from Brest, or any other Ports of France, in the Course of the last three Months.

This information, he said, was 'of so much Importance that any reasonable Expence to obtain Accurate & Authentick Accounts will be allowed on this Occasion.' He had Dorset pursue the question the next month, instructing him that it was 'highly necessary to obtain the earliest Information of the Intentions of the French Court, relative to the Force they propose leaving in the East Indies.' What the Administration wanted, he said, was 'the most explicit Declaration . . . of the Number of Ships, they mean to keep in those Parts;' and he asked for the names of these, and details of their force.[6]

The nations did not reach immediate agreement, however; and Carmarthen pressed the matter on Dorset again in March. Then, early in April, the British heard that the French had given three *flûtes* to their merchants trading to the East. Pitt now told Carmarthen that he wished 'very much to know whether You have had any Answer from Paris on the Subject of the French Force in the E. Indies — and whether any step has been taken towards the Dutch.' Carmarthen had the Embassy officials ask again, and this time the French indicated a willingness to reduce their eastern squadron to a minimum. Pleased, Carmarthen then told Hailes that

> it will be extremely necessary to ascertain the Naval Force, which the Dutch propose keeping up in India. The French having already suggested the idea of making a still greater reduction in the marine of the two Crowns to remain in those Parts, I told the Comte d'Adhemar that we could not make any alteration in the plan already established for that purpose, till we knew the intentions of Holland, upon the subject.

Hailes replied on 10 June, that the Dutch ambassador had said that he would seek instructions on the point.[7]

The business dragged on. Carmarthen again asked Dorset for information about the French force on 2 July. At last, in October, the nations seemed on the verge of resolving the question amicably, when Vergennes expressed willingness to reach agreement without the Dutch, and suggested that each nation keep one 64-gun ship of the line, two frigates, and one corvette on the India station. Carmarthen was pleased. 'Nothing,' he effused,

could be more agreeable to His Majesty than the very friendly proof of the
sincere disposition of the Court of France to cultivate and perpetuate the present happy state of harmony between the two Courts.

Less trusting than Dorset and Carmarthen, Pitt discussed the situation
further with Howe.[8]

Pitt was distrustful because he and his colleagues had received reports
which they could only take as auguries of war. In February, Carmarthen
told Dorset that he had heard 'that a treaty actually subsists between
France and the United Provinces, the great if not the sole purport of
which is to endeavour to drive the English from the East Indies.'[9] This
report was premature, but the French certainly were interested in
cementing their wartime alliance with the Dutch; and the British could
not but find this ominous, for they knew, as Carmarthen said, that their
rivals' profound purpose in doing so would be to raise a great force in the
East.

The French continued to negotiate with the Dutch for a treaty across
the year. Hailes reported in June that it would be one of alliance, and
not just of commerce, and that, 'tho' believed to be in great forwardness,
none of the particular stipulations are known.' The next month Dorset
said that the nations had run into difficulties in their negotiations. The
Ministers were not to be lulled, and Carmarthen replied:

> As far as any progress has been made in the projected alliance between France
> and Holland, the most serious consequences to this country (in regard to our
> oriental possessions) are to be guarded against, the mutual guarantee of
> foreign possessions being plainly concerted with a view to future hostilitys with
> us in that quarter of the world.

Soon afterwards, the Foreign Secretary obtained a draft of the proposed
treaty; and on 26 August Dorset reported that 'the French Cabinet now
presses very much the conclusion of the Treaty of Alliance with the
Dutch, according to the plan proposed.' The difficulty of Holland's being
in conflict with Austria, France's partner in another treaty, delayed the
French concluding the negotiations at this time, however.[10]

As they hung fire over a treaty with the Dutch, the French pursued
other moves which the British could only find threatening. In April,
Hailes said that he thought the French were interested in establishing 'a
[communication] with India by the way of Alexandria, Suez, and the
Red Sea;' and Dorset also reported this in July.[11] Early in July, too,
Dorset passed on a report that the French were about to obtain the island
of Gottenburg from Sweden, in return for a West Indian one and other
inducements. Carmarthen, who had heard this elsewhere, simultaneously advised that

> Every circumstance of the arrangements lately made between France and
> Sweden must likewise be in the highest degree interesting to this country, as
> the permitting the French to have a depôt for naval stores &c. in the northern

seas must in its consequence be highly pernicious to the other maritime, nay even to the rest of the commercial powers of Europe, and from the situation of Gottenburg, may in a short space of time affect Great Britain in the most alarming degree.

Three weeks later, Dorset reported that the French King had given his Swedish brother the island of St. Bartholomew in the Antilles, 'in consideration of his having consented to allow Gottenburg . . . to be an entrepot for the French trade in the Baltic.'[12]

The French accompanied their acquisition of Gottenburg with a surge of activity in their ports. In September, Hailes sent details of works at Cherbourg aimed at giving a command of the English Channel. The next month, Dorset reported that the French had just launched three two-decked ships at Toulon, and had others under construction.[13]

Dorset said that the French were proceeding in their shipbuilding 'with no great alacrity,' but the British ministers nonetheless found these developments alarming. The Armed Neutrality of 1780 had shown only too well how success in war turned on a secure supply of the Baltic's naval stores; and, taking for granted that the French would attack the British first in India in any future war, they saw an inevitable and intimate connection between these European events and France's general desire to strenghten her 'system of politics in the East Indies.'[14]

They therefore sought to counter France's public moves. Since Copenhagen was the 'entrance and key of the Baltick, thro' which all naval stores must pass,' Pitt tried to get Russia and Denmark to join in a 'permanent and solid connection' to oppose the Swedish-French axis. And, he saw that Harris was instructed to

> obtain information about the French forces in the Cape of Good Hope or in any other Dutch territories in the East or West Indies, and to furnish details of any agreement on the subject between the Republic and France or whether the Republic had asked for the removal of French troops and, if so, what the response had been.[15]

At the same time, they moved to obtain surer knowledge of France's hidden intentions. On 14 October, Captain Arthur Phillip asked the Admiralty for a year's leave, so that he could go to Grenoble to settle some 'private Affairs.' This reason was a blind covering one of public significance — one month later, Evan Nepean recorded paying Phillip £150, 'to enable him to undertake a Journey to Toulon & other ports of France for the purpose of ascertaining the Naval Force, and Stores in the Arsenals.'[16]

While the French had given no cause for overt protest, they had given much for alarm, and the British were anxious. India was central to Pitt's plans for national revival; and the British capacity to defend their commercial establishment there was weak indeed, especially if they had to do so against the French and Dutch forces combined.

II   *The British consider their naval position in the East*

Pitt and his colleagues soon had report to justify their suspicions and raise their anxiety. In December they heard that the French, following a plan of de Suffren, were settling Acheen on the northern tip of Sumatra. De Suffren considered that possession of this port, together with that of Trincomalee, would give France the 'keys to Hindustan.' The British shared this view, and Carmarthen wrote urgently and secretly to Hailes for details. Acheen, the Foreign Secretary said, was 'of the utmost importance to British Interests should it ever fall into the Hands of France, or Holland,' for 'Trincomalé on the Western & Acheen on the Eastern side of the Bay of Bengal would indeed render the safety of the British Interests in that part of the World to the most alarming degree precarious.'[1]

As they waited for Hailes to reply, Pitt began a far-reaching review of the nations' strategic position in the East. On Christmas Eve, he asked Howe's opinion of a series of reports and proposals—among others, Lacam's to build a harbour in Bengal; the East India Company's for settlements at Acheen and the Nicobar Islands; and Matra's for New South Wales.[2*]

Howe replied immediately. He considered Lacam's 'a wild scheme.' He thought the Nicobar Islands 'much the most eligible Station for Ships of War, were commercial purposes less in contemplation for fixing at Atcheen;' but that 'it would require a long time before Magazines could be formed for Keeping a Squadron on that side [of] India, all the Year.' Moreover, Bolts may already have formed a settlement there. The length of the navigation to New South Wales, 'subject to all the retardments of an India voyage,' did not encourage him 'to hope for a return of the many advantages in commerce or War, which Mr. M. Matra has in contemplation.'[3]

---

* Pitt's letter to Howe is presently unrecovered, but from Howe's letters to Pitt and Sydney of 25 and 26 December, we may know its probable date, its tenor, and the substance of the enclosures that accompanied it.

Howe gave Pitt his views on a series of proposals for strategic and commercial moves in the East on the night of Saturday 25 December 1784. In doing so, he cited Paper B—Mr. Sulivan's Memoire, and Paper I—Major Rennell's description of the Nicobar Islands; and as well, he referred to Lacam's idea to build a harbour for Calcutta.

The same day (25 December), Sydney gave Howe Matra's, and perhaps Young and Call's, proposals for New South Wales. Howe returned these the next day, observing incidentally that they 'are copies only of the former sent to me on the same subject, on Friday Evening.'

From this, then, we may assume that Pitt asked Howe's advice on 24 December, and that he sent at least nine enclosures, dealing with New Harbour in Bengal, the Andaman and Nicobar Islands, and New South Wales.

In mid-January, Hailes said that the Acheen report seemed without foundation, but the Administration continued to receive others equally ominous. Harris wrote from the Hague on 4 January that he thought he would be able to obtain details of 'any project hostile or otherwise . . . relative to The East-Indies' formed there, but added that he could not guarantee to learn

> what is passing at Versailles, where the Forces & Funds of The Dutch East India Company may be applied to views of conquest or aggrandizement before The Company itself has any Information on the subject.[4]

Phillip reported that the French were paying 'the greatest attention' to their navy. They were outfitting thirteen ships-of-the-line at Toulon, and eleven frigates and storeships. They were recruiting additional shipwrights, and importing naval timber from Albania.[5]

On 1 February, Harris observed that 'the Situation of Europe appears never to have been so critical, at any Epoch since the breaking out of the Thirty Years War, as it is at the present Moment.' With this consciousness, the Administration extended their counter-moves. Hailes employed a spy, de St. Marc, who claimed he would be able 'to give copies of all material dispatches sent by the French Court to India, & also to furnish constant accounts of the number & destination of the Ships at Rochefort.' Dundas interviewed George Baldwin, a Levant merchant on 'the expediency of opening the passage to India by Suez.' Pitt sent Jenkinson to talk to Thompson about the strategic situation in the East, who recommended

> an inquiry into the state of the Isles of the *Andamans*, as a protection for our fleets to secure & defend *Coromandel* & *Bengal*,

and stressed the potential importance

> of De Voltas in South Africa for our India men.

Thompson then developed his ideas on Das Voltas Bay, and gave them written up to Sydney on 21 March.[6]

The Court of Directors threw further fuel on the fire of British anxiety, when they passed on a copy of Bussy's 1782 instructions, where the French had written their Indian aspirations very large. So, too, a few weeks later, did Phillip, Hailes, and Harris. In a report which Nepean received on 10 May, Phillip said that the Toulon arsenal was 'in very good Order and very superior to what it was when I saw it before the War.' On 12 May, Hailes reported on the state of the French navy, and gave details of the forces which the French were sending to Pondicherry. Three days later, Harris passed on a purloined document in which a French agent described how they were working to isolate the British in Europe before launching a land and sea war against them in Asia. 'Our political manoeuvres are and must be directed principally against our

Maritime Rival,' this agent asserted; and added that these manoeuvres had the object of achieving a rupture at the earliest opportunity, and of 'laying the way for decisive blows on the coast of India in concert with the United Provinces.'[7]

These reports led Pitt and his colleagues to consider further how they might strengthen the nation's position in the East. In April, the Commissioners for India (Dundas, Grenville, Mulgrave, and Walsingham) met in secret session, and, with Cabinet approval to do so, instructed the Bengal government to survey the Nicobar Islands. While these could not become commercially important, they observed, 'their situation would give the greatest alarm to our possessions, and the most effectual check to our Operations in a future War' if they were occupied by an enemy. Indeed, the commissioners said, 'an anxious desire to hold possession of them would alone indicate in any other power a System of Hostilities.' Aware that the Danes and the Austrians had been interested in these islands, they asked the Bengal Government to settle one circumspectly, in order to establish 'a right of Possession,' and recommended Nancowery Harbour as a likely site; and they told the Company to send their instructions 'in the most secret manner.'[8]

In May, Nepean had Pitt and Dundas's confidant John Call give Thompson's Das Voltas Bay proposal into the House of Commons Committee investigating the transportation question; and Call then obtained from the Committee the recommendation that, if circumstances warranted it, the Administration might settle the area to 'promote the Purposes of future Commerce or of future Hostility in the *South Seas*.' In June, the India Commissioners asked the Bombay Government to occupy Diego Garcia, and to advise 'the best manner of settling it [so as] to make it a place of refreshment for Ships.'[9]

The British diplomats and spies continued to send details of unfavourable developments. In April, Calonne, the French Comptroller General, re-established an official East India Company. Since the Treaty of Versailles had provided for the French renewing their eastern trade, the British were expecting this. What disturbed them was the kind of aid which the French Government gave the merchants. On 2 June, Hailes sent de St. Marc's report that a 64-gun ship had sailed *armé en flûte* for Bourbon. On 21 July, the embassy secretary reported that the French were planning to send out two more *flûtes*. On 4 August, he reported an *arrêt* (proclamation)

by which the property of the Ship of war, the Dauphin, is transferred by the King to the East India Company, under whose direction she is to make a voyage to China. . . . Ships of force, or Ships capable of becoming Ships of Force, [he pointed out] bear with them a suspicious appearance, and should any of the sixty four Gun Ships intended to be laid up, as it is said, be hereafter converted to the Service of the Company, I shall be apt to think that the establishment is meant to make designs much more hostile than Commercial.[10]

Now, too, the French mounted an ambitious expedition to complete whatever exploration Cook had left undone in the Pacific Ocean. It required no paranoia or imaginative invention to see that this voyage might also have political and commercial consequences. Indeed, the French themselves provided for such, when they instructed La Pérouse to report on the forces and trade of the European colonies he would visit, on the commercial potential of the products of the land in and about the Pacific, and on the purpose of any settlement the British may have formed in the southern half of this great ocean.[11]

While the French spared no expense to make La Pérouse's voyage a monument to scientific endeavour, the British diplomats and spies reported that it had another purpose. Dorset wrote in early May that he had heard on some authority that the navigator had

> orders to visit New Zealand with a view to examine into the quality of the Timber of that Country, which is suppos'd by the account given of it in Capt. Cook's Voyage may be an object worthy of attention.

De Suffren thought that ships might sail from Mauritius to New Zealand with little difficulty; and it was rumoured that the French were thinking of 'establishing some kind of settlement there if it shall be found practicable.' A month later, he wrote that

> sixty Criminals from the Prison of Bicêtre were last Monday convey'd under a strong guard & with great secrecy to Brest, where they are to be embarked on board M. de La Peyrouse's Ships & it is imagined they are to be left to take possession of that lately discover'd Country.[12]

At de Castries's urging, the French Government now returned to the question of establishing a route to India via Suez. Dorset reported at the end of June that there was 'much reason to believe that the French Cabinet have serious designs of making an Establishment in Egypt whenever a favorable conjunction shall offer itself.'[13] The Ottoman Emperor had banned Christians from navigating the Red Sea; and the French sought to circumvent this interdiction by negotiating directly with the dissident Egyptian Beys. Typically, they also had their emissaries reconnoitre Egypt against a possible future invasion of it.

These moves spread a French presence over much of the globe, and while they were part of a general expansionist policy, they all bore specifically on India, the fulcrum about which French aspirations turned. How the re-establishment of an official company to conduct trade in the East did so is of course immediately obvious. La Pérouse's voyage did so because a supply of New Zealand naval stores would have added to Mauritius's strategic capability, and information on the north Pacific fur trade might have led to the new company's developing a profitable line. And Egypt, of course, was particularly relevant to India — as one of the Commissioners observed when Carmarthen passed Dorset's reports to the India Board,

> France in possession of Egypt would possess the Master Key to all the trading Nations of the Earth. Enlightened as the times are in the general Arts of Navigation and Commerce, she might make it the Emporium of the World. She might make it the Awe of the Eastern World by the facility she would Command of Transporting her Forces thither by Surprize in any Number and at any Time — and England would hold her Possessions in India at the Mercy of France.[14]

III *The French prepare for war*

As before, Pitt and his colleagues both sought additional information about these latest French moves, and acted to counter them. The India Board asked Carmarthen to ask Sir Robert Ainslie at Constantinople for details of the French activities in Egypt. In August, acting on the Beauchamp Committee's recommendation, Sydney asked the Admiralty to send Thompson out in the *Grampus* and *Nautilus* to survey the Das Voltas Bay region, in order 'to fix upon a proper Spot for making a Settlement.' Via Nepean, Banks suggested that a botanist go out to help assess the area's suitability; and the Admiralty agreed to this. The Navy Board put some of the *Nautilus'* stores on the *Grampus* for later transfer at sea, so as to disguise the length of the survey ship's intended voyage. The Admiralty Lords gave their secret instructions to Thompson, and Banks's to the gardener A. P. Hove, on 15 September; and Thompson sailed soon afterwards.[1]

The Administration received proposals for another place on the African coast as they mounted this survey. In May 1785, bad weather had forced the captain of the homeward-bound Indiaman, the *Pigot*, to take shelter in Gromarivire Bay (now St. Francis Bay), which lies some 550 kilometres east of the Cape of Good Hope. There, the ship's company found great hospitality from a Dutch farmer, who fed them for a month from his extensive herds and flocks, and his abundant crops. To the travellers, the area seemed paradisal — the climate was healthy, the soil wonderfully fertile, and there were no wild natives or beasts.

The experience showed two of the party that one of the bays to the east might be an excellent site for a new base. One was Lieutenant Henry Pemberton, who proposed this to Dundas. Pemberton saw that a port on this coast, well-supplied from the fertile hinterland, would be of great assistance in the expansion of the nation's eastern trade. Ships and men could refresh there; a protected harbour would offer ships shelter year-round; and forces stationed there could swiftly mount attacks on either the Cape or Mauritius in wartime. Moreover, the Administration could use the felons sentenced to transportation to establish the settlement, since the savage Kaffirs who inhabited the bordering areas would discourage escape. Pemberton presumed 'that the possion of a port on this Coast will be considered as an object of National importance.'[2]

The other was William Dalrymple, now Colonel. After reconnoitring the district carefully and travelling overland to the Cape he sent his wife a description, and asked her to

> draw up a Memorial immediately in my Name, and submit it to my friend Mr. Devaynes, and the Minister, that a Settlement on the Caffre Coast wou'd be of the most important consequences to Britain and the India Company;

and this his wife dutifully did.[3]

Dalrymple represented that the climate was wonderfully healthy, that the soil was fertile, and that there was a plenty of game and fish. He pointed to St. Helena's vulnerability, and said:

> We shou'd in a few years derive every advantage from a Settlement here, that the Dutch have from the Cape; and in time of War, and returning home, wou'd refresh here: With this additional advantage that the French wou'd not be so likely to capture our Ships, as they cou'd not know whether they wou'd touch at St. Helena or at the Settlement.

He suggested that the Administration send a small expedition to survey the coast, 'in Order to find a proper place for a settlement. . . . In this Plan I clearly foresee the greatest advantages to my Country,' he concluded,

> and to be the founder of this Colony is my ambition — We have lost America, and a half way house wou'd secure us India, and an Empire to Britain — We are at a loss where to send our Convicts — to send them to this Country, wou'd indeed be a Paradise to them, and Settlers wou'd croud here — It is the finest Soil I ever saw, with a divine Climate.

Devaynes gave Dalrymple's proposal to Pitt and Dundas, telling the latter that he thought the idea 'of very material Importance,' for such a settlement might be 'of the greatest Utility to us & Prejudice to our Enemies.' If they were to do anything, however, they should do it *secretly out of hand.* Accordingly, he said, he had not told his 'Court or any other Person' of the proposal. Pitt saw that such a settlement might 'answer in some respects the purposes of the Cape,' and 'serve also as a receptacle for convicts;' and he had Devaynes convey the plan also to Grenville and Howe. Devaynes then told Dundas that Dalrymple wanted a frigate, a transport, a tender, and three or four hundred men, and was anxious to set out; and asked him to give his opinion directly to Pitt. Presumably because they already had the Das Voltas Bay survey in hand, however, the Administration did not act further on Dalrymple's scheme.[4]

In September, too, the Administration sent General Cornwallis to Berlin, to listen to Frederick the Great's views on the European situation, and to assess the prospects of Britain and Prussia's developing a joint policy to counter the French activities. The crabbed old monarch told Cornwallis with some relish that 'the balance of power, which England had so long and so strenuously supported, was lost;' that France, Spain, Austria, and Russia 'were in alliance;' that England and Prussia 'were *isolés*, without any ally whatever,' and that, alone, they were no match for the 'mass' he described; that England 'would have to contend with the fleets of France, Spain, Holland, and perhaps Russia;' that Holland 'was in the power of France,' who intended to govern her with an ambassador.[5]

Crabbed Frederick may have been, but he had good sources of information; and the British could only share his alarm at the rising French influence in Holland. After summer consultations with Pitt and Carmarthen, Harris returned to his tasks there with renewed vigor and urgency. He wrote to the Foreign Secretary on 19 August,

> I have not been inattentive to what made a very material part of the Instructions I received from Your Lordship on leaving England — and I have been endeavouring, as far as the Shortness of time would permit, to discover if it was possible, not only to Separate the Interests of The Dutch East India Company from those of France, but, to unite them with those of Great-Britain.

He had assured the Dutch representatives of the Company whom he had met, he continued, that Britain had no plans for commerical expansion in the East Indies, that would be harmful to their interests, and he had underlined this point by tentatively suggesting that Britain might not exercise the right accorded her by the late Definitive Treaty, of free navigation in the Eastern archipelago.[6]

In September Harris made a friendly contact with the Zealand directors of the Netherland East India Company, and soon afterwards, he developed a close understanding with Boers, the Company's solicitor. The directors suggested that one way for Britain to increase her influence over their Company would be to arrange for the English Company to make them a large loan, for which they would offer three ships with cargoes of tea as security. If their Company's financial position did not soon improve, they said, they would be forced to accept the terms which the Patriot-controlled States-General were making a condition of financial help. Harris and Carmarthen were in favor of the English Company's making the loan, but Pitt ruled against it, unless the Dutch one could offer something clearly advantageous in return.[7]

Despite Harris's efforts, things continued to go badly for Britain in the autumn of 1785. With French help, the Austrians and the Dutch settled their dispute over the Scheldt. This cleared the way for the French to pursue again the treaty of defensive alliance with the Dutch, which they now did with great vigour.

In September and October, the so-called Comte de Grimoard urged upon both de Castries and Vergennes his idea that France and Holland should reach a 'particular and secret Treaty,' both to protect and further their interests in Asia, and as a prelude to some form of union. This idea found fertile soil in de Castries's outlook, for the Maréchal was obsessed with the idea of humbling the British in the East. He considered that, by themselves, the French would find it very difficult to dislodge their enemy, but that, in combination with the Dutch, and especially with the use of the Dutch bases, they might have good success. They would, however, need to effect three alterations in the Dutch Company's circumstances to obtain this success. First, the Company would need to relinquish its authority over the military and naval administration of its colonies, and to give it instead to an independent supervising officer. Second, this officer would need to be French. Third, the Company would need to increase its forces in the East, if possible to a superiority over the British ones. De Castries thought that if the two nations either agreed each to maintain six warships and six thousand men, or Holland twelve ships and France twelve thousand men, at their eastern bases, they would have a force sufficient to overwhelm the British at Bombay, Madras, and Calcutta.[8]

Vergennes, who had been looking towards a commercial treaty rather than a military one, sought to calm de Castries's ardour by replying that, in view of the nation's circumstances, the King desired only peace; and that they therefore must avoid any action which would conflict with this end 'as necessary as it was noble.' In keeping with this outlook, he sought to reassure the British, by telling Dorset that they intended to maintain only a small squadron in the East. Vergennes must have known the hollowness of his assurance, however, for even as he offered it he had de Castries's telling analysis of how a treaty of defensive alliance would radically alter the naval balance in that part of the world. France and England, the Maréchal pointed out, had agreed 'verbally' to keep up only a token naval force, but Holland had not done so, and might therefore maintain a squadron. If Holland did this, Britain would have the bitter choice either of keeping to her agreement with France, or of increasing her forces, which would justify France's doing the same. In either circumstance, the combined French-Dutch forces would be superior.[9]

With the general opinion of Cabinet against him, Vergennes had to give way. He sent Grimoard to Holland to establish links with the leading Patriots, and he instructed the French representatives to settle a treaty of defensive alliance with their Dutch counterparts. This they quickly did. On 9 September, Harris told Carmarthen he was attending to the 'flinging Delays and Difficulties in the way of the french alliance; but a week later, he had to report 'a manifest intention to make us feel the close Intimacy which Subsists between The Republic and the Court of Versailles.' Events continued to turn unfavourably for the British as the French pressed the negotiations forward in October. On 8

November Harris wrote that 'all appearances' indicated that the nations would 'inevitably and expeditiously' conclude a treaty; and he saw small hope of 'saving' Holland.[10]

Harris read the situation well. The French and Dutch representatives signed Preliminary Articles on 9 November. After a momentary hesitation, the British Administration sought to prevent the States-General formally ratifying the treaty. Carmarthen told Harris on 17 November that he should take all possible means to prevent this 'measure so alarming to the interests of this Country.' The diplomat reported on 29 November that he had been unable to discover if there were any secret articles to the Treaty, but commented that none was necessary, since it obliged Holland to follow France 'in all her Operations.' On 6 December, Carmarthen wrote that Pitt wanted him 'to redouble *every possible effort* within the next Fortnight, if the Stadtholder's Timidity has not rendered all opposition to the French Alliance already desperate.' Harris then presented a memorial to the States-General, assuring them of Britain's regard and interest, but a majority of the Dutch provinces accepted the Preliminary Articles, and the French and Dutch exchanged acts of ratification at Versailles on 21 December.[11]

The treaty of defensive alliance between France and Holland signified the nadir of Britain's influence in Europe in the 1780s, for it confirmed the island power's isolation from her continental neighbours, and it raised the gravest threat to her position in India. Pitt knew that it might be the reef on which his schemes to revive her fortunes might founder; and that he would need to pass it safely if he were to bring his cargoes home. The search for a passage soon led him into scarcely-known waters.

CHAPTER 6

The diplomatic struggle for India
1786

I The results of French diplomacy

The results which the British suspected and feared from the French-Dutch alliance soon appeared. On 13 December, Harris reported that the Patriots were urging the Dutch East India Company to increase

> to a very considerable amount, their Land-Forces in Asia. They wish them to have four thousand Men in garrison at the Cape — Three Thousand at Trincomalé, as a proportionate Number in the other Establishments — In short, to Substitute nearly, a thousand European Soldiers where, formerly, they had only one Hundred.

He repeated that events in Holland required the 'utmost attention to the East-Indies, & confirm what has been Said of the Designs of France to aim her first blow at us there.' A few weeks later, in response to rumours that the Dutch also intended to increase their naval forces in the East Indies, he asked the Dutch Minister if this were so, observing 'that it would not become England to See any Power, however friendly, with a Naval Force Superior to Her own in the Indian Seas.'[1]

In January 1786, the Zealand directors approached Harris again. Unless the British could offer a loan at once, they said, the Company would be forced to capitulate to the States General. Harris replied that neither his Government nor the English East India Company would be able to advance 'a Single Florin' until they had assurances that

> in return for this essential Assistance from England, none of these innovations in the East Indies (So near taking place, in favour of France) Should ever be adopted here.[2]

The Zealand Directors could not, of course, promise this. Largely through their efforts, however, the Dutch Company postponed for a year a decision on the proposals for reinforcing their garrisons. Harris reported this with satisfaction on 13 January. A week later, though, the climate changed again, and he had to advise that the States General had decided to give France two battleships.[3]

Boers, the Company's solicitor, now approached the British diplomat, to repeat

> that unless England hastened to make Some friendly overtures to the Dutch East India Company, its Situation was so distress'd that it would be, inevitably, obliged to fling itself intirely into the hands of the present Governors of this Country, for Support.

As before Harris asked for 'positive assurances . . . that the Company would never act in opposition to the Interest of Great Britain;' and Boers pointed out that, even if the Directors might be persuaded to give these, their Company's charter did not allow them to make such agreements with foreign powers. Boers then told Harris of the Patriots' plans to vest final power over the Company's affairs in a Board of Control, which would consist of persons favourable to France. As Harris reported, it required

> no very deep reflection to See that the moment it has taken place, the Dutch will increase both their Naval and Land Forces in the East, and adopt every measure the most favorable to France, and most inimical to England.[4]

With a loan seemingly out of the question, the pair discussed what other measures there were by which Britain might give the Dutch directors 'Spirits & Encouragement,' without which they would probably accept the reform the Patriots were proposing. Boers pointed to several, but said that the only one that would have 'a very powerful effect' was that one at which Harris had hinted the previous year —

> a Declaration, That there did not exist, on the part of England, any intention, in virtue of the Article of the last Treaty of Peace which grants a free Navigation in the Indian Seas, to establish a Spice-Trade, or in any Shape whatever, to interfere with that The Dutch East India Company has so long carry'd on exclusively, with the Molucca Islands.[5]

Before the British Government had the opportunity to analyse and respond to Boers's views, the Patriots succeeded in having the Council of the Netherlands East India Company accept the addition of two directors from the States General. Harris reported this on 3 February, and at the same time set forth his view of the situation in considerable detail. 'The intentions of France in forming a Connection with this country are too evident to admit of a doubt,' he told Carmarthan privately.

> The Patriots are in the plentitude of Power & concur heartily with the Court of Versailles in all its operations & designs — If the direction of the East India Company falls into their hands (& I much fear it will) you may be assur'd that all its force, wealth & resources (without any regard being paid to its commercial interests) will be employ'd against us in India the moment France chuses to give the signal . . . .
> The most effectual way of defeating their designs would be to anticipate them:

to do by them, while we have the force in our hands what they certainly will do by us whenever it is in theirs; to attack & destroy the Dutch Settlements in the East, to take possession of their Spice trade and to crush while it is yet time the existence of a power, who is on the eve of becoming our most formidable enemy.

He added publicly that

The Government of this country (or rather the faction which usurps its Government) during the course of the last year, and more especially Since the disputes between The Republic and The Emperor took a favorable turn have been, repeatingly, pressing the Company to increase, to a very considerable amount, their Army Establishment by proposing to them to take into the Service Several of the Corps The States-General intended to reform, on the conclusion of the Peace.[6]

Things then developed as Harris feared they would. He reported on 14 February that the Patriots had won control of the Netherlands East India Company council. At the same time, though, he picked up a most exciting rumour, which suggested that the Dutch forces in the East had revolted against the States General, and had asked for British protection. 'I am most anxious', he wrote to Carmarthen again a week later,

for a confirmation from you of the news I sent you last post from India — I cannot doubt its veracity as to the general substance but am inclined to think the particulars mistated — How fine a thing it would be to take the Cape, Ceylon, Batavia, Amboina, Bandi, Ternate, Timor etc. etc.

The information was not authentic. Carmarthen replied on 24 February,

the Accounts received in Holland, & said to be brought by M. de Kersaint from the East Indies, agree in substance with those we have had from France. No great credit, however, appears to have been given to them by those who are conversant with the Affairs of India.[7]

More disturbing news was soon to hand. Harris had prepared his weekly despatch on 7 March, when he received new information 'relative to the future Operations of the Dutch & French in Asia, with which Your Lordship cannot be too soon made acquainted.' 'France has intimated to those of the Faction in whom she places the greatest Confidence,' he said,

that a Rupture with England in Asia is not of a very distant Period. That it is therefore of the utmost Consequence that no Time should be lost in augmenting the Naval & Land Force of the Republic in that Quarter of the World. That the waiting for the Deliberations of the East India Company would (by the Delay it would create & the Publicity with which it would be attended) — defeat the great Object of such an Augmentation. And that it was highly essential the States should take on themselves both the ordering & the Expence of this Measure.

In consequence of these Insinuations the leading Patriots have come to a Resolution *among themselves* to send as soon as they can be got ready, Four Ships of the Line, & Four Frigates, with as many Troops as the Ships will hold over & above their Compliment, to the Cape, where they are to remain for further orders. . . . The Ships are to be taken from those in the greatest forwardness at Amsterdam. And the Soldiers are to be raised from the Regiments lately formed.

Mons. de Cotleuri, whose Name I have more than once mentioned, is the Person the French employ to carry through this great Part of their Negotiation. His language is that our power in India is exorbitant, & our Intentions hostile to a Degree. that we must be kept down there at any Rate; . . .

[Mons. de Coetloury] has whispered in the Ears of some of his most intimate Confidants, that notwithstanding the Failure of their last Attempt in Bengal, France is preparing new Troubles for us in India, & that Her Measures will be too well concerted to leave any Doubt of their Success.

He assures the Patriots that his Court will not be behindhand in reinforcing both her Fleet & Army in India, and that in a very few Weeks a Squadron with Troops on board will be ready in one of their ports . . . to sail for the Mauritius.

The Foreign Office received this despatch in the early morning of 10 March. Carmarthen immediately gave it to Pitt and the King; and he replied to Harris on the same day, that 'the Designs of France & Holland in the East Indies cannot be too constantly or too minutely attended to;' and that Harris should continue to gather all possible information about them.[8]

This the British Ambassador did with great assiduity. On 21 March, he reported that 'the french agents at Amsterdam, in conjunction with those of the faction, are unremitted in their endeavours to hasten the Reinforcement to be sent to India;' and that

Two Ships of 64 Guns and Four Frigates are, actually, getting ready, with the avowed Intention of being sent to India — and it is probable that Two more of 64, which, as it is said, are meant to relieve the Squadron in The Mediterranean will have Secret orders to follow the same Route.

Carmarthen sent this information to Howe. Three weeks later, Harris reported that

Mons. Cotleuri went, a few days ago, to Amsterdam, with a plan from the french Ministry for the Dutch Company not only to take 6000 french Troops into their Service, but, to erect Several Strong Fortifications in different parts of their Settlements, and to confide the construction of the works to french Engineers.

He added that 'the States General have determined to Send four more Frigates (2 of 36, and 2 of 44) to India. The whole of their naval force there, will, then, be Nine Frigates, and Three Ships of the Line,' Carmarthen sent this information to Pitt as well as to Howe.[9]

By now, Harris was in despair. 'The french influence here,' he wrote home at the end of February, 'is at its highest pitch—and bears down everything before it.' 'It is not on the cards,' he said a month later, 'to reclaim this Country. Everything, both foreign and domestick, concurs to throw it into the arms of France.'[10]

Dorset's reports from France gave the Administration no more cause for optimism. On 2 February, he wrote that the French Government had ordered 'as speedily as possible, 22 Ships of the Line;' and that they had purchased a 'Forest of Timber proper for Masts, about sixty leagues from Riga,' which naval inspectors would soon visit. 'In short,' he observed, 'France is at this moment straining every nerve to put her Navy on the most formidable foot.' A week later, he said that the French were determined to realize 'the advantages that their new Alliance with Holland seems to promise them in the East,' and intended to send eight Indiamen, a 64-gun ship, and a frigate out from l'Orient in March. Carmarthen sent this information to Pitt and Howe.[11]

Dorset and Harris's reports inevitably fed the Administration's fears about the likely size of the French and Dutch naval forces in the East. On 17 February, Carmathen instructed Dorset to represent to the French Government that, in view of the lately-concluded alliance, the French and Dutch squadrons should count as one, and together not exceed the strength that Britain and France had agreed to. The Administration would not come to a final agreement, the Foreign Secretary said,

> until we are assured that we shall not be obliged to keep up a force double to that, which we have hitherto understood France was equally bound not to exceed, for instance one 64, 2 Frigates & a Cutter, was the force France appeared disposed to agree upon. If Holland has the same force, England must have 2 64's. 4 Frigates, & 2 Cutters in order to be upon a footing of equality with two nations who by their late treaty must be considered (in those seas particularly, perhaps) as forming one consolidated power.

A week later, he asked Harris to make similar representations to the Dutch.[12]

The hope that France and Holland would agree to this proposition was of course a forlorn one from the first. Vergennes assured Dorset informally on 9 March that Britain had 'no reason to be alarm'd at the connection with Holland, as the Treaty, which has been enter'd into between the two Powers is only defensive.' He made the inevitable formal reply on 1 April, that the King had found it impossible to entertain the British request. Two weeks later, Harris reported that the Dutch intended to add four frigates to their squadron in the East. Then, rubbing salt on raw British nerves, France announced that she would oppose interference by any other foreign power in Dutch affairs with force.[13]

Now, too, came details of French activities in the near East. Sir Robert Keith sent Joseph II's report that 'France is firmly determined to strike a bold stroke by making Herself Mistress of all Egypt.' The Emperor said that he knew this 'with Certainty from more Quarters than one,' and that 'Mons.' Toff himself told me at Paris that he had travelled through all Egypt by Order of his Court to explore that Country in a military light, and to lay down a Plan for the Conquest of it.' Carmarthen sent this letter to Pitt. Harris reported that the treaty which the French had concluded with the Beys allowed their East India Company to send goods home via Suez. Sir Robert Ainslie wrote that the French were 'busily employed' in what he hoped were

> fruitless endeavours, not only to rival the [East India] Company's Commercial Connections towards the Persian Gulph; but also to establish Political Connections, in order to secure themselves exclusive privileges, and an Important Influence.[14]

France certainly managed her diplomacy well in the three years after the end of the war. By the treaties with Sweden, Holland, and the Egyptian Beys, she laid a comprehensive basis for consolidating her position in Europe, and for expanding it in the East. Fox may have embellished, but he did not invent, when he charged that France's conduct 'had been such as no human wisdom could have exceeded.'[15] That she had realized her objectives so much better than had Britain was due in part to the inherent weakness of Britain's situation, and in part to the incompetence of the British Foreign Secretaries. And this success, of course, made Pitt's task of reviving Britain's fortunes so much the more difficult.

II *Pitt moves to meet the threat*

Pitt and his closest advisers did not need Fox's fulminations to know that the situation in Europe and the East in the spring of 1786 called for urgent measures if Britain were not to be reduced to a mendicant nation; and they moved decisively to avoid this fate. They did so on a number of fronts. Taking up a policy that Dundas had urged across the previous two years, Pitt amended the India Act, so as to give the Governor-General of Bengal supreme civil as well as military control, and the ability to act independently of his Council; and they persuaded Cornwallis to accept appointment. Pitt extended his supervision of foreign affairs, drafting many of the despatches which Carmarthen sent to Paris and the Hague. In doing so, he endorsed Carmarthen and Harris's idea that Harris should intervene more forcefully in Dutch affairs; and he provided funds to support this intervention. Mulgrave developed strategic counters to the French moves in Egypt and the East. Pitt himself became profoundly involved in Indian affairs, and chaired all the

Board of Control's secret sessions between June and October, when he, Dundas, and Mulgrave oversaw despatches with great care. Last, Pitt implemented the policy he had earlier framed, of using the convicts to increase the nation's capacity to defend its empire.

Pitt and Dundas's gaining Cornwallis's agreement to become Governor-General was a considerable achievement. Shelburne had obtained the soldier's provisional consent in 1782, and North and Fox had sought it again the next year. Pitt had had Sydney offer him the military command in April 1784, and then, in May, the civil one as well, but Cornwallis was dissatisfied with their Act's not removing the limitations on individual power which had bedevilled Hastings, and he politely withdrew himself from consideration in August. The pair had renewed their request in February 1785, with an offer to amend the Act, but again, Cornwallis declined politely.

A year later, the Administration sought Cornwallis out once more. 'The proposal of going to India has been pressed upon me so strongly,' he told a friend,

> with the circumstance of the Governor-General's being independent of his Council, . . . having the supreme command of the military, that, much against my will and with grief of heart, I have been obliged to say yes.

He met Pitt and Dundas in lengthy sessions in March and April, to discuss the policies which they wanted him to implement; and they amended the India Act, to give him the powers he wanted. The politicians and the soldier built up a considerable rapport. Cornwallis remarked to Dundas later, 'It is not extraordinary that we have anticipated your wishes, or coincided with your opinion on most . . . subjects, as I had the advantage of talking them over so frequently with you in London.' He sailed for India at the beginning of May.[1]

Early this month, too, Harris was able to report with satisfaction that the Dutch East India Company had rejected the Patriots' proposals to strengthen their settlements' fortifications, and to employ six thousand French troops. A few days later, however, he had to say that six new directors had been installed in the Company's Council. Then, as he worked to stiffen resistance to changes in favour of France in the administration of the Company, he found that the resolution of many of his Dutch friends faded.[2]

Only among the Zealand officials was there a firm purpose to resist the encroachments of the Patriots and the French. In mid-May, Van de Spiegel, the Pensionary, told Harris that Zealand was prepared to defy the States General and oppose the reforms if Britain would offer protection—in short, that

> Zeland is ready to consent that their Share of the East India Company shall be annex'd (*incorporée* was the word) to That of England; to Whom They will

make over a participation of *all the Rights* They hold by Charter, both in Europe and Asia, provided the whole Trade is carried on under The English Flag, and that England will consent to afford the same protection (*la même sauvegarde*) to the Zeland ships in India as to its own.

Harris personally saw some possibilities in this extraordinary offer; but he knew that the acceptance of it could not but lead to war, and that,therefore, his Government would not encourage it.[3]

Rather than pursuing it, then, he arranged with Van de Spiegel to urge the Stadtholder to take a positive stand against the Patriots. As part of the plan, he proposed a declaration of Britain's friendly intentions. The British Cabinet approved of this idea, and Harris then told the States General that 'His Brittanic Majesty disavowed all intention of interfering in the domestic concerns of the Republic,' but earnestly wished that 'the Government should be preserved in those hands to which it has been intrusted by the Constitution, and founded on principles established by the unanimous consent of the whole nation.' This had a better reception than Harris hoped for; and he wrote a few days later that 'My Memorial Seems, from the Impression it makes, to have perfectly answered the purpose for which it was intended.'[4]

Harris now stepped up his covert moves, too. At the beginning of June, he asked Carmarthen for £1,500 'to feed the arrière-ban of our new party.' Ten days later, he put the sum needed 'to gain over inferior dispensers, *Dutch borough-mongers* and those who have influence in the streets and highways' at £2,000. Early the next month, he raised his request to £2,500, asking that the money be paid into his private accounts in England, so that he might disguise its source. Pitt met these requests.[5]

As Harris worked abroad, Lord Mulgrave planned at home. Born in 1744, Constantine John Phipps had entered the Navy in 1760, and had served with his uncle Augustus Hervey during the Seven Years War. In 1776, he and his close friend Joseph Banks had sailed in the *Niger* to Labrador and Newfoundland, where they patrolled and botanized. Then, in 1768, he entered the House of Commons, where he voted with the 'King's Friends.' In 1773, he took the *Racehorse* and *Carcass* in search of a northern passage to India, and reached 80°N above Spitzenburg before the ice forced him back. He became the second Baron Mulgrave on the death of his father in 1775, and two years later took a Commons seat in the Lord Sandwich's interest, when Sandwich also appointed him to the Admiralty Board. At the end of December 1783, he sought this patron's agreement to his joining Pitt's Administration. In April 1784, Pitt appointed him joint Paymaster General of the forces, and to the Committee of Trade and the India Board. His keen interest in naval affairs resulted in his soon becoming Pitt's expert on strategy. In 1785, for example, he gave the Minister a lengthy consideration of the Navy's peacetime establishment, and he and his fellow Commissioners ordered surveys of the Nicobar Islands and Diego Garcia.[6]

With the diplomats' reports on French activities there, Mulgrave
turned his attention to the Near East in the spring of 1786. Developing
on Dundas's beginning with Baldwin the previous year, he drew up a
paper discussing the advantages in security, dependability, and speed
which they would derive from firmly-established lines of communication
overland to India. To obtain these advantages, Mulgrave thought that
they should have lines to Bombay through Leghorn and Venice, and
Constantinople and Cyprus, to Cairo, and along the Red Sea, on the one
hand; and, on the other, through Venice and Vienna, Constantinople, Aleppo, Baghdad, Busra (and perhaps Muscat). They
might employ local agents in the Arabian towns, but should have a
European one at Cairo, and Baldwin seemed the best-qualified candidate.[7]

Repeating and enlarging on Mulgrave's views, the India Board (Dundas, Walsingham, Grenville, and Mulgrave) then decided to send
Baldwin as Consul to Egypt, in order 'forthwith to negociate such a
Treaty as shall put His Majesty's Subjects, at least on an equal footing
with those of the French King.' They presented their plan to the East India Company and Carmarthen on 19 May, sending the latter as well a
'Draft of Instructions' for Baldwin.[8]

Now, too, the Administration took up the convict question again. In
January, Nepean had Campbell estimate the likely cost of transportation
to New South Wales. In February, in answer to Mr. Bastard's query
about whether they intended to transport to Africa, Pitt said that as this
required 'great deliberation, it must be proceeded in with caution;' and
he added, that if 'the mode prescribed by the act should not be thought
literally practicable, his Majesty's servants would very soon substitute
another mode of punishment in its stead.' By early May, however, the
ministry had decided to continue with transportation, for Pitt then told
John Rolle,

> Tho' I am not at this Moment able to state to You the Place, to which any
> Number of the Convicts will be sent, I am able to assure You that Measures
> are taken for procuring the Quantity of Shipping necessary for conveying
> above a thousand of them. And I have every reason to suppose that all the
> Steps necessary for the removal of at least that Number, may be compleated in
> about a Month. The Plan may I am in hopes, afterwards be extended to
> whatever farther Number may be found requisite.

He asked Rolle to tell Bastard this.[9]

Pitt's announcement to Rolle reflects his decision to build a base to
serve as a place of refreshment for the India ships, and as a strategic
outlier to the subcontinent, for the 'measures' he referred to were
preparations to implement Thompson's Das Voltas Bay scheme. At the
beginning of May, 'in consequence of Mr. Pitt's desire,' Nepean asked a
number of merchants to estimate 'the Expence of conveying to Cape

Voltas on the Southern Coast of Africa some of the Convicts under sentence of Transportation.' Macaulay and Gregory gave him their estimate on 10 May, and Calvert his on 1 June. Nepean then asked Steele to assess these, observing,

> It seemed to me to be Mr. Pitt's intention at all events that if Cape Voltas was not found to correspond with our expectations for the Settlement of the Convicts that some other Spot should be fixed upon to the Southward of the Line, and as that is his determination, it might not be improper to Contract for Cape Voltas under certain conditions, that if it should be thought adviseable before the departure of the Ships from hence to fix upon some other place, that such Ships should in that case be hired at so much per Ton per Month.

Steele passed the estimates on to the Navy Board, who reported that the merchants' terms were reasonable.[10]

The spring of 1786, then, saw the emergence of a comprehensive British policy aimed at countering France's diplomacy in Europe, and her expansion in the eastern world. This policy had two strands, distinct, but interwoven — a more active diplomacy in Europe and the Near East, to balance the French gains; and, in case of this one's failure, the strengthening of strategic resources in and about India. Both involved a co-ordinated use of various resources, with Harris's expertise, the nation's money, and Baldwin's Levant experience in the warp of the first; and Mulgrave's strategic insight, the Admiralty's resources, and the convicts' labour, in that of the second. This policy emerged as Pitt took a much more immediate hand in the business of the Home and Foreign Offices and the India Board, and it bore his stamp.

III *Crisis in Europe and the East*

The situation in Europe and the East worsened before Pitt, Dundas, and Mulgrave's policy could take effect. In letters which reached the Board of Control late in March, John Macpherson, temporarily Governor-General of Bengal, warned of the arrival of a *flûte* at Pondicherry, and of French interest in the Andamans.[1] Then, in mid-June, the Administration received Macpherson's reports of incidents in Bengal which boded great ill.

These incidents ostensibly arose from conflicting interpretations of the Thirteenth Article of the Versailles Treaty, by which Britain agreed to restore to France the factories and territories she had held in India before 1749, and guaranteed a 'free, certain, and independent commerce' along the Orissa, Coromandel, and Malabar coasts, and in Bengal, such as she had enjoyed before.[2]

Because it was not specific enough, this article soon gave rise to contention. Previous to 1783, the British had had a monopoly of the salt, saltpetre, and opium trades in Bengal; and, as well as being barred from these trades, other Europeans operating there had done so under British and native customs regulations, which included inspection of cargoes, and payment of duties. In agreeing to the French regaining 'a free, certain, and independent commerce' in Bengal, the British did not consider that they had also agreed to their losing either their traditional trading privileges, or their control over trade.

The French, at least in India, saw the matter rather differently. They took the Thirteenth Article to allow:

1. The free, certain, and independent Trade, Export and Import, . . . in every part of India, and in every Article, Salt and Saltpetre included, absolutely free from duty;

and

2. The free, certain and independent entrance of French Ships and Boats in the Ganges, without being liable to be searched or visited.[3]

Asserting what he claimed as his nation's right, Dangereux, the aptly-named French agent in India, sent the cargo vessel l'*Auguste-Victor* up the Ganges towards Chandernagore in late November 1785. When the captain attempted to pass the British fort at Budge Budge without stopping, the British, who had reports that the ship had a cargo of salt, fired across her bows. The French captain then stopped, and allowed the British to search his ship, who found that it did not in fact have the rumoured cargo. Two weeks later, the captain of the frigate l'*Espérance*, which was leaky and in urgent need of repair, also attempted to pass the British fort at Budge Budge. The British fired on her too, and her captain stopped, but the delay proved too much for the ship's strained timbers, and she sank.

With considerable eloquence, and great indignation, Dangereux then discussed the matter of these 'insults' with the Bengal government;[4] and the British authorities, remembering their instructions not to provoke the French, were conciliatory. They apologized for the Budge Budge officers' falsely believing that the l'*Auguste-Victor* had a contraband cargo, and they offered to replace the frigate. On the other hand, they insisted upon their construction of the Thirteenth article. And as these were but the latest and most sinister of a series of disputes arising from the divergent interpretations of that vexing Article, they decided to seek a comprehensive settlement of the conflict with the Vicomte de Souillac, the French Governor-General at Mauritius.

For this mission, the Bengal Government chose their Paymaster, Colonel Charles Cathcart, who knew the Viçomte. They instructed him to be accommodataing about the restoration of old rights, but to insist that they would not relinquish their requirement that the French pay customs duties on goods sent to or from Chandernagore, which was established by 'immemorial custom' and 'express Summary from the Country Government.' As well, he was to convey their determination to maintain

ambiguities over an article in treaty suggesting that it could override GB. rights.

the monopolies of the saltpetre, opium, and salt trades, which they held 'on the Ground of ancient Custom,' and which nothing but 'the most positive Instructions from Europe' would persuade them to give up.

Cathcart was to assure de Souillac of the 'extreme anxiety' of the British in Bengal to fulfil the obligations prescribed by the Treaty of Versailles; and if he succeeded in negotiating a settlement, he was to return to Bengal. However, if the French Governor-General did not receive him cordially, *or if he saw any other signs of imminent French hostilities*, he was to sail directly to Europe, and report to the Company and the Administration. He sailed in February.[5]

The Bengal government told of these developments in a series of letters which reached the Secret Court and the Board of Control in mid-June. They painted an alarming picture, describing the

> Intrigues in which the . . . Agents of France appear to be employed for the Increase of their Power,

and suggesting that Dangereux had contrived the Budge Budge incidents in order to give France a pretext for war. They also described the weakness of Britain's naval situation in the East. 'The French have ships at Mauritius,' they pointed out,

> They have Cruisers in the Gulph of Persia, — and they sometimes have Frigates on the Coromandel Coast. The Dutch too have a Fleet in India, while the English are without any, or at least will be so on the expected Departure of the Ships now commanded by Captain Hughes.

In the absence of a British squadron, they asserted, two enemy warships could stop them supplying Madras and Bombay; and since these presidencies

> must depend in a great Measure on us for the Means of carrying on War, we shall be involved in the most serious Dilemma if, at the Commencement of Hostilities there shall not be a British Marine Force in India equal to that of our Enemies.[6]

Now, too, the Administration received a report from Hailes in Paris tending to confirm the Bengal officials' alarming views. He had continued to attend to the question of French interest in Acheen, he said, and while unable to learn anything definite, he had heard of a proposal, which came either from France or Holland, that Austria should cede the Nicobar Islands, and the Danes their factories on the Malabar coast. 'From the importance of such views,' he told Carmarthen,

> I take the earliest opportunity of sending your Lordship intimation of my intelligence. I need not remark upon the advantages of the Situation of the Nicobar Islands, commanding the entrance into the Streights of Malacca, and if join'd with Trincomalé, likely to render truly formidable the French and Dutch power in the Bay of Bengal. I doubt not but your Lordship will be in-

J

clined as well as myself to give credit to this Account, should you not (as I have not) hear anything of the prosecution of the French Plan for a settlement at Acheen.

The Foreign Secretary sent this information to Pitt, and to the Admiralty and India Boards.[7]

Pitt, Dundas, and Mulgrave responded first by asking Carmarthen to have Hailes take the matter up with Vergennes. This Carmarthen did on 5 July. Hailes replied four days later that Vergennes, who had not yet received accounts from India, wished to have the British ones, and was accommodating.[8]

With this information, and cautiously awaiting details of Cathcart's negotiations at Mauritius, the Commissioners for India then met in secret session on 19 July, to draft a preliminary despatch to the Bengal Government. They praised the Indian officials for their restraint, and in general approved of their stand. They enclosed copies of Carmarthen and Hailes's letters on the matter, observing that

> from the tenor of this answer we are led to hope, that the disputes which have taken place in India, did not arise from any preconceived plan or instructions from Europe, to create difficulties in the execution of the Treaty.

And, they issued explicit instructions on how the Bengal officials were to proceed in the interval while the home government discussed the operation of the Thirteenth Article, so as not, 'by concessions on your part, [to] weaken any ground it may be intended to maintain.'[9]

Carmarthen sent copies of the British reports, and of the Board of Control's instructions to the Bengal Government, to Hailes on 4 August, telling him that he should not

> enter into a particular Discussion of the several Points involved in this Business, as to commit in any Degree, this Country in respect to its future Conduct, without further Instructions from hence.

He should brief Eden, who was then in Paris negotiating a commercial treaty with France, but Eden, too, must be most circumspect in using any of the material in his present discussions. The Foreign Secretary ended this instruction by pointing to the circumstance 'which must never be lost sight of' — France's interests in India, 'whatever Her Pretensions may be, should in Point of Justice, as well as Policy, be considered by us, as purely & simply Commercial;' while Britain's, 'from her Territorial Rights, necessarily include the greatest Objects of Political Concern, as well as those merely dependent on Commerce & Navigation.' Hailes acknowledged this instruction a week later, and in return gave details which again pointed to Dangereaux's having deliberately contrived the Budge Budge incidents in order to provoke war.[10]

As Pitt and his colleagues waited anxiously for news of Cathcart's proceedings, they found their hopes for another project disappointed. On 23

July, the *Nautilus* reached Spithead, for T. B. Thompson to report that he had found 'no Bay, River, or Inlet' in Das Voltas Bay's supposed latitude, only a 'barren & rocky' shoreline; and that he had then followed this frequently fog-bound coast north to 16°S, 'without finding a Drop of fresh Water, or seeing a Tree.' He had not found a suitable harbour, and had seen only 'savage & shy' natives. Clearly, Das Voltas Bay was anything but the desirable situation that explorers' accounts had led his uncle to think; and the Administration could not send the convicts, or anyone else, there to build a naval base.[11]

Now, too, came reports from Harris to confirm Macpherson and Hailes's view of Dangereux's actions, and to make the need to strengthen Britain's strategic resources about India urgent in the extreme. The diplomat wrote on 1 August that he had 'good reason' to think that the French ambassador had received 'Some very important Instructions, relative to the future plans of the French in The Dutch-East-Indies and that Something Ministerial on this subject will soon appear.' He was led to believe, he said, that 'its tendency will be to place French garrisons in The Dutch Settlements in Asia.' Harris wrote farther to this point three days later, saying that

> The Court of Versailles is to represent, ministerially, to The Republic the defenceless State of the Dutch Settlements in India—and to insinuate that if Their High Mightinesses expect France to fulfil the Article of the late Treaty by which She guarantees to Them their possessions in that part of the Globe, it is absolutely necessary to put their military establishment there upon a more respectable footing—that is to Say (according to a plan, given in Some time ago), to raise it to 14,000 European Troops.
>
> The States, on receiving this Representation, are to Send it to the East India Directors. These are to repeat what They have already Said—'that the exhausted State of their finances puts it out of their power to increase their expences, and that They cannot Supply a fund for more than 9,000 men.'
>
> To this The States (Supposing the power of the Pensionaries equal to the Work) are to reply 'that They will furnish the money'—and France is to lend the 5,000 men deficient in the complement, which are to be carried out by the Rhingrave De Salm—who is to take upon him the Supreme command of all the Dutch Forces in Asia.

The Foreign Office received both these despatches on 7 August, and sent them on to Pitt. Then, in a letter of 8 August, which arrived four days later, Harris said that 'the crisis which, in my opinion, is to determine the political existence of This Republic is drawing nearer and nearer every hour.'[12]

Then, on 15 August, Cathcart reached London. He gave the Secret Committee a letter with five enclosures detailing his proceedings at Mauritius; and he reported directly and secretly to Sydney on these, and on the French naval forces in the East. Sydney sent an account of his interview with Cathcart to the King at 3.25 p.m. on 16 August. Three hours later, George expressed his satisfaction with the peaceful settlement of the dispute, but also observed that 'France certainly under the name of flutes can soon collect a considerable naval force in the East Indies.'[13]

Cathcart's coming to London presents a puzzle. The Bengal Government had told him to return if he succeeded in his negotiations, to go to England if unsuccessful, *or if he had signs of war*. He did succeed in reaching an accord with de Souillac, but he nevertheless sailed home. His enclosures to the Secret Committee, and Sydney's account of their interview, unfortunately seem not to have survived; but George III's explicit reference makes it reasonable to assume that he went to England because he found a naval build-up at Mauritius.

Such report, of course, coming so close upon Macpherson's from India, and Harris and Hailes's from Holland and France, could not but have confirmed Pitt and his advisers in their view that the French were preparing to drive the British from the East. In this atmosphere, and knowing that they could not proceed with the Das Voltas Bay Scheme, they decided to establish a convict colony at Botany Bay, on the coast of New South Wales.

CHAPTER 7

Botany Bay and the first fleet
1786-1787

I   *The Administration considers alternatives to Das Voltas Bay*

AUGUST 1786

Sun		6	13	20	27
Mon		7	14	21	28
Tues	1	8	15	22	29
Wed	2	9	16	23	30
Thurs| 3	10	17	24	31
Fri	4	11	18	25	
Sat	5	12	19	26	

August began inauspiciously for Great Britain. On the second day, as the *Annual Register* recorded for posterity,

As the King was alighting from his post-chariot, at the garden entrance of St. James's, the woman, who appeared very decently dressed, in the act of presenting a paper to his majesty, which he was receiving with great condescension, struck a concealed knife at his breast, which his majesty happily avoided by drawing back. As she was making a second thrust, one of the yeomen caught her arm, and, at the same instant, one of the king's footmen wrenched the knife from her hand. The king, with great temper and fortitude exclaimed, 'I am not hurt — take care of the poor woman — do not hurt her.'

The same day she underwent an examination before the privy council, when it appeared that her name was Margaret Nicholson, daughter of George Nicholson, of Stockton-upon-Tees; and that she had lived in several creditable services. Being asked where she had lived since she left her last place? She answered franticly, 'She had been all abroad since that matter of the crown broke out.' — Being asked what matter? She went on rambling, that the crown

was her's — she wanted nothing but her right — that she had great property — that if she had not her right, England would be drowned in blood for a
thousand generations. Being further asked where she now lived, she answered
rationally, 'At Mr. Fisk's, stationer, the corner of Wigmore-street,
Marybone.' On being questioned as to her right, she would answer none but a
judge, her rights were a mystery. Being asked, if she had ever petitioned? She
said, she had ten days ago. On looking back among the papers, such petition
was found, full of princely nonsense about tyrants, usurpers, and pretenders
to the throne, &c. &c.

Mr Fisk being sent for and interrogated, said she had lodged with him
about three years; that he had not observed any striking marks of insanity
about her — she was certainly very odd at times — frequently talking to
herself — that she lived by taking in plain work, &c. Others who knew her, said
she was very industrious, and they never suspected her of insanity.

Dr. Monro being sent for, said, it was impossible to discover with certainty
immediately whether she was insane or not. It was proposed to commit her for
three or four days to Tothillfields Bridewell. This was objected to because it
was said she was a state-prisoner. At length it was agreed to commit her to the
custody of a messenger.

Her lodgings being examined, there were found three letters about her
pretended right to the crown, one to Lord Mansfield, one to Lord
Loughborough, and one to General Bramham.[1]

This unseemly event inevitably engrossed the Home Secretary's attention in the next days. He had first to supervise a close examination of the
woman, to determine her motives. In the evening of 3 August, he informed the King that she appeared to be insane, that two magistrates
were searching her lodgings, and that Nepean had gone to interview
General Bramham.[2] Then he had the petitions from a nation shocked at
this dreadful attempt on their sovereign's life and grateful for his mer-
ciful deliverance to receive and lay before the King; after which, of
course, he had his Majesty's gracious thanks to return.

After repeated interrogations, Nepean and Fraser (who ran the secret
service in Europe) decided that Margaret Nicholson was not the agent of
a foreign government; and the doctors decided that she was insane. (It
seems that she became disordered after a lover deserted her.) The Great
Cabinet of the Privy Council confirmed these findings in a lengthy inter-
rogation on 8 August, and announced them to the nation.[3]

It was all very trying. 'Deeply impressed with the protection of the
Allmighty,' George took a country tour to Oxford, to restore his and his
family's agitated nerves (and also to avoid being in London on his
profligate heir's birthday). Lord Sydney, too, retired to the country for a
restful weekend after this 'disagreeable and alarming event' which — as
he told a correspondent — 'You will easily imagine must have taken up
my whole time & attention.'[4]

With this portend of the disjointed time exorcised, the Administration
turned their attention to the other, much more serious, ones which they

were receiving—Sir James Harris's reports of the plans to send French troops to the Dutch settlements in the East, and T. B. Thompson's disappointing one on the south-west African coast.

These reports placed the Administration in a considerable quandary. On the one hand, Harris's indicated an ever more urgent need to strengthen the nation's position in the East; on the other, Thompson's showed that they could not implement their scheme for doing so at Das Voltas Bay. If Pitt were to continue with his idea of using the convicts to build a new naval base south of the line, he would need to find another site along, or just off, the India route; one with a satisfactory harbour, a healthy climate, a fertile hinterland; no or few native inhabitants (or at the very least benign ones), one not possessed or claimed by another European power.

These varied requirements, of course, reduced the field from which the Administration might choose; but by 7 August, they had four immediate prospects. The first was the Caffre Coast, which Pemberton and William Dalrymple had recommended the previous year as having good harbours and a fertile hinterland. After their Das Voltas Bay experience, however, the Administration could scarcely have proceeded to settle this coast without confirming its suitability with a survey by an experienced naval officer and a botanist; and it would, of course, have taken at least another year to have the results of this survey. As well, the area's proximity to the Cape, and the presence of Dutch farmers in the intervening territory, would have justified Holland's claiming a prior right to possess; and various circumstances show that Britain wished to observe the decorum then prevailing amongst European nations on this point.

The second and third prospects emerged from proposals from Captain John Blankett. Writing to Howe on 6 August, Blankett said as he understood that the *Nautilus* had returned 'without the success there was reason to expect,' he supposed

> the finding a proper place to send our Convicts may again become *a Naval question*

(my emphasis). From this general perspective, Blankett saw that the Administration had two objects to achieve in disposing of the convicts—to get rid of them

> at the smallest expence possible to Government; [and] to make their future labour & subsistence serviceable to the State.[5]

Blankett suggested that either Tristan da Cunha or Madagascar might meet the need. In citing the South Atlantic islands, he passed on the report of his boatswain that the prevailing winds gave outward-bound ships a favourable passage there, and that land and sea offered rich food supplies. These remote islands were not clearly a suitable site for a colony, however, for they were small, they lacked anchorages, and they were very cold in winter. The possibility of Bolts's having already claimed them for Austria was an additional impediment (if one were needed); and the Administration showed no real interest in them.

As they had also done in mid-1785, however, they showed considerable interest in Blankett's other suggestion. Blankett thought that they might obtain a 'limited district not to be extended' from the natives of Madagascar, for which they should pay an annual rent (so as to consolidate and continue 'a mutual interest of the Parties'). They might transport the convicts annually on the outward-bound Indiamen, for as these sailed largely cargo-less, Government would thereby have a ready conveyance, and shipowners a gratuitous revenue. As Madagascar was fertile, the Administration might maintain the convicts cheaply there. They might admit local women to the settlement as expedient. The settlers might develop an extensive and profitable trade in the island's products—in timber, salt, and slaves to the Cape; in rice, salted provisions, butter, cheese, hides, and slaves to the Portuguese settlements on the east African coast; in salted provisions, timber, and gum to India. They might also develop one in European manufactures (cutlery, bracelets, guns, etc.) with the natives. These trades would help the settlement become self-sufficient, and lessen the expense to which the Administration would be put in maintaining it, but they would be incidental benefits. The main ones that the British might derive from the move would be, first, 'an Entrepôt between Europe & Asia, for the refreshment of all Ships going to & from India, as has been fully proved from the first Navigation of those Seas;' and second, 'a great resource & recruit for the Navy in India in any future War.'

Blankett told Nepean privately on 10 August that he had suggested Madagascar to Howe, adding that he had 'reason to think that if it becomes a Naval question that Idea will be adopted,' and that 'I just hint it to you, in case you have any other plan which it might cross.' Howe responded four days later. Blankett's boatswain's having been to Tristan da Cunha, he said, carried more weight with him 'than all which has been avered by almost all the ancient Navigators from foreign Countries.' 'The recent Experience of their Inaccuracy in the instance of the Sloop returned a short time since from Africa', he said, increased his doubts 'of the reliance to be placed on the generality of their assurances.' However, he conceded the usefulness of surveying 'those Tracts which have not been revisited lately,' so as to have a better understanding of their potential. Blankett then thanked Howe for this reply, and assured him that he spoke of Madagascar from personal knowledge, as he had spent six weeks there. Again, he offered a profound insight into the Administration's motive for establishing a colony of convicts when he repeated that he had concluded that their disposal might be a 'Naval question,' and now identified this view as the 'Minister's, (i.e., Pitt's).'[6]

The likely 'naval' advantages of a settlement on Madagascar were, of course, those which Blankett described, but there were a number of obstacles to the Administration's adopting his proposal. Blankett was an experienced officer, whose opinions the politicians valued greatly, but he had not made a regular survey of the island's potential sites. Neither had he had a botanist with him, to make an expert assessment of its fertility and its products' potential utility. The Administration would have had to survey before they could have decided to colonize. This would have been costly and time-consuming; and even if they had thereby found a suitable site, they would have had to overcome the objections of an East India Company haunted by the spectre of illicit trade before they could have proceeded—as Blankett himself conceded, it was 'probable the India Company would make obstacles to such an establishment.' The French, too, might very well have objected, for they had intermittently maintained settlements there. Though interested, the Administration hung fire.

The fourth prospect was Botany Bay, on the coast of New South Wales; and this, on 19 August 1786, Pitt and his colleagues decided to colonize.

II *The attractions of Botany Bay*

Historians have for long considered that the Pitt administration decided to colonize Botany Bay suddenly and in some despair, with the sole aim of ridding the nation's prison and hulks of the too-numerous transportees. The very opposite is, in fact, true—Pitt and his colleagues took this decision after an extensive and careful consideration; and their broad motive for it was the same as that for their earlier interest in Das Voltas Bay: Botany Bay was a place where they might use the convicts' labour to increase the nation's capacity to protect her position and commerce in the East.

This seems rather strange to us, of course, who possess an instinctive consciousness of Australia's geographical isolation. Yet, given their perspectives and requirements, there was much about Botany Bay to recommend it to Pitt and his advisers. First, it offered a sheltered anchorage, and was amenable to fortification. Cook described it as 'Capacious safe and commodious,' with 'steep rocky clifts next the Sea' (and therefore 'tollerably well sheltered from all winds'), and an entrance through narrow-set heads. It had a channel giving 12-14 feet of water at low tide, and anchorages of from 5 to 7 fathoms.[1]

Second, the area had the potential to meet the colonists' needs, and those of the ships that might visit. There were native resources—on land, a sort of 'wild Spinage,' a kind of cherry, 'large quantities' of quails and parrots; about the bay, a plethora of shellfish and fish. A number of streams entered the bay, and the land about offered a prospect of infinite improvement. As Cook and Banks described it, there were areas of swampy ground, but also others of woods and 'Lawns' (i.e., grass lands). The woods were

> free from underwood of every kind and the trees are at such a distance from one another that the whole Country or at least great part of it might be cultivated without being oblig'd to cut down a single tree.

Away from the marshes, the soil was 'a light white sand' that produced 'a quantity of good grass;' and there were areas of a 'much richer' 'deep black Soil,' which bore 'besides timber as fine meadow as ever was seen,' and which might produce 'any kind of grain.' Colonists might cultivate these tracts 'in the Ordinary Modes used in England,' Banks said. 'In this Extensive Country,' said Cook,

> it can never be doubted but what most sorts of Grain, Fruits, Roots, &c^a of every kind would flourish here were they once brought hither, planted and cultivated by the hand of Industry, and here are Provender for more Cattle at all seasons of the year than ever can be brought into this Country.

The trees offered an abundant supply of fuel and building material; and the stone was also 'very proper' for building.[2]

Third, the climate appeared healthy. Cook observed that the Aboriginals of New South Wales lived 'in a warm and fine Climate and enjoy[ed] a very wholsome Air.' Matra told the Beauchamp Committee that they had found the climate 'perfectly agreeable to European Constitution.' Clearly, Botany Bay would be no white man's grave in the manner of Gambia or Batavia.[3]

Fourth, the British might occupy the area without violating either the dictates of humanity or the decorum of European politics. Banks thought that the coastal districts were very thinly inhabited, and the vast interior ones most likely deserted. He and Cook had encountered only a few Aboriginals during their stay at Botany Bay, never more than '30 or 40 together.' Though given to hostile gesturing, these had seemed not 'at all to be feared.' They had only the most insubstantial of dwellings, and appeared nomadic. He believed that they wandered

> like the Arabs from place to place set [their shelters] up whenever they met with [an area] where sufficient supplys of food are to be met with, and as soon as these are exhausted remove to another leaving the houses behind, which are framd with less art or rather less industry than any habitations of human beings probably that the world can shew.

They had no discernible social or religious organization. According to European notions, New South Wales was *terra nullius*, to be occupied on the basis of first discovery, without purchase from the indigenous inhabitants. Cook's discovery and charting of the coast, and his formally

of NSW

possessing it, being the first recorded by a European, gave Britain first right amongst her neighbours to settle it.[4]

Fifth, though it was not adjacent to the established routes, the British did not conceive of Botany Bay as being inconveniently far from the Indian sub-continent, for they thought of it as at least as much on the edge of the Indian as of the Pacific Ocean. Matra described New South Wales as extending 'from the 44.th degree of South Latitude, to the 10.th and from 110, to near 154 degrees of Longitude.' It was 'about a Months run to the Cape of Good Hope; five weeks from Madras, and the same from Canton; very near the Moluccas, & less than a Months run to Batavia.' From it, they might attack the Dutch in the East Indies by a 'safe, & expeditious Voyage,' and the Spanish in Manila with equal facility. The colonists might also obtain livestock from Savu and the Moluccas, which were 'very near New South Wales.' Young told Pitt that Botany Bay lay 'not more than about Seven Hundred Leagues' from the coast of China, 'nearly the same distance from the East Indies; from the Spice Islands about five hundred Leagues, and about a months run from the Cape of Good-hope.' (He lengthened these distances in later versions, but retained the import.) The Beauchamp Committee interviewed the East India Company's shipping clerk so as to obtain an estimate of the likely cost of transporting to New South Wales. When newspapers announced the Administration's decision to colonize, they described New Holland as being 'in the Indian Seas.'[5]

Sixth, by settling New South Wales, the Administration would render *actual* the *preliminary* right of possession which Cook had established, and thus preclude the French or the Dutch from occupying it, and thereby adding to British problems in the East.

Seventh, the islands in the south-western Pacific Ocean offered the prospect of a supply of naval stores for the eastern marines. These prospects ranged from New Caledonia to New Zealand, but centred on Norfolk Island, about sixteen hundred kilometres to the north-east of Botany Bay. This small island is of volcanic origin, with two peaks of about three hundred metres, and is some 36 square kilometres in area. Its coastline is abrupt and jagged, and offers a reasonable landing at only one spot. Shoals and reefs cluster about it. La Pérouse, who was unable either to anchor or land there, described it as 'only a place fit for angels and eagles to reside in.'[6]

If an eyrie of eagles and angels, though, Norfolk Island had other attributes in the late Eighteenth century. Cook and Wales reported that it was 'uninhabited and near akin to New Zealand,' that the native flax, (*phormium tenax*), so covered its shores that it was 'scarce possible to get through it,' and that the 'Spruce Pines' which grew there 'in vast abundance and to a vast size, from two to three feet diameter and upwards,' were superior to those of New Zealand and New Caledonia for 'masts, Yards, &c.' Here was an island, they said, 'where Masts for the largest

Ships' might be had; and Cook fashioned one tree into a yard for the *Resolution*.[7]

Cook's report of Norfolk Island inevitably increased the interest in the prospect of obtaining naval stores from the south Pacific which his and Banks's earlier descriptions of New Zealand's timber and flax had first engendered, and which Banks's failure to establish the *phormium tenax* at Kew did not dampen. After Cook's second voyage, J. R. Forster gave some specimens of the fibre from this plant to a 'Foreign Lady' to work, and the result was 'a degree of fineness and whiteness which could be little expected.' When Forster showed the results to the Admiralty, they asked Cook

> to bring from New Zealand, if you should touch there in the course of your present intended voyage, a quantity of the seeds, and if practicable, some of the Plants of the beforementioned Hemp or Flax, that farther Experiments may be made of it.

Cook evidently followed this request, for while he does not mention it again, King recorded one landing on the north-west coast of America because 'we wanted earth . . . for some New Zealand plants of flax.'[8]

At some time in the late 1770s or early 1780s, people tested the *phormium tenax*, for James Matra was able to represent in 1783 that

> in Naval Equipments it would be of the greatest importance; a Cable of the Circumference of ten Inches would be equal in Strength to one of eighteen Inches made of European Hemp. Our Manufacturers are of the opinion that Canvas made out of it, would be superiour, in Strength & Beauty to any Canvas of our own Country.

There were practical tests, too, for Sir George Young had samples of cordage, and of canvas 'which had been worn & tried in the foot or clew of a Cutter's Mainsail.'[9]

As a consequence of this attention, those well-placed to do so formed the opinion that the New Zealand hemp was potentially a most valuable raw material. Brook Watson told a Canadian correspondent in 1785, 'Could the Flax of New Holland be introduced and accord with your soil, 'twould be better than the mines of South America to Spain;' and in 1789, as he helped the Board of Trade assess the Abbé Bruelles's process, he told Hawkesbury that

> The more I consider the Nature of Hemp, the Capability of our Country to produce it and the Consequences of its being so produced and the peculiar Advantages which would accrue to Our Manufactures from bringing it to them in its best Form, by the Mode recently discovered for doing it — the more anxious I am for its being carried to the highest Pitch of Improvement. To this Desire Your Lordship must attribute the repeated Applications with which I trouble You. The Specimens of New Zealand Hemp which I have seen are so far superior to any other I have beheld that I most earnestly entreat Your

Lordship to take the best and most speedy Means for procuring some of its Seed from that Country; if taken from the Plant it must be put in a Heap to heat for some Days, then dried schreened and put into Bottles well corked to keep out the Air.[10]

About this time, too, Banks finally succeeded in establishing the plant at Kew. A few years later, at the King's request, he included a specimen, and worked samples as well, in the collection he sent to Catherine II of Russia; and his comments indicate his profound and sustained interest in the plant's possibilities. 'Much has been said by all who have visited New Zealand,' he wrote,

> on the prodigious strength of the fibres of the *Phormium tenax*, usually called New Zealand Flax; I have seen a Fishing Seine more than a hundred fathoms long entirely made of its leaves, divided into narrow Ribbonds without any twisting: in the box with the drawing a small bundle of this Flax manufactured by the Indians is sent, it is part of what I procured when I visited New Zealand in 1769. In 26 years keeping it must have lost much of its original strength, but it is still very tough: as this Plant which is brought from a climate much resembling the South of France or Portugal may certainly be cultivated in some part of the extensive dominions of Russia, & possibly in a Country where Hemp is a staple, become an article of commerce, His Majesty is pleased to order that one of them should be added to the Dutchesses Collection.[11]

Authors and publishers presented this information about the Pacific's resources to the British public repeatedly in the 1770s and 1780s. Initially, newspapers and journals gave brief details of the islands and their productions. Then, Hawkesworth conveyed Banks's comments on the timber and flax of New Zealand; and Sydney Parkinson offered his description of the *phormium tenax*. Cook described his sailing routes; and also New Caledonia, the Isle of Pines, Améré, and Norfolk Island. He included plates of the New Zealand spruce and flax, and of the trees on the Isle of Pines, partly in the hope that these might be useful to seamen. The Forsters, Marra, and others echoed Cook's descriptions. Compilers then repeated this information in lesser detail, in collections of voyages and travels, geography books, and some scientific works. By the middle of the 1780s it was something of a commonplace that the New Zealand flax

> might prove of more real benefit to [Britain], could it be thoroughly introduced, than the productions of all the islands which our circumnavigators have discovered for a century past.[12]

Finally, that they might decide to colonize it without further investigation no doubt also recommended Botany Bay to Pitt and his advisers. As Howe's comments to Blankett show, after Das Voltas Bay the Administration realized the likely unreliability of old report; and this consideration of course did not attend that which they had of Botany Bay.

Cook and Banks had surveyed, botanized, and observed the New South
Wales coast only sixteen years before; and Cook was the greatest, and
most accurate, explorer of his age (or of any other), while Banks was pre-
eminent in European science, and a trusted adviser. The Pitt Administration could have had no reason to suspect that their descriptions
might be unreliable. 'Do you think Government would run any Risk in
Attempting this plan without further Examination than you or any body
you know could give them of that Country,' the Beauchamp Committee
had asked Matra, who had replied, 'I think they would not.'[13]

The Administration had an estimate of the likely cost of transportation to New South Wales to add to the reliable descriptions of the region,
too. Nepean had obtained this at the beginning of the year, when, beginning from Matra and Young's suggestions, he had sketched sending out
one 40-gunship, a tender, and two transports with some six hundred
convicts and three Marine companies, and had asked Duncan Campbell
for figures for transporting the convicts out, feeding and clothing them
in New South Wales for a year, and equipping them for agriculture. On
the basis of the transports returning empty, and the round voyage taking
fifteen months, Campbell thought that the cost of carrying each convict
outwards would be more than £50; but he commented, 'Should the Ship
be Permitted to take in a Load at China for Britain in that case the Contractor might be able to obtain a handsome profit by the Voyage, & of
course to Relax in their terms.'[14]

It would not be right to claim that Pitt and his colleagues saw a colony
at Botany Bay as being as desirable as one at an efficacious Das Voltas
Bay would have been. Botany Bay was off the shipping routes, and the
costs of transporting to there were inevitably greater than they would
have been to south-west Africa. Botany Bay was clearly a second choice,
made when the first proved abortive. Still, it had its attractions, especially those of naval stores and general strategic position; and, given
the Administration's general purpose for the convicts, these made it a
satisfactory prospect.

III   *The decision to colonize New South Wales*

While the chronology of the Administration's August 1786 decision to
colonize Botany Bay remains clouded in places, there are enough details
extant for us to reconstruct substantially what happened.

T. B. Thompson reached Spithead in the *Nautilus* on 23 July, and he
reported to the Home Office the next day. As Blankett's letters to Howe
and Nepean show, news of his disappointing report soon spread, but, no
doubt for a variety of reasons in addition to the disruption to business
which Margaret Nicholson's attack caused, the officials did not begin for-

mally to reassess the prospects of their plan for the convicts until the week beginning 14 August.

The Home Office dealt with a good deal of colonial business in this week. First, they quickly considered Thompson's report, and dismissed him on 15 August.[1] Then, the next day, Sydney had Cathcart's reports on his convention with de Souillac and on the French naval buildup at Mauritius, and passed these on to the King. On this day, too, Sydney had Fawkener, the Clerk of the Privy Council, arrange for Hawkesbury to reach town 'on Friday morning early enough to hold a Committee of Trade before the Levee, to consider of Lord Dorchesters Instructions.' Pitt, Sydney, Hawkesbury, Carmarthen, Grenville, and Effingham met in Council on Friday 18 August, and approved the Home Office's draft of these instructions.[2]

At the same time, Nepean assembled the basis for a decision for Botany Bay. While Cook, Banks, and Matra's accounts showed that this site had the necessary physical attributes for a convict settlement, and that the nation would gain strategically from one there, the likely cost of transporting to, and maintaining a settlement there was clearly a considerable impediment. Nepean thereafore had his colleagues in the Treasury examine Campbell's figures. After consulting with the Admiralty and Navy Board officials, these reported that the Administration might transport to Botany Bay for less than Campbell suggested if they themselves victualled the crews of the transports, as well at the marines and the convicts, during the voyage, and if they settled on crews of fifty rather than seventy, and added thirty marines to each as a guard. On this basis, they estimated the cost of sending out a warship and tender, two transports, two companies of marines, and six hundred convicts, and of feeding, clothing, and equipping these convicts for one year, at £39,187.[3]

This estimate was not a complete one, for it did not include the cost of a superintendent, or that of victualling the marines. Nepean accordingly then added these, and others as well. First, he increased the projected marine force to three companies (180 men), and included the sum of £500 for the superintendent's salary, to arrive at a cost of £17,669 for maintaining the colonizing party for the first year. He estimated that they should save one half of the cost of victualling the marines and convicts in the second year, so that the cost of the settlement should then drop to £14,449; and that 'the Service of the Tender after the Second Year or even the 40 Gun Ship will not be necessary, so that the expence of the Establishment at the end of 3 Years will probably not exceed £7000 per Year.' He allowed £45 for carrying each convict out, £1000 for their tools, and £1300 for 'Stock to be purchased & Seeds,' to arrive at a cost of some £30,000 for beginning the colony.[4]

Then, seeing that one person could scarcely superintend six hundred convicts unaided, he sketched a civil staff establishment of:

						Yearly Salary.		
						£	s.	d.
The Naval Commander to be appointed Governor or Superintendent General	...	...	...	...		500	0	0
The Commanding Officer of the Marines, to be appointed Lieut. Gov. or Dep? Superintendent			...	...		250	0	0
The Commissary of Stores and Provisions for himself and assistants (to be appointed or named by the Contractors for the Provisions)		...	...	...		200	0	0
Pay of a surgeon ...	...	...	...	£182	10	0		
D? of two Mates.	...	...	...	182	10	0		
						365	0	0
Chaplain ...	...	...	...	...	...	182	10	0
						£1,497	10	0

Adjusting some figures, he then determined that it should cost the Administration £29,300 to begin the settlement, £18,669 to maintain it during the first year, £15,449 during the second, and below £7000 during the third — that is, over three years and eight months, about £32 per convict per year, or some £4 more than that of keeping him on a hulk.[5]

Nepean's arriving at this — in view of the expected return — acceptable cost cleared the way for a firm proposal to send the convicts to Botany Bay, and this took form as the 'Heads of a Plan for effectually disposing of Convicts, and rendering their Transportation reciprocally beneficial both to themselves and to the State, by the Establishment of a Colony in New South Wales.' Considerable mystery still surrounds the authorship, purpose, and significance of this crucial document. Though it survives in several copies, these are all final versions in clerks' hands.[6] No draft has yet appeared, so that we lack conclusive proof of who composed it. Nepean's position, and his constant and profound involvement with the convict business, however, make it most unlikely that anyone else did. Even if he did not do so wholly, he must have contributed largely to it, and the internal and circumstantial evidence of his authorship is so strong as to justify definite ascription.

Nepean framed the 'Heads' alert alike to the need to satisfy the British public's sense of its humanity, and Pitt's rather conflicting desire to increase the nation's strategic capacity in the East and at the same time restrain expenditure. New South Wales seemed 'peculiarly adapted to answer the views of Government,' he said. Its climate was salubrious, and its soil fertile enough to sustain an agriculture. The colonists might obtain livestock from the Cape of Good Hope and the Molucca Islands. With industry, they should become self-sufficient in food in three years, so that the cost of maintaining the colony would then diminish greatly. In any case, the difference in cost between placing the convicts at Botany Bay, and that of keeping them on the hulks, when set against the 'great object to be obtained by it,' was 'too trivial to be a consideration with

Government.' As well, New South Wales's remoteness meant that the convicts could scarcely return to Britain without permission.

The expedition to establish the colony should consist of a warship and a tender of about two hundred tons and convict transports; of officers and three companies of marines; and of convicts. After escorting the transports out, the officers would use the warship and tender to obtain livestock, and perhaps Polynesian women to redress the sexual imbalance. The marines, who would maintain order amongst the colonists and protect them from the natives, should include 'Carpenters, Sawyers, Smiths, Potters, (if possible) and some Husbandmen.'

The advantages apart from that of ridding the kingdom of the convicts were strategic and economic. First, the cultivation and manufacture of the *phormium tenax* 'would be of great consequence to Us, as a Naval Power;' and they might also obtain 'any Quantity of Masts and Ship Timber, for the use of our Fleets in India.' Second, by cultivating spices ('Asiatic productions'), the colonists might soon 'render Our recourse to our European Neighbours for those Productions unnecessary.'[7]

Sydney presumably took the 'Heads' to the Cabinet meeting on Saturday 19 August. No records of that meeting have yet appeared,[8] but we may reconstruct the likely terms of the ministers' discussion. On the one hand, they needed to resume transportation. On the other, Harris's report that French troops were to garrison the Dutch settlements in the East, and his comment that 'the crisis which . . . is to determine the political existence of This Republic is drawing nearer and nearer every hour,' and Cathcart's information about the French *flûtes* at Mauritius, indicated that they needed to move immediately to secure the nation's position in the East. They would be able to do so in several distinct ways if they sent the convicts to Botany Bay—a settlement there would give them a base from which they might send squadrons against the Spanish on the west coast of South America and in the Philippines, the Dutch in the East Indies, and even the French at Mauritius; from the area, they might obtain a supply of naval materials for the Indian dockyards; they would pre-empt any plan the French might have lurking behind La Pérouse's voyage to settle the region. Howe again indicated this strategic context of the decision when he asked Blankett if he would be

> willing to undertake the direction of the plan (under suitable appointments) in case the conduct of any similar [i.e., to the proposed Madagascar one] Voyage of discovery & Settlement of the Convicts should be tendered for his acceptance?[9]

Though formally a Cabinet one, the decision to colonize Botany Bay was very largely the work of two men. As Nepean's letter of 10 June, and Blankett's letters of 6, 10, and 16 August show, it was Pitt who developed the idea of using convicts to build a strategic outlier to India; and he both supervised the implementing of this idea, and attended to par-

K

ticular details himself, in the months between the decision and the sailing of the First Fleet. He received William Richards's proposal for the Administration and the East India Company to share the cost of the return voyage, he discussed this informally with the Company Chairmen, and he had Rose take it up formally with them. He had Pretyman and Wilberforce find a chaplain. While the Treasury Board was in recess between 20 August and 25 October, he authorized the Secretaries to expend the necessary funds. In December, he asked Nepean to obtain statements of expenses from the Admiralty, Navy, and Ordnance Boards; and Middleton in return asked Nepean to tell him that he would have the Navy Board's 'as soon as possible — probably this Evening or early tomorrow.' He discussed the colony's legal structure with Camden. He obtained Banks's first scheme for the breadfruit voyage, which involved Phillip's sending one of the convict transports from Botany Bay to Tahiti. He then discussed the scheme with the West Indian merchants who were pressing for it, and with the East India Company.

As Under-Secretary of the State department responsible for the convicts, Nepean had the greatest and most immediate responsibility for organizing the Administration's disposal of them. Evan Nepean was one of those Eighteenth century men who, like Cook, rose to positions of responsibility and eminence as a consequence of their competence and industry, rather than of wealth or interest. The son of a Plymouth shipwright, he was (in Edward Thompson's words) 'an amazing man — slow yet sure — calm & of few words — sober & laborious.' Shelburne brought him to the Home Office in March 1782, and he served there under five Secretaries for the next twelve years, until he went with Dundas to the War Office. He won the praise of all who worked with him for his application to and his command of his multifarious duties, which included administering the diplomatic service in the Barbary states, and the secret service in France and Spain. He also won Pitt's friendship, who trusted him implicitly, and, in 1804, appointed him to the Admiralty Board. Tired and ill, Pitt often in his last years called at Nepean's house, where he would 'take a chair in a corner, and, laying aside state and gravity, would gambol and play with the boys.' In his personality as well as in his position, Nepean was not Prince Hamlet but an attendant lord — one who applied policies rather than one who began them. In the disposal of the convicts, he was the prism which refracted the light of Pitt's intentions to others.[10]

Nepean's first task was to have the Home Office formally announce the decision to the Treasury, so as to obtain the necessary funds, and he drafted a letter for this purpose on 21 August. Borrowing from previous communications concerning the convicts, he began this by citing the crowded state of the prisons and the imminent danger of epidemic. The *Nautilus'* survey, he continued, had shown that Das Voltas Bay was not a

Sir Evan Nepean, 1st Baronet
By Gainsborough (?). *Courtesy of Sir Evan Nepean and the
National Library of Australia*

suitable site for a convict colony, and the Administration had chosen
Botany Bay instead. He asked the Treasury to

> take such measures as may be necessary for providing a proper number of
> Vessels for the conveyance of 750 Convicts to Botany Bay, together with such
> Provisions, Necessaries and Implements for Agriculture as may be requisite
> for their use after their arrival.

The colony would be under the command of 'an Officer and proper
assistants;' and three marine companies would be sent. The Home
Office would ask the Admiralty for a warship and tender. The Navy
Board would victual the crews of these, and the marines, during the
voyage, but the Home Office was to support them after their arrival.
They intended to give the commander two years' supply of food for the
colonists, who would also need building and agricultural implements,
clothing, and shoes, as listed. They would need garden seed, and seed-
grain, bedding, and surgical instruments and medicines. The
commanding officer would need to issue bills drawn on the Treasury for
provisions and livestock on the way out. He would also need to barter for
livestock at 'the Islands contiguous to the new intended Settlement.' Nepean concluded by asking that the Treasury 'cause every possible Expedition' to prepare and despatch the expedition.[11]

Nepean assembled a series of papers to accompany the announcement — the 'Heads,' his list of provisions, estimate of clothing,
and sketch of the staff establishment, Middleton and Steele's list of tools,
and Macaulay and Gregory's offer to transport for twenty-eight guineas
per person. He then *back-dated* his announcement to 18 August, had the
clerks copy it and the other papers, had Sydney sign it, and sent it off to
the Treasury the same day. There, obviously with Pitt's concurrence,
the Secretaries recorded having received it on 18 August, having read it
to the Board on that day, and the Lords having approved the request
before they adjourned for two months.[12]

This formality arranged, Nepean, and Rose and Steele set about
organizing the colonizing expedition. Steele told the Navy Board of the
scheme of 26 August, and asked them to engage shipping for transportation. The Navy Board accordingly advertised for tenders on 1
September, and thereafter placed a great variety of other necessary ar-
ragements in train. Nepean drafted the formal announcement to the Admiralty on 31 August. He omitted the stock opening, instead asking
directly for the warship and tender, which should be 'fitted for Sea with
all possible expedition,' and for the marines, who should if possible be
volunteers. As the officers, sailors, and marines would go upon a service
'entirely unconnected with Maritime Affairs,' they were to be under the
immediate direction of the Home Secretary after their arrival at New
South Wales. Sydney signed the copied version, and Nepean enclosed
the 'Heads.'[13]

Nepean recurred to the epic formula about convicts when he wrote to the East India Company to obtain their permission for the move. Observing that the Company's territorial grant 'appeared' to comprehend New South Wales, he requested the merchant agreement 'previous to the actual execution of the measure,' pointing out that this would 'not only be acceptable to His Majesty, but [would] be a means of preventing the emigration of Our European Neighbours to that Quarter, which might be attended with infinite prejudice to the Company's Affairs.' Sydney signed the letter, and Nepean sent off a copy of the 'Heads' with it.[14]

The Administration found an officer to head the venture in these days, too. Blankett evidently did not want the job, but by the end of August the Home Office had chosen his fellow adviser, Captain Arthur Phillip. This choice evidently caused some tension amongst the ministers, for Howe replied waspishly to Sydney's announcement of it that 'the little knowledge I have of Captain Phillip would [not] have led me to select him for a service of this complicated nature.'[15]

Phillip was well-qualified for the task, however. He had ferried Portuguese convicts to Brazil; he had made the voyage to the East; he had farmed; he was experienced in survey; and he had, in his secret service, shown himself to be just that 'discreet' officer Nepean thought necessary. There are enough hints for us to conclude that some of the Administration at least wished to reward him for his service, and that he saw his appointment in this light.

In late October, with the commissions for the colony's establishment issued, and the mounting of the First Fleet well in hand, Nepean also informed the Irish Government of the scheme. He did not now enclose the 'Heads,' but he did run through the plan's attractions. The site of the colony would be Botany Bay, 'or some other place contiguous thereto' on the coast of New South Wales. From Cook's account, and from that of those who had sailed with him, this appeared

a Country peculiarly adapted for a Settlement, the Lands about it being plentifully supplied with Wood and Water, the Soil rich and fertile, and the Shores well stocked with Shell and other Fish.

There were 'very few' natives in the area. Phillip would be Governor. About 750 convicts would be sent. The Administration would support the colonists at first, but they should soon become self-sufficient, for they would obtain cattle from neighbouring islands, and begin cultivation as soon as they arrived.

'Besides the removal of a dreadful Banditti from this Country,' Nepean observed,

many advantages are likely to be derived from this intended Settlement. Some of the Timber is reported to be fit for Naval purposes particularly Masts,

Governor Arthur Phillip
By Francis Wheatley. *Courtesy of the Mitchell Library, Sydney*

which the Fleet employed occasionally in the East Indies frequently stand in need of, and which it cannot be supplied with but from Europe. But above all, the Cultivation of the Flax Plant seems to be the most considerable object. This Plant has been found in that Neighbourhood in the most luxuriant State, and small quantities have been brought to Europe and manufactured, and, from its superior quality, it will it is hoped soon become an Article of Commerce from that Country.*

The 'Heads of a Plan' and Nepean's letters of formal announcement are together most instructive of the Administration's motives for the colonization of New South Wales. Nepean was the official most responsible for organizing both the First Fleet and the colony, and he worked to Pitt's explicit direction to do so. His comments clearly show that, in deciding to send the convicts to Botany Bay, Pitt was implementing his scheme to use their labour to increase the nation's strategic capacity in the East. The rag and bone shop of Australia's beginning was perhaps not so foul as we have for so long supposed.

---

* Nepean to Sackville Hamilton, 24 October 1786, HO 100/18:369-72. Characteristically, Nepean did not sign this draft, but it is in his hand; and Hamilton replied to him on 2 November, thanking him for 'the Intelligence respecting the intended Settlement at Botany Bay which I had the Honor to receive by your Letter of 28.th October' (HO 100/18:391).

Nepean evidently omitted the last paragraph quoted above from his letter of 28 October. (He indicated this by annotation—'This clause left out in the Letter written to M.r Hamilton'—in his draft: the final version has seemingly not survived.) Since some writers have found the omission significant, it is perhaps worthwhile to discuss it briefly.

I see four abstract explanations for the omission:

(1) It indicates that the Administration had lost interest in the *phormium tenax*;
(2) Nepean, on reflection, thought the statement of motive not germaine to his purpose of informing the Irish Government of the British one's plans for disposing of the convicts;
(3) Nepean thought he should not advertise the naval stores motive for strategic reasons;
(4) He thought he should not do so because of the unsettled state of Anglo-Irish relations.

Nepean's seeking information about how to work the *phormium tenax*, and persons qualified to do so, in the days when he wrote to Hamilton, as well as the Administration's instructions to Phillip (below, pp. 138-41), presumably render 1) invalid. 2) is possible. The Administration's secrecy about the *Nautilus* survey and the extent of their claim to New South Wales perhaps give 3) some plausibility. Altogether, though, I think 4) the most likely explanation for the omission, for the Irish Parliament would likely have received any news of a threat to their staple export to England most unhappily.

The significant point surely is that this paragraph, whether or not finally sent, conveys Nepean's sense of the expedition's non-'convict' purpose.

IV   *Naval stores and the First Fleet*

The crisis in Holland did not arrive as quickly as Harris predicted, but his reports across the rest of 1786 and into 1787 continued to show a situation fraught with danger for Britain. He wrote on 5 September, for example, that it was evident 'that France is bent either on annihilating this Country as a Power or on reducing it to the state of a French province.' Hailes continued to report disturbingly from France, too. On 7 September, he wrote that France's views seemed less directed 'to a participation of our power in India, than to the entire subversion of it.' The French were worried, he said, that the wealth which the British would derive from their eastern 'Trade and Possessions' would allow them to redeem their national debt, and thus greatly increase their strength in Europe. The next month, he sent details of the treaty which the French had concluded with the Egyptian Beys.[1]

Now, too, developed a threat to Britain's supplies of naval stores. Early in the year, Alleyn Fitzherbert, the British Minister to Russia, had presented the Russian Court with a draft of a treaty to replace the commercial one then expiring; and the Russians had given him a divergent one in return. Negotiations had then languished, and after Pitt reconstituted the Board of Trade in late August, he and Hawkesbury made its first task the examination of the various terms proposed for the new treaty.[2]

The trade in naval materials was inevitably a central consideration. Edward Forster and Godfrey Thornton, Governors of the Russia Company, told the Board how, 'of Hemp, little comes from any other Country, of Flax, a small Quantity comes from the Prussian Dominions, the rest from Russia;' and that, if Russia were to sell elsewhere, 'it must be to sell again for the consumption of Great Britain, and in that case she probably would not receive so good a Price, or be so well paid.' The Board then asked the Navy Board to supply details of prices of masts, hemp, flax, and other stores since 1763.[3]

As the Board had this examination in hand, it received most disturbing information. Richardson, the East India Company's Accountant, wrote to Lord Hawkesbury on 8 September, giving 'Facts that disgrace a commercial Country not in darkness.' Richardson reported that, acting in the interests of 'another' nation, agents had placed orders both in Britain and Russia for all available supplies of Petersburg hemp—so that, whereas in March the price was £23 per ton, it had now become £31-£32 per ton. This had given an 'unexpected check' to trade, he said, since shipowners had lost in duties, British rope-makers were idle because of the lack of raw material, and especially, thirty-four India ships had that year been chartered to carry hemp at the old price; and as each ship would need an average of 30 tons, the rise in price would mean 'a considerable loss' to their owners. On behalf of these owners, Richardson asked Hawkesbury if the Navy Board could release 1,000 tons from its stores for the owners either to buy at a reasonable rate, or to replace in the following year. Such a step, he thought, would benefit commerce and manufacturers, would cause the prices to drop, and would give renewed employment to rope-makers.[4]

Hawkesbury told Richardson to ask the Navy Board 'for Hemp from His Majesty's Stores,' and the Board of Trade then took the matter up. On 21 September James Mitchell reported that the Russian merchants who controlled the supply at home had had their London agents buy up all available supplies, thus achieving a monopoly of the British market. (And it was later found that the merchants had acted with Catherine's concurrence.) Mitchell thought that an immediate solution might be for the Navy Board to release some of its stocks, but he added:

> as to future means: I leave to your Lordships Wisdom & Commercial Knowledge: to me the Prospect is dark, and the Evil without remedy, whilst Petersburgh shall remain the almost only Market of that necessary commodity for the completion of a maritime Equipment. We must depend on Russia, unless we cultivate our own Plains, or promote the growth of Hemp in some other Quarter of the globe, to rival that Emporium of Commerce in naval stores.

This crisis, potentially very damaging commercially and strategically, faded soon after, as an over-abundant Riga harvest forced the Russian merchants to lower their prices. But the British of course remembered the threat.[5]

In this atmosphere, the British pressed forward with their colonization of New South Wales. Working under Pitt's general supervision, Nepean, Rose and Steele, Stephens, Middleton, and Phillip busied themselves with the mounting of the First Fleet in September and October. Many of their arrangements were, of course, those practical ones necessary to the sending some one thousand persons some twenty thousand kilometres across the world's oceans to begin the European planting of a new continent; and, inevitably, these strongly reflect the fact that most of the colonists were convicts. At the same time, however, some separately show the Administration's strategic motive for the move.[6]

We see this motive first in their choice of Arthur Phillip to govern the colony. We see it second in the Admiralty's choice of warship and tender. The *Berwick*, soon renamed the *Sirius* ('from the bright star in the southern constellation of the Great Dog'), of about five hundred and forty tons, had been built for the India trade. She was of a 'round full built,' and mounted twenty guns, with a spar-deck above. The Admiralty had used her as a storeship during the American war, and, like the *Endeavour*, she was 'exceedingly well calculated' for her coming service about New South Wales. The *Supply* was a brig used to carry naval stores from yard to yard. She was 'a very firm strong little vessel, very

flat floored, and roomy, mounted eight guns, and had a deep waist.'
This build meant that, while she might be a poor ocean sailer, she would
be suitable for ferrying livestock and naval stores once at New South
Wales. At Phillip's request, the Administration added eight cannon to
the ships' armament, so that he might equip a small fort. Also instructive
is the Administration's appointment of John Hunter as second captain of
the *Sirius*. Hunter was a skilled surveyor, and his presence meant that the
examination of coastlines and sailing routes would not depend on
Phillip's being able to leave the settlement.[7]

We see the strategic motive next in Nepean's equipping the colonists
to manufacture the *phormium tenax*. Via Brook Watson, the Under-
Secretary received Captain Twiss's reference for Lieutenant Dawes.
Twiss, who had commanded the Engineering Corps in Canada and who
was then working for the Navy Board, said that his young protege was
skilled in astronomy, and that

> whatever You desire him to do respecting the Flax, from new Zeland, or any
> other important Article of Commerce, which that Country may produce, his
> future Conduct will prove that his Abilities, and Application, are worthy Your
> Protection.

Dawes accordingly sailed with the First Fleet. Though we presently lack
evidence of it, we may presumably also ascribe the presence there of
Roger Morley, a 'master weaver,' to Nepean's efforts to send out
qualified people. Whether by design or accident, there were also hemp
dressers, rope-makers, and weavers, among the First Fleet convicts.[8]

At the same time, Nepean sought information about the *phormium
tenax*, so as to be able to instruct the people he was sending to work it.
William Sharrow, a Birmingham manufacturer, supplied some such on
24 October. Sharrow's letter has seemingly not survived, but from Nepean's reply, we may see that the manufacturer discussed difficulties the
Administration was likely to encounter in importing this product. The
Under-Secretary wrote on 27 October,

> if you could at your leisure, within the course of a Week or ten days, commit
> to paper your thoughts upon the Management of the Flax plant, so as to serve
> as an Instruction to the People who may be employed in its Cultivation, and
> tend to remove those objections to its importation which you suggest, it will be
> considered as a further obligation.[9]

Sharrow replied that he would do 'everything in [his] Power to Com-
municate the Improvem.t of the Flax Plant, to make it elligable for Importation, w.h Certainly is a Great National Object.' He saw that 'the
Plant on Arrivale of the Convicts will Imploy Men Women & Children;'
and he asked for a sample, so that he might 'Improve it in Differant
Manner's for Sundry Manufactory's, & Convince you the Real Value of it
According to the Presant price of Silk. Flax & Hemp.' He wrote again

soon afterwards, repeating his request for a sample, and asking if his 'Report & Instructions will do the Middle of next Month [i.e., December].'[10]

We see the strategic motive, too, in Banks's contributions to the venture. The great naturalist included European hemp and flax in his list of seeds, marking them 'For Commerce' (i.e., export);[11] and he planned to obtain specimens of *phormium tenax* and breadfruit.

Banks had tried unsuccessfully to establish the exotic flax at Kew in the 1770s, when, encouraged by merchants who saw the prospect of a cheap staple for their slaves, he had also toyed with the idea of establishing the breadfruit in the West Indies. Now, he saw that the colonization of New South Wales presented an opportunity to realize both projects. His first plan for the voyage that the star-crossed pair Bligh and Christian later made famous was for Phillip to outfit one of the convict transports at Botany Bay, and send her, first to New Zealand, for 'as many of the Flax plants as will Fill two tubs & no more,' and then, to Tahiti, for the breadfruit. He gave this plan to Pitt in March, together with instructions for 'Gov. Phillip which were to guide him in framing instructions for the Mast.' of the Vessel;' and he engaged David Nelson, a gardener, to go out with the First Fleet. Phillip consequently asked Nepean to see that his instructions included 'That I send one of the Ships to Charlotte Sound, in the Island of New Zeland, for the flax plant, & to the Friendly Islands for the Bread fruit;' and Pitt discussed the scheme with the East India Company, and with the West Indian merchants. Banks then came to see that he might have the ship much better fitted out for its task in England. He altered his scheme accordingly, and asked that Phillip 'send home the Flax Plant.'[12]

Despite the great mass of his papers extant, the full extent of Banks' hand in the decision to colonize New South Wales remains surprisingly obscure. He had been the first to suggest such a colonization, and, with Cook dead, he was the most authoritative source of information about the south Pacific. He had clearly encouraged Matra to present his proposal in 1783, and he was intimately involved in mounting the *Nautilus* survey in 1785. In 1787, he was entirely responsible for planning the breadfruit expedition, and he oversaw the fitting out of the *Guardian* in 1789. He had a very large hand in the planning of Vancouver's expedition, and in that of Flinders a decade later. From the mid-1780s onwards, as Mackay has said, Banks carried forward Britain's 'presiding genius of exploration.'[13]

Such things as his drawing up the list of seeds for the First Fleet, and his obtaining these, his first scheme to obtain the breadfruit, his wishing to have the naturalist Francis Masson join the expedition at the Cape, and Phillip and Hunter's subsequent attention to him, suggest that Banks played this role in 1786, too. Indeed, one anonymous commentator a few years later identified him as the prime agent, saying that the Solomon of the Royal Society found means to persuade the great men in office, that the Hemp, or a Substitute for it, was of such prodigious strength, that a single hair would hang even all his Council, and that the timber of the Colony would afford masts for our navy.[14]

Given the author's jaundiced view of his subject, it is now difficult to know what precise weight to give this report. Still, the evidence we have of Banks's interest in the *phormium tenax*, of his having the Administration's ear, and of his hand in similar ventures, is sufficient to suggest that it conveys an essential truth.

The Administration originally hoped to despatch the expedition by the middle of October, and they made good progress at first; but then, as difficulties grew, they had to postpone their expectations to mid-November, then to mid-December, then into the new year. Finally, all was adjusted, though, and the King issued his instructions to Phillip on 25 April.

These instructions, which Nepean drafted, are again of great importance in our understanding of the Administrations' intentions with the colonization. They begin by asserting the nation's sweeping territorial claim to New South Wales between the latitudes of 10°S and 43°S eastwards from 135° of Longitude, and to 'all the Islands adjacent in the Pacific Ocean;' and by announcing the intention to send some 780 convicts and a marine guard to form a settlement at Botany Bay. Phillip was to collect materials for the colony en route, at Teneriffe, Rio de Janeiro, and the Cape of Good Hope. On arrival at Botany Bay, he was to disembark the civil and military establishments, the convicts, stores, and provisions, with 'every possible exertion,' so as to free the ships under charter to the East India Company to proceed to China. Immediately upon establishing a settlement, he was to 'proceed to the Cultivation of the Land,' and to take whatever the convicts produced into the public store. He was to send Hunter in the *Sirius* and *Supply* to the Savu, Molucca, and Society Islands to obtain supplies of live stock; and he was to use these supplies to establish a 'competent' stock, so that he might supply the settlement from its own resources. He was to render the settlement self-sufficient partly with the view of supplying 'a farther Number of Convicts which you may expect will shortly follow You from Hence.' He was to endeavour to live in harmony with the native population, to bring women from Polynesia, to grant land to the industrious and deserving, and to forbid private trade.

As well as of the exigencies of their mode of colonization, the Administration also advised Phillip of their profound objectives. By settling Botany Bay, of course, he would establish an effective possession of that part of the coast of New South Wales. He was also, however, 'as soon as Circumstances will admit of it,' to send a 'small Establishment' to Norfolk Island, 'to secure the same to Us, and prevent its being occupied by the Subjects of any other European Power.' (Though they did not say so explicitly, it was of course for its naval materials that the Administration saw Norfolk Island as 'a spot which may hereafter become useful,' and hence instructed Phillip to take possession of it.)

Moreover, as cultivation and livestock would soon flourish in the settlement, it could not be 'expedient' that all the convicts 'should be employed in attending only to the object of Provisions.' He was therefore to set some to cultivating flax:

> As it has been humbly represented unto Us that Advantages may be derived from the Flax Plant which is found in the Islands not far distant from the intended Settlement, not only as a Means of acquiring Cloathing for the Convicts and other persons who may become settlers, *but from its Superior Excellence for a variety of Maritime purposes, and as it may ultimately become an Article of Export*, It is therefore Our Will and Pleasure that you do particularly attend to its Cultivation, and that you do send home by every opportunity which may offer, Samples of this Article, in order that a Judgement may be formed whether it may not be necessary to instruct you further upon this Subject (my emphasis).

He was also to survey the coasts and islands within his jurisdiction, in order to obtain knowledge for future operations:

> Whereas We are desirous that some further Information should be obtained of the several Ports or Harbours upon the Coast and the Islands contiguous thereto within the Limits of Your Government, You are, whenever the Sirius, or the Supply Tender, can conveniently be spared, to send one, or both of them, upon that Service.[15]

Phillip took the eleven ships in his squadron to sea on 13 May 1787, with the expectation that he should, after three years or so, return from a colony 'in such a State as to repay Government the Annual Expence, as well as to be of the greatest consequence to this Country.'[16]

CHAPTER 8

Endeavours and alarms
1787-1792

I   *British strategic planning and European diplomacy*

As they mounted the First Fleet and Phillip took this to New South
Wales, the Administration continued with other moves to counter the
French initiatives in Europe and the East. In October and November,
Blankett renewed his discussions with Howe and Nepean about
Madagascar, now extending his assessment of the nation's naval needs
in the eastern seas. Warning of the French forces there, he said that the
Andaman Islands, Negrais, Aracan, Sirian, Morgui, Junk Ceylon
(Phuket), Quedah (Kideh), Pulo Pulang, Rhio (Riau), Pedir, Diamond
Point, and Tapanovly (Tapanuli) were all supposed to offer harbours,
but that the British presently had little, if any, certain knowledge of
them. All were reportedly capable of sheltering a fleet, and, if so, the
possession of one or more would allow the India squadron to winter in
the Bay of Bengal. Again he indicated the context of the Botany Bay
decision, when he said that his information might prove useful 'Should
any circumstances render the continuing the proposed settlement in
New Holland inconvenient in future.'[1]

Unaware of this advice, of course, but acting according to what, from
the long discussions he had had with them before he had sailed, he knew
to be Pitt and Dundas's intentions, Cornwallis took up the search for
sites for a naval base early the next year. In March 1787, he told Dundas
he intended to survey the Islands in the eastern Bay of Bengal, for 'good
& secure Harbours for Ships of War.' Kyd, whom he sent to do so, made
a brief examination of the Andamans, and did not like their lack of
agriculture. He found that Nancowery Harbour had disadvantages. He
was greatly impressed, however, with Penang (Prince of Wales Island),
where the East India Company was forming a settlement, for it had a
good climate, a sheltered and capacious harbour, agriculture, and an 'inexhaustible stock of Timber.' Cornwallis sent Dundas this information,
saying that he would pay the Sultan of Quedah for the island, and send
Kyd to fortify the Company's settlement there.[2]

The Commissioners for India had, previously, asked the Bengal and
Bombay Governments to investigate the Andaman and Nicobar Islands,

142

and Diego Garcia but, scarcely attracted by surveying voyages, which were uncomfortable and offered little or no return for their expense, the Company officials had given these requests only scant attention. In a despatch which reached the Board of Control at the end of March 1786, the Bengal Government replied that the Nicobars were hilly, rainy, and therefore unhealthy, offered no anchorages, were small and gave 'few Articles of provision,' and were, because of the monsoon, inaccessible for several months of the year. If the Danes and the Imperialists saw them as having commercial value, they said slyly, 'We are not sure that it would not be wise policy to permit these Nations to continue in their Delusion.' They could see that a station in this region might offer advantages in war, however; and they thought the French might be contemplating settling the Andamans, which offered reasonable anchorages, but which also had wild and savage inhabitants, no agriculture, and a heavy rainfall.[3] Later in the year, the Board heard from the Bombay officials that Diego Garcia was 'nothing better than a convenient Station for surveying and exploring the numerous Islands and shoals about, and to the Southward of the Line,' and that they could not maintain a settlement on it, or fortify it, without an enormous and continuing expense.[4]

Pitt, Dundas, and Mulgrave were most dissatisfied with these reports, and, as Cornwallis was independently renewing the quest, at Mulgrave's urging, they re-examined thoroughly the nation's naval position in the East. 'It is of the greatest importance,' they considered,

> to ascertain the most proper Stations for the Shelter refitting, refreshment or protection of Squadrons and Ships of War, as well as Convoys or East India Ships during the different Seasons under various circumstances in the East Indies, in case of a future War; as well as the places most worthy of attention either for offensive or defensive operations in the extensive possessions of this Country in that part of the World.'[5]

They proposed, therefore, to send out to India a well-qualified person, who would examine all places which had seemed worthy of attention in the past, and any others the Governor-General might suggest. The person sent was to have whatever help Cornwallis could offer, from either the King or the Company's resources. In particular, he was to inspect Diego Garcia, Tapanovly Bay and Acheen on Sumatra, Penang, and the Nicobar and Andaman Islands, in order to discover

> the ease and convenience of access in different Seasons, the circumstances which may make them capable of defence by Fortification, where that might be necessary, with the relative circumstances of strength and expense; the facility of procuring water, or refreshments, for a larger or smaller Force, the healthiness of the place.

He was not to confine his enquiries to 'Military or Naval objects', but was also to report 'any Observations [that] should occur to him, which may tend to the extension or security of the Commercial Interests, and Navigation of the East India Company.' And he was to give Cornwallis 'a full State of the whole; whose judgment & determination must guide ultimately the measures of Government and the India Company.' Dundas then told Cornwallis privately of this plan.[6]

Before the Administration could mount this survey, however, the long-threatened storm of European politics struck. On 28 June, seeking a solution to her country's political impasse, the Princess of Orange set out secretly for the Hague with the aim of persuading the States General to restore to her husband the Stadtholder the command of that city's garrison. A detachment of the Patriots' Free Corps unceremoniously arrested her on her way.

To all parties, war seemed the almost inevitable outcome of this 'insult' to the King of Prussia's sister. Pitt tried to lessen this prospect late the next month, when he sought and obtained France's agreement to the proposition that neither nation should arm its fleet without first informing the other of this intention. At the same time, however, Nepean sent Blankett and another officer fluent in French (Le Geyt) to Brest 'to enquire into the state of the French Squadron at that Port;' Pitt sent Grenville to the Hague to make an independent assessment; and Pitt wrote to Cornwallis that

> the first Struggle will naturally be for the foreign dependencies of the Republic, and if at the outset of a War we could get possession of the Cape & Trinquemalé, it will go farther than anything else to decide the fate of the Contest.[7]

Grenville reported at the end of August, confirming both Harris's assessment of the situation, and the India Board's sense of Trincomalee's importance. On 9 September, on his sister's behalf, the King of Prussia demanded both apology and satisfaction from Holland, and gave the Dutch four days to reply. On 13 September, Eden wrote that the French Foreign Minister had said his nation would come to Holland's aid in the event of a Prussian invasion. Simultaneously, Carmarthen told Eden that Britain could no longer delay arming her fleet; and Pitt told him that the French must either give up 'their predominant influence in the Republic, or they must determine *to fight for it.'* The British prepared for war.[8]

Surprisingly, this did not come. The Duke of Brunswick led the Prussian army into Holland on 18 September, and the Patriots gave way with scant resistance. At the end of October, in the face of the Prussian supremacy, the British mobilization of the fleet, and Grenville's firm statement of Britain's determination to intervene if France gave military support to the Patriots, the French formally renounced their interest in Dutch affairs; and the Stadtholder thankfully resumed the direction of his nation.

Pitt, Dundas, Mulgrave, and Grenville worked busily to realize the chance which this alteration gave to secure Britain's position in the East. Dundas began to consider what offers they might make to regain Dutch friendship at the beginning of September.[9] Two months later, borrowing heavily from Francis Baring, he drew up a paper on the 'Considerations on the Subject of a Treaty between Great Britain & Holland rel: to their Interests in India.'

The chief of these considerations were, of course, those now quite familiar ones, of Britain's need of a port offering year-round shelter to her shipping in the Bay of Bengal, of Trincomalee's being by far the most suitable such port, and of the advantages of having a general access to the Dutch bases in the East; and these informed Dundas's long and masterly analysis of Britain and Holland's respective interests. Dundas saw that 'a Treaty with the Dutch is preferable to [one with] any other Country, as she can promote the sale of our Products and Manufactures in a superior degree; and at the same time contribute very important political assistance.'

Each nation had one principal object. Britain's was *'to maintain and preserve the Empire which she has acquired, in comparison of which even trade is a subordinate or collateral consideration'* (my emphasis). Holland's was 'in the first instance, to secure to herself the monopoly of the Spice Islands; and Secondly, to extend her general trade by every means in her power.' Holland was not herself strong enough to threaten conquest, and, indeed, in the distressed state of her economy, would welcome what commercial help Britain might be able to give; and as Britain might be vulnerable to attack by France and Holland combined it was sound policy

> to detach Holland from France in India, either as an active or passive friend, and to induce her to be warm and zealous to Great Britain. Any reasonable indulgence or sacrifice that can be made for that purpose (although a precise equivalent may not be obtained) will be wise and amply justified by the event.

Britain should, therefore, not take up the right to a free navigation in the East Indies, and she should return Negapatam, which the Dutch had 'very much at heart'. In return, Britain should require, at least, a guarantee of access to Trincomalee and the Cape of Good Hope; and, at best (though this was clearly a hope for the future) the cession of both harbours.[10]

These views then became the heart of British diplomacy towards Holland. Mulgrave quickly drafted the 'Heads of a Treaty of Defensive Alliance and Mutual Guarantee of Territories & Commerce at the Cape of Good Hope, and in the East Indies,' to propose to Holland, and presented as well some 'Observations' on these. Dundas, Mulgrave, and Grenville met as the India Board on 20 December. After going over Mulgrave's *projet*, they drew up a commentary on it for Carmarthen, recommending that Britain give back Negapatam to the Dutch, and assure them of their long-held monopoly of the spice trade. In return, Britain should ask for Trincomalee and Rhio, and should retain the right to navigate amongst 'the islands to the Eastward of the Easternmost part of Sumatra.' (They pointed out that they used this rather vague description so that British war and merchant ships 'may avail themselves of the different passages through the Islands to China as the seasons and other circumstances may require.').[11]

Pitt then pressed this project upon the Dutch, at the same time agreeing to lend 2,000,000 guilders to the Zealand chamber of the Netherlands East India Company. Despite not having reached agreement on all points, Britain and the United Provinces signed a treaty on 15 April 1788, and Pitt gave the money between May and October.

II *The search for naval security in the East*

As they brought the Dutch from the French to the English camp and thereby lessened the likelihood of an early French attack on India, Pitt, Dundas, Mulgrave, and Grenville continued to see a need for reliable information about harbours and coasts in the eastern seas, but they had to ride out a storm from another quarter before they could return to the task of obtaining this. In November 1788, George III suffered a serious attack of porphyria, which left him demented for some months. While he perhaps did not address the oak in the Great Park at Windsor as the King of Prussia, his behaviour during his illness was commonly of this sort; and Pitt and his friends had to summon all resources to avoid the regency which threatened, for the Prince of Wales would soon have dismissed them in favour of Charles James Fox and his friends.

As the King's recovery made their position more secure, the politicians returned to questions of naval need in the East. In January and February, drawing on information supplied by Middleton, they developed a distinctly new scheme for the naval defence of India. As much as possible in future, they would mount this from Indian resources. They would establish a ship-building centre, most probably at Bombay, where they might add two docks to those already in use. Here, they would build guardships, and while the Indian yard would continue to need some European materials, they would use local ones as much as possible — teak in hulls and for lower masts, coir cables, and local cloths for smaller sails. They would extend the local force of artificers, and would meet the costs of this programme from local revenues.[1]

This was a bold move, and the reasons which underlay it were powerful ones. The traditional mode of supplying the Eastern marines from Europe was not only extremely expensive, but also most fragile in wartime. As the Commissioners pointed out:

few of our Naval Stores except those of Metal are produced in Great Britain. We have our Hemp, our Masts, Deals, Plank and part of our Iron from abroad at a very considerable expence, independant of freight. We have at present an Interest in India. We want to make it useful to us in a way that will not impoverish the Country; and we are willing to spare as much as possible our own Oak Timber for 50 or 60 Years to come. Whatever helps therefore India can afford, Whatever Supplies we can prudently draw from it, we should readily accept, and freely use. Nor should any Article be sent out from England for the equipment of India Guardships, that can be procured on the Spot; or in the adjoining Settlements. The only reason for giving the preference to articles from England is the increase of Seamen. But we shall want them still more in India; and it would be absurd to offer any reasons against resolving to raise them in the Country where they are to be employed.

In March Mulgrave took details from Sir Richard King concerning navigation to the Coromandel coast and the advantages and disadvantages of the European stations about it. According to King, Negapatam was healthy, its anchorage was safer than Madras or Pondicherry's, and ships could obtain ample refreshments there. The best station to intercept ships coming from Europe during the south-west monsoon was off the Friar's Hood in northern Ceylon, which was only two days sail from Negapatam. Any ships bound in this season for Karical, Tranquebar, Pondicherry, or Madras had to pass 'within sight of Ships lying off Negapatam.' In a 'naval light,' King thought Negapatam 'of the utmost Consequence to any Nation not possessed of Trincomalé.'[2]

In October, the Commissioner took up the survey of the eastern seas again. Appointing Lieutenant Moorsom to the *Ariel* sloop, they instructed him first to examine the 'different circumstances' which might qualify Diego Garcia 'for an harbour, or as a place for refreshment and repair, &c or as a central situation for correspondence.' He was next to survey Tapanovly Bay, Acheen , Pulo Pinang, Junk Ceylon; and then, to assess Lacam's scheme for a harbour near Calcutta. Early the next year, Dundas officially asked Chatham, Pitt's brother and now First Lord of the Admiralty, to instruct Commodore William Cornwallis on the purposes of the survey; and the Commodore then sailed with the *Ariel* among his squadron.[3]

Earl Cornwallis had meanwhile been acting in India to facilitate this survey, which he knew to be truly the nation's need, as well as his superiors' wish. In December 1788, he sent Lieutenant Blair to survey the Andamans and Nicobars again; and six months later this officer reported that he had found a number of suitable harbours. He thought one, Port Andaman, on the west coast of Great Andaman, would accommodate the largest fleet, it was sheltered from both monsoons, had a good supply of water, could be strongly fortified, and trees suitable for masts, and probably for hulls, grew about it. He said of another, Port Cornwallis on the south east coast of Great Andaman, that it was 'hardly possible to conceive a more secure and perfect Harbour,' and that it could hold fifty ships of the line. It was as well perfectly sheltered, it could be well-fortified, was 'easy of access in either Monsoon,' and was well placed vis-a-vis Calcutta. Its one disadvantage was that it had only three meagre brooks, so that settlers would need to build a reservoir.[4]

As he waited for his brother, Commodore William Cornwallis, to arrive and confirm Blair's report, the Governor-General claimed the Andamans for Britain, and sent Blair with a party of labourers and local convicts to begin making Port Cornwallis into a naval base. During the previous two years, Cornwallis reported to the Board in August, he had made use of all the means in his power 'to obtain an exact knowledge of the adjacent Islands and Coasts;' and he thought that if, on further trial, the Andamans proved a satisfactory base, he would relinquish Penang, and relocate the Company's settlement there to Port Cornwallis.[5]

Pitt, Dundas, and Mulgrave had great hopes for the survey, and it did produce good and satisfying information.[6] Moorsom reported that Diego Garcia's harbour provided shelter, and that settlers might use the local timber to build forts; but also that the island offered limited supplies, having only water, fish, turtle, coconuts, and three kinds of timber. It was 'advantageously situated' to be a place where a squadron sailing from Europe might pick up news of the enemy in India; but it might only be useful as a transit for communications between the Indian presidencies if the enemy had cut their usual lines of communication.[7]

Commodore Cornwallis reached Bengal in mid-September, and Moorsom three weeks later. Then, taking Kyd and Colebrook with them, they sailed in December to survey the Andaman and Nicobar Islands, with Cornwallis afterwards going to Penang, and Moorsom to Sumatra. Seven months later, the anxious Commissioners had the Governor-General's report that the Commodore 'speaks very favourably of Nancowery Bay in the Nicobars, and thinks our new Harbour in the Great Andaman a very fine one;' and that Penang would never answer as a refitting station for warships. A few weeks later, they received an unsolicited report from Blair that the Commodore was 'perfectly satisfied' that Port Cornwallis was 'a place of infinite national importance.'[8]

With this survey in hand, Pitt, Dundas, Mulgrave, and Grenville turned their attention to the south Atlantic. Starting from the instructions which the East India Company had given to the Captain of the *Swallow* a half-dozen years earlier, in June 1789 they planned a survey of Isla Grande, Tristan da Cunha, and the southwest and southeast coast of Africa, for a suitable site for a port. Two months later, they received Banks's recommendation that Archibald Menzies should report on the botanical aspects of these places; and Grenville, now Home Secretary, announced the scheme to the Admiralty, who set about equipping the *Discovery* for the task.[9]

III *Phillip follows instructions in New South Wales*

As Pitt and his colleagues moved to obtain authentic information about navigation towards and in the Indian Ocean, Phillip was pursuing his charge at the other edge of this strategic waterway with fine determination.

After refreshing and gathering supplies at Rio and the Cape, Phillip had reached Botany Bay in the *Supply* on 18 January, for the rest of the fleet to join him within three days. Finding, contrary to expectation, that Botany Bay offered only very indifferent anchorage, little fresh water, and sandy soil, he and Hunter examined the coast northward, to discover Port Jackson's excellence. Less visionary and more professional perhaps than we have supposed in his reporting, he described this as 'the finest Harbour in the World, in which a thousand Sail of the line may ride in the most perfect security;' and drew Dundas's approval because of 'the advantages which must always be derived from a Port so capacious and secure as Port Jackson.'[1]

Phillip hoisted British colours in Sydney Cove on 28 January 1788, and disembarked the colonists in the next days. On 7 February, they assembled to hear David Collins formally proclaim the Colony by reading the Governor's commission, and the letters-patent establishing civil and criminal courts in New South Wales.

Having commenced settlement and taken formal possession of New South Wales, Phillip moved on three fronts to realize his instructions, and make the Colony of the greatest consequence to Britain. His difficulties on the first of these — the establishment of herds and agriculture — have of course been often described. And the colonists' situation was indeed, as Phillip soon observed, 'very different from what might have been expected.' The area about Port Jackson was in general barren, with the topsoil often scarcely covering the sandstone. There were richer pockets, however, and these Phillip set the convicts to cultivating. But the convicts were lazy, and the marines declined to supervise them in their labours. Few of the colonists knew much about building or agriculture. The party's tools quickly proved of inferior quality. Most of the first-sown seed failed to germinate, and there was much thieving from the general store and the gardens that did appear. Careless slaughter by the Europeans, lightning, Aborigines, dingoes, and poison grass soon reduced the number of sheep. The two bulls and four cows which Phillip hoped to breed into a herd wandered away from a careless stockman, and weren't recovered. Savu was too distant to be a convenient source of livestock. Port Jackson yielded fish only intermittently.[2]

When Phillip represented the colonists' situation and wants in clothing, tools, seed, livestock, artificers and agricultural supervisors, the Administration moved immediately to remedy them, despatching new supplies, nine agricultural supervisors, and twenty-five convicts selected for their experience in building or agriculture and gardening, in the *Guardian* in September 1789. The *Guardian* loaded wine at Santa Cruz, and livestock at the Cape, then struck an iceberg in 41° East Longitude on 13 December. After heroic struggle, Lieutenant Riou brought her back to the Cape, where a storm wrecked her. In reiterating his account of these difficulties in mid-1790, Phillip observed that many of them 'could not have been guarded against, as they never could have been expected;' and it was then truly, as he also said, 'rather a Matter of Surprize that a regular Settlement exists, than that it is not in a more flourishing State.'[3]

Still, Phillip remained hopeful in the face of all. In July 1788, he told Sydney that though New South Wales offered 'no great resource to first Settlers,' and though 'more labour is required than was expected,' he thought that with more aid the colony would become 'a Valuable acquisition.' In September, he had 'no doubt but that a very few years will make this Settlement a very desirable one, & fully to answer the end proposed by Government.' In mid-1790, after he had received fresh supplies of livestock, and managed to increase agricultural production, he was able to assure the Administration that the colonists would not 'starve' (though 'Seven eighths,' he said, deserved nothing better).[4]

Aided by Pitt, Dundas, and Grenville's decision in September 1790 henceforth to supply the colony as much as possible from India, this improvement then continued steadily. When Phillip sailed for home in December 1792, there were some two hundred and eight acres under wheat, twenty-four under barley, one thousand eleven hundred and eighty-six under maize, one hundred and twenty-one of gardens, and one hundred and sixty-two cleared; there were twenty-three cattle, eleven horses, one hundred and five sheep, and forty-three pigs in the Government stock; and there were thriving gardens on Norfolk Island. There was then no doubt but that the colony would survive and prosper.

Neither did Phillip neglect his other strategic tasks as he struggled to make the colony self-sufficient, and the ways in which he pursued these show how central he considered them to the whole endeavour. On 1 February 1788, only five days after he removed the fleet to Port Jackson, he told King that he should go to Norfolk Island; and on 12 February he gave this officer instructions which read in part,

> after having taken the necessary measures for securing yourself and People, and for the preservation of the stores and provisions, you are immediately to proceed to the cultivation of the Flax Plant, which you will find growing spontaneously on the Island.[5]

King and his party, which included 'two persons who pretended to some knowledge in flax-dressing,' and in whose equipment were 'tools for dressing flax,' sailed in the *Supply* on 15 February, and arrived off

Norfolk Island on 1 March. After making several reconnoitres, King undertook an extensive tour of the island on 4 March, and landed his men and equipment on 6 March. On 7 March, he commenced clearing ground for cultivation. He noticed the pines immediately, describing them as being 'of an incredible growth,' but curiously, he failed to recognize the *phormium tenax* before the *Supply* sailed for Sydney (8 March).[6]

King's initial failure to discover the flax did not destroy hopes for obtaining naval stores from Norfolk Island, though it did dampen them somewhat. One officer wrote from the island on 7 March that Cook's descriptions did not do justice to the pines, which 'are beyond any thing of the kind I ever saw.' The carpenter of the *Supply* was similarly impressed. Phillip reported home that

> Lieut! King describes this island as one intire Wood, without a single Acre of clear land that had been found, when the Supply left them, and says, that the Pine Trees rise fifty, and sixty feet, before they shoot out any branches, there are several other Kinds of Timber on the Island, which as far as he could examine it, was a rich black Mould, with great quantities of Pumice Stone. the trees are so bound together by a kind of supple Jack that the penetrating into the interiour parts of the Island was very difficult. several good springs of Water were found, and I apprehend His Majesty's Ships in the East Indies, may be supplied from this Island with Masts, & Yards, which will render it a very valuable acquisition. The cultivation of the Flax Plant, will be attended to, when People can be sent to clear the Ground.[7]

Affairs on Norfolk Island soon promised a fairer prospect. The surgeon recognized the *phormium tenax* on 17 March, and King began working it immediately. (At the same time, he proceeded with cultivation, and with the cutting and sawing of timber.) When the *Supply* next visited the island, in late July, as well as being able to respond optimistically to Phillip's queries about the little colony's prospects of becoming self-sufficient, King was able to say that he had found the flax, and that while he had not yet succeeded in working it, nonetheless he had 'no doubt' that it 'would make good cordage, canvas, and linen.'[8]

King could not report favourably on the prospects of a landing place, since he had found no anchorage that would be at all times secure, even for a vessel of 30 or 40 tons. However, at this point he did not regard this lack as an insurmountable difficulty. He supposed that

> forty men might make a very lasting pier in six months where boats might land with the greatest ease, & from whence masts etc. might be sent off, & *ships of the line launched from it*, if the pier is made of a sufficient breadth (my emphasis).

And he saw the productions of the island as being

timber for the construction of vessels, pines for masting them, and, when the flax-plant can be worked, a sufficiency of cordage for the navy of Great-Britain, which needs no cultivation, as the island abounds with it.[9]

Phillip responded enthusiastically to this information. He wrote to Sydney on 28 September 1788:

The Flax Plant (some roots of which I shall send by the Sirius to the Cape, to be forwarded to England) is found very luxuriant all over the Island, growing to a Height of Eight feet: unfortunately, the Person I sent who calls himself a Flax dresser, cannot prepare it, as this Plant requires a different treatment in the dressing, to what the European flax plant does. Your Lordship will I presume order proper Persons to be sent out, by which means that Island will, in a very short time be able to furnish a considerable Quantity of Flax. The Pine Trees, in the Opinion of the Carpenter of the Supply, who is a good Judge, are superior to any he has ever seen, and the island affords excellent Timber for Ship building, as well as for Masts and Yards, with which I make no doubt but His Majesty's Ships in the East Indies, may be supplied, as likewise with Pitch and Tar; the only difficulty being the Want of a good landing place; and I have not the least doubt that one will be found in some of the small Bays; or if not, Mr. King proposed blowing up two or three of the small Rocks which make the Reef dangerous: but if disappointed in both, there will be no danger in the Summer time; and I am assured by the Master of the Supply, it will be safer for a Ship to load with Masts and Spars at Norfolk Island, than it is in Riga Bay, where so many Ships load yearly.[10]

King's activities on Norfolk Island in the last months of 1788 continued to justify some optimism about the fulfilment of the general purpose. In late October, he sent off a cargo of 'Balks, plants [and] spars' to Port Jackson; and presumably Phillip referred to items in this cargo when he wrote 16 November,

Two lower Yards were cut at Norfolk Island for the two Store Ships, and the Masters have my Directions to deliver them at Deptford Yard: by those Spars they will be able to determine the Quality of the wood.

On 9 December King was able to write:

During the last 12 days landing has been as safe as at a Wharf in the Thames. A Vessell might have been launched from hence with great ease & safety & lain these 12 days in the Road in perfect smooth water.[11]

By mid-1789, however, when the *Supply* visited again, it had become apparent to those on Norfolk Island that they would not succeed readily in establishing it as a source of naval materials. King had still not been able to work the flax, and (as Collins later put it)

the pine trees, of the utility of which such sanguine hopes had been entertained, were found to be unfit for large masts or yards, being shakey or rotten at thirty or forty feet from the butt; the wood was so brittle that it would not make a good oar, and so porous that the water soaked through the planks of a boat which had been built of it.[12]

Despite these setbacks, Phillip strove until he left to establish a supply of naval materials. When he sent Major Ross to Norfolk Island as commandant in place of King in March 1790, Phillip told him,

> you will cause the Convicts to be employed in the Cultivation of the Land in such Manner as shall appear to you the best calculated to render that Settlement independent as far as respects the Necessaries of Life—paying such Attention to the Cultivation of the Flax-Plant, as your Situation will admit of; & which is to be the principal Object when the Necessaries of Life are secured to the Settlers.

He stressed the importance of this object when he also told Ross to

> point out such Means as may appear to you the most likely to answer the Views of Government, in the cultivation of the Flax-plant.[13]

British interest in the possibility of obtaining naval materials from Norfolk Island continued for a number of years. In response to Phillip's request for a person qualified to work flax, the Home Office sent out Andrew Hume, who arrived in 1790. Hume applied himself to the task, and the next year sent Phillip some specimens of cloth, but at the same time said he was 'much in want of proper material, as well as proper people for the purpose of carrying on the manufactory.'[14]

Curiously, Dawes seems not to have contributed to these efforts. Rather than sending him to Norfolk Island, Phillip put him in charge of artillery and engineering at Sydney, where he built an observatory, and a battery and magazine on the west point of the Cove.

In these years, too, Phillip set his officers to making those observations of the coasts north and south of Port Jackson, of the islands adjacent in the Pacific, and of routes to the East Indies, that all knew to be so 'necessary for the Good of His Majesty's Service.' Hunter charted Port Jackson, Botany Bay, and Broken Bay. Bradley charted Norfolk Island. Ball surveyed Lord Howe Island. Hunter and Ball drew up directions for those who would follow to these spots at the world's edge. Shortland tried a route above New Guinea and through the Molucca Islands when he took the First Fleet transports home. Hunter crossed the Pacific between Cook's routes when he went to the Cape of Good Hope for supplies in 1788/9, so as to seek out yet undiscovered islands; and he gathered information on the passage below Van Diemen's Land when he returned. When he took the crew of the *Sirius* home in the *Waaksamheyd* in 1791 he, too, went above New Guinea, observing carefully.

By accident rather than design, Phillip and his officers had some valuable help in this endeavour. As they made their way to Canton to collect their cargoes of tea, the captains of the *Lady Penrhyn*, *Scarborough* and *Charlotte* sighted the Kermadecs, and, the Marshall and Gilbert Islands. Then, between 1788 and 1792, as a consequence of the *Bounty* embroglio, Bligh and Edwards gained surer knowledge of the Cook and

Fijian Islands, the New Hebrides, and Torres Strait. By the end of Phillip's term, the British were well on their way to knowing the main features of navigation in the seas about New South Wales.

IV   *The Nootka Sound crisis*

The sudden turn-about in Dutch affairs in the autumn of 1787 diminished the immediate need of these measures, of course. However, less than three years later, another political crisis arose that showed the British their timeliness, and how they might use the new knowledge and resources resulting from them.

This second crisis developed first at Nootka Sound, another of those spots on the margin of the Pacific Ocean which Cook brought to European consciousness. There, the British sailors had traded with the Indians for sea otter furs, to sell them at great profit in Kamschatka. British merchants quickly saw the potential of this trade. In 1785, at the Administration's insistence, the East India and South Sea Companies licensed a group to trade in furs between there and Asia north of Canton; and by 1789 these, British adventurers from Bengal, British interloping under cover of the Portuguese flag from Macau, Russians, and Americans, had ventured or were venturing to the northwest American coast.

Alarmed by this untoward activity on a coast over which they claimed sovereignty, the Spanish moved to confirm their claim by presence and occupation.[1] In February 1789, Flores, the Viceroy at Mexico City, sent two vessels under the command of Martinez to make

> dispositions for the cutting of lumber and the construction of a shed to serve as barracks and shelter from the inclemencies of weather, an assembly place to meet with the Indians, and a trench to defend yourselves from their invasions in case they attempt such

at Nootka, so as to create at least the pretence of a 'formal establishment' there; to explore the coast up to 55°N latitude; and to point out to the expected Russian and British expeditions the priority of Spanish exploration and occupation.

Martinez reached Nootka Sound at the beginning of May, to find in the vicinity two American ships, and two ships (*Iphigenia* and *Northwest American*) operated by British merchants under Portuguese colours, whose commander John Meares had established a camp there the previous year. Martinez arrested the crew of the *Iphigenia*, then expelled them. He confiscated the *Northwest American*, so as to use her in the survey, and sent her crew to Mexico. Then, in June, he first turned away, then seized the *Princess Royal*, one of the pair of ships carrying Chinese artificers and materials for shipbuilding that the British merchants licensed to trade had sent to establish a permanent factory. And he seized the *Argonaut*, whose captain, Colnett, asserted that the English company had sent him as Governor to fortify an establishment, build vessels for the coastal trade, and exclude other nations from it, and, as well, that Cook had given the British a prior right to possess. Martinez sent this ship and crew under guard to San Blas on the Mexican coast, and set about building a winter camp. At the end of July, however, he received unexpected orders to return south.

Garbled news of these events reached London at the beginning of February 1790. Then, ten days later, the Spanish ambassador told Carmarthen (now the Duke of Leeds) of the incidents, asserted Spain's priority of discovery and occupation, and denied Britain's right to trade on the north-west American coast. When Banks refuted the Spanish claim to priority, the Administration moved to strengthen their hand, deciding 'to lay the foundation of an establishment for the assistance of His Majesty's subjects in the prosecution of the Fur trade from the North West Coast of America.'[2]

The developed scheme involved sending the *Gorgon*, a 44-gun ship then being prepared to carry troops and supplies to New South Wales, and the *Discovery*, the sloop intended for the survey of the south Atlantic, to Port Jackson, where Phillip would supply a party to undertake the settlement. These ships would rendezvous in December at the Hawaiian Islands with the frigate which Commodore Cornwallis would simultaneously despatch from India. The squadron would proceed to the north-west American coast in the (Northern) spring, where the officers would demand or enforce satisfaction from the Spanish, establish the settlement, and survey the coast from 40°N to 60°N. When winter came, the *Gorgon* would return to New South Wales, picking up some Maoris en route so that these might instruct the colonists on Norfolk Island in the mysteries of New Zealand flax dressing. Following Mulgrave's preliminaries, Nepean conveyed the scheme in its essentials to the Admiralty at the end of February, and then, in March, he drafted appropriate instructions for the captains of the ships, for Phillip, and for Commodore Cornwallis.[3]

As the Administration hastened to fit the ships for sea, Meares arrived from Macau with more details of the clash. His inflated representation of his acts of possession there, increased the politicians' determination to assert 'the Rights of [British] subjects to exercise their Navigation and Fisheries, as well as to land and form Establishments on all *unoccupied* Coasts of the American Continent and Islands.' They put off their scheme to send the warships, and instead protested in the strongest terms.

When Spain did not concede immediately, the British prepared for war. Cabinet considered Meares's evidence on 30 April; and then, ordering a 'hot' press, Pitt mobilized the fleet. On 7 and 8 May, the

Board of Control (Pitt, Dundas, Mulgrave, and Campbell) drew up instructions concerning the routes which the ships due to sail from Canton in January and February 1791 should use in the event of war. The Secret Court then issued these; and Dundas wrote to Cornwallis privately, that all their accounts from Spain portended 'a Resolution to go to War.' On 21 May, the Commissioners told the Governor-General that he was to invade the Spanish possessions in the East on first news of war.[4]

Grenville wrote to Commodore Cornwallis concerning their plans for the China ships on 5 June. The next day, Hood told him that the Admiralty intended to send him 'a good seventy-four and two or three stout frigates;' and that Blankett and Troubridge, who were to go in the *Leopard* and *Isis* to Canton, would join him after they had escorted the merchantmen from the China Sea. The Admiralty formally instructed the Commodore to take Blankett and Troubridge (now in the *Thames*) under his command at the end of July, and the captains then sailed.[5]

The Administration's choice of Blankett to command the escorts is again instructive. Like Phillip, Blankett was multilingual, he had been a strategic adviser since the early 1780s at least, he was skilled in survey, and he had served as a spy. His having previously prepared a lengthy report on the Seas of Japan of course added to his qualifications. Clearly, in choosing Blankett for the task of escorting the Company ships from China, Pitt, Dundas, Mulgrave, and Grenville were not simply choosing a run-of-the-mill officer available because of seniority or another mundane reason. As they had done when they sent Phillip to New South Wales, they now sent a 'discreet' officer on a task of considerable consequence to their general efforts to strengthen the nation's strategic position in the East.

Blankett reached the Cape at the end of October. When circumstances allowed him to do so safely, he reported that the colony there was in general very fertile, but that the colonists had to import all kinds of timber; that they were profoundly discontented; and that, if they were to revolt and to establish a free port, this would be most consequential to Britain. 'America & Africa,' he wrote,

> might be furnished from thence with all the produce of India & China, & many ports of Europe and Asia would find a vent & return for many of their productions, without being subject to the risque & expense of a longer Navigation. [You] will see at one View all the Advantages that would arise to the Cape, were it made the Entrepôt of European and Asiatick Commodities.

From the Cape, he sailed via Timor into the China Sea, to examine this route's suitability. Then, with the crisis with Spain resolved, he surveyed the China coast northwards of Macau, while Troubridge investigated the Pelew Islands.[6]

After several months of negotiations, and in the face of Britain's naval superiority, Spain gave in. In October, the two nations signed a convention, by which Spain agreed to restore

> the buildings and tracts of land situated on the North-west Coast of the continent of North America, or on islands adjacent to that continent, of which the subjects of His Britannic Majesty were dispossessed about the month of April, 1789,

and to compensate the British traders for their losses. Both agreed to permit each other's subjects to navigate, fish, trade, and settle 'places not already occupied' in and about the Pacific Ocean.

With their interest aroused, the Administration now continued with their scheme to survey the north-west American coast. Nepean told the Admiralty of the intention to pursue it in January 1791, Grenville sent on the King's instructions a month later; and then, in another two weeks, he passed on Banks's instructions for Menzies. Vancouver then sailed to survey and chart, first the Hawaiian Islands, and second, the north-west coast of America, in order to obtain 'a more complete knowledge' of any north-west passage, and of 'the number, extent, and situation' of any European settlements there. As befitted one who had gone to the edge of the world's oceans with Cook, this he did with surpassing dedication and brilliance in the next four years.[7]

In its execution, this expedition showed many of the features of that originally planned by Nepean. Vancouver sailed via the Indian and the south-western Pacific Oceans, touching at western Australia and New Zealand. Lieutenant Hanson in the *Daedalus* re-supplied him on the north-west American coast in the autumn of 1792, then loaded cattle and sheep at California, and sailed for New South Wales. En route, he called at New Zealand, and induced two Maoris to go with him, so that the colonists might have their advice on flax-dressing. Phillip had sailed for home before Hanson arrived, but Grose immediately sent the Maoris to King at Norfolk Island, who found to his disappointment that it took only 'one day' for these to convey the little Knowledge they had.[8]

By 1792, then, the officers whom the Pitt Administration sent to obtain information which they might have 'recourse to on every occasion, whether for the Objects of Peace or War,' had much advanced British knowledge of navigation in the southern Atlantic, the Indian Ocean and the China Sea, and the south-west and north-east Pacific, and of the strategic resources of the islands in and coast about these seas. The Administration had established bases in New South Wales and the Andaman Islands; and they had sketched a procedure for using these to advantage. They were moving to make greater use of local resources in the defence of the nation's eastern establishment. They were, in short, better equipped that their predecessors in the 1770s had been to protect that establishment from the fury of the French storm, soon to break again.

CHAPTER 9

A strategic outlier
1793-1811

I *British strategy and the New South Wales colony*

Pitt and his colleagues first found the French Revolution a favorable
rather than unfavorable development in European affairs. As the French
examined their new situation at the turn of the decade, they showed
some interest in adopting a constitution on English lines; and this prospect promised a vindication of the view Pitt had put when defending his
commercial treaty of 1786, that no nation was 'unalterably' the enemy of
another. Even if future events might not validate the prospect, the
ministers thought that a France politically and economically disarrayed
could scarcely threaten as she had even three years before.

After Louis XVI and Marie Antoinette's attempt to flee in June 1791,
however, the Revolution took a course unfavorable to Britain. Radical
groups gained control of French affairs, declared a republic, and raised
nationalistic fervour, while *émigré* nobles and priests, and sympathetic
European monarchs schemed to restore royalist rule. At first Pitt declined to support either side (and indeed, in early 1792 he still anticipated fifteen years of peace.) As the Republicans launched their
blood-dimmed tide, however, and as British radicals became restive, he
came to view the situation much less sympathetically. In November
1792, he told the Stadtholder that Britain would come to Holland's aid if
France attacked.

The Republicans declared war on Holland and Britain on 1 February
1793, and Pitt had then to cope with the threat. Britain's needs were both
defensive and offensive, of course: she had to preserve herself from invasion and her links with and possessions in the West and East Indies; and
she had, as Dundas put it, simultaneously to humble the power of
France and enlarge her own wealth and security. Consulting principally
with Dundas ('every act of his being as much *mine* as *his*,' he told Grenville in 1794), Pitt turned to the strategy with which his father had had
such success in the late 1750s, when he sought allies to contain or defeat
the French armies in Europe, and sent naval squadrons and expedi-
tionary forces to maintain Britain's hold on her colonies and weaken
France's on hers.[1]

158

This strategy of sapping France's ability and will to fight in Europe by capturing her colonies and destroying her shipping and trade, of course, turned on Britain and France's inherent strengths and weaknesses. Britain was a small country, with limited resources, and a population of some fourteen millions. France was much larger, she had more resources, which she could immediately augment by engulfing her neighbours, and she had a population of some forty millions. Britain could not hope to raise armies to match the French ones, nor maintain alone those which she could place in Europe. To pursue a continental war, she needed allies. Her island situation and firm mercantilist system, however, had led her to develop extensive and competent marines. Though also a colonial power, France had not given the same attention to her marines, which habitually succumbed to the British ones.

A major effect of the strategy was to perpetuate the circumstances which gave rise to it. In 1793-4, the British captured French bases and islands in Canada and the West Indies, and Pondicherry in India. The French balanced these losses with gains in Europe, when they mounted huge armies which progressively defeated the allied ones. By the end of 1794, they had forced the British from the Continent, and expanded into Holland. The British responded by capturing the Cape of Good Hope, Trincomalee, and Malacca in 1795, while France compelled Prussia and Holland to make peace and Austria to wind down her campaign, and enlisted Spain as an ally. In 1796, the British took Colombo, Amboina in the Moluccas, and the Banda Islands, while Bonaparte swept through Italy, defeating the Austrians and closing the ports to the British, and Spain declared war on Britain. British squadrons shattered the Spanish fleet off Cape St. Vincent in February 1797, and the Dutch one in October, but in this latter month the French forced the Austrians to the peace of Campo Formio. In 1798 the French attempted to break the pattern, when they sent Bonaparte across the Mediterranean to capture Egypt as a prelude to striking at India, but Nelson destroyed the French fleet at Aboukir Bay, and the British then confined the army to Egypt. Pitt organized a new coalition of European allies, but Bonaparte returned to France in August 1799, proclaimed himself First Consul, and soon had the French armies defeating the Allied ones again. In August 1800, Bonaparte obtained Russia's help, when Czar Paul organized the Second Armed Neutrality and closed the Baltic to Britain. Nelson opened it again, when he destroyed the Danish fleet at Copenhagen the next April, and British forces then compelled the French ones in Egypt to surrender. At a profound impasse, the belligerents reached an uneasy peace in March 1802.

As this outline shows, the general circumstance of the British-French struggle between 1793 and 1802, as of the generic one throughout the Eighteenth century, was that Britain, the maritime power, controlled the seas, and had a general authority in the West and East Indies, while France, the land power, dominated the European continent. In this circumstance, Britain needed non-European sources of naval and other strategic materials, and bases from which her squadrons might operate; and this need meant a strategic role for the infant Colony in New South Wales.

Phillip's preparations for the Colony's playing this role had not progressed as well as he and the Administration had expected, and his successors had to continue them even as the drama began. At the opening of hostilities, 'the procuring livestock for the settlement [was] of all other considerations that which [might lead] most directly to put it in a situation to maintain itself;' and both home and colonial authorities continued their efforts to achieve this. Late in 1792, Lieutenant Hanson loaded the *Daedalus* with eighteen cattle and fourteen sheep at Monterey, then gathered one hundred hogs at Tahiti, but only four sheep and eighty hogs remained alive when he reached Sydney the next April.[2]

Neither did two private attempts at this time at increasing the colony's stock have better success. In October 1792, Grose and his fellow officers engaged Captain Raven of the *Britannia* to obtain supplies at the Cape. Raven loaded three horses, thirty cattle, and twelve goats, but twenty-nine of the cattle and three of the goats died before he reached New South Wales again in June. Late in 1792, too, Matthew Bampton, a Bombay trader, freighted the *Shar Hormuzeir* with five horses, twenty-five cattle, two hundred and twenty sheep, one hundred and thirty goats, and assorted foodstuffs and other goods, but he lost all the cattle, half the sheep, and other of the stock on the way.[3]

One reason for these animals' not surviving was that they were unaccustomed to 'dry food,' and the officials and merchants next dealt with this problem. In mid-1793, consulting with Lieutenant Bowen, who had sailed out on the *Atlantic* in 1791, the Home Office instructed Grose to load the *Daedalus* with fodder and the items put on the First Fleet ' for traffic and barter,' and send her the shorter distance to Timor, the Moluccas, or Java for stock. At it turned out, Vancouver needed the *Daedalus* back, but, following Bowen's ideas, the Administration then purchased two ships (*Supply* and *Reliance*) specifically to use for bringing stock to the colony.[4]

At the same time, Grose contracted with Bampton for more stock from India, and, having taken special care, the merchant landed one hundred and twenty-nine cattle at Sydney in May 1795. Late in this year, the colonists had the pleasing knowledge that beasts might thrive in New South Wales, for a party discovered the herd, now enlarged by progeny to forty, that had wandered from their keeper in 1788. In September 1796, on learning of the British capture of the Cape of Good Hope, Hunter sent Kent and Waterhouse there in the *Supply* and *Reliance*. Kent landed five horses, twenty-seven cattle, and thirty-five sheep in May 1797, and Waterhouse followed the next month with three horses, forty cattle, and one hundred sheep (including some merinos). With these shipments as a base, the colonists began to develop herds and flocks.[5]

The colony's agriculture took hold at the same time. The Administration had instructed Phillip to make small grants of land to convicts and soldiers who chose to remain after serving their terms, which he had done. On Phillip's departure, however, Grose made larger grants to *serving* officers, and allowed them liberal access to convict labour. Though unauthorized, and much to the officers' private advantage, this new policy also brought public results, as the recipients expanded the colony's production. The cultivation of the fertile Hawkesbury flood plains soon assisted this expansion.[6]

The combination of successful importation, the breeding of animals and an extension of agriculture brought a striking improvement in the colony's circumstance. As John Macarthur told his brother in mid-1794,

> The changes that we have undergone since the departure of Governor Phillip are so great and extraordinary that to recite them all might create some suspicion of their truth. From a state of desponding poverty and threatened famine that this settlement should be raised to its present aspect in so short a time is scarcely credible.[7]

Though caterpillar plagues, droughts, and floods brought periodic reverses, the colony now made steady progress towards self-sufficiency. In August 1799, Hunter reported that the Government, officers, and settlers together had some one hundred and thirty-eight horses, seven hundred cattle, five thousand sheep, two thousand seven hundred goats, three thousand four hundred hogs; and six thousand one hundred acres under wheat, eighty-two under barley, two thousand five hundred under maize, and 'large tracts of garden-ground.' A year later, King reported further increases, observing that the colony had 'a tolerable abundant quantity of breeding cattle,' and that it might be possible to begin culling the Government herds for fresh meat in three years. At the end of 1801, he wrote that more than half of the six thousand inhabitants supported themselves, that he had opened a trade with Tahiti in pork, and that, in view of there being

> at some distance large tracts of a fine country that might be cultivated to great advantage, [and the] whole surface [being] perhaps unequalled for grazing-ground, either for sheep or horned cattle,

he could foresee the time when the colony might supply itself with food.[8]

King also made a beginning at cloth manufacture. In mid-1800, he asked Foveaux on Norfolk Island to continue working the *phormium tenax*, and to make an experimental planting of European flax. At Sydney, he set dressers and weavers amongst the Irish convicts to

M

cultivating the European variety, and 'every woman that can spin' to manufacturing what these others grew. He also investigated a native fibre-plant growing in the Hawkesbury Valley. By the end of 1801, these efforts had produced '279 yards of fine and 367½ of coarse linnen,' and he sent samples home.[9]

In these years, too, the British significantly extended their knowledge of adjacent coasts and seas. In February 1797, making its way to Port Jackson with supplies, Campbell and Company's *Sydney Cove* was wrecked on Preservation Island, off the north-east tip of Tasmania. When he reached the settlement some six months later, the captain reported that the tides and currents in the area indicated a strait from the southern Indian to the southern Pacific Ocean. Hunter had speculated that this might be so from his first year in the colony, and he of course knew that this strait, if it offered safe navigation, would provide a much more convenient route than that about the south of Tasmania. He therefore sent, first Bass, and then Flinders, to confirm its existence and to chart it, and this the pair did in a series of voyages in 1798 and 1799.[10]

In 1799, too, the Administration built and fitted out the *Lady Nelson*

> for the purpose of prosecuting the discovery and survey of the unknown parts of the coast of New Holland, and of ascertaining, as far as is practicable, the hydrography of that part of the globe.

The next year, they appointed Lieutenant Grant to command her, instructing him to pay

> especial regard to the examination and accurate delineation of all such harbours as [you] shall discover and judge to be commodious for the reception of shipping, and also of such shoals and other dangers as [you] may from time to time meet with,

and, having Hunter's first reports of it, told him to attend to the Bass Strait area on his way to Sydney.[11]

Grant sailed along much of the coast of Victoria, and reached Sydney in December 1800, and the captains of the *Margaret* and the *Harbinger*, following the same route from the Cape, immediately afterwards added to his information. King sent Grant back to extend his survey, and then, Lieutenant Murray, and outward-bound captains soon took advantage of the results. By the end of 1802, the Bass Strait route was the preferred one for ships approaching the colony from the west.[12]

The Governors extended the settlement's defences, too. In 1798, Hunter improved Dawes's battery, and built another on Bennelong point opposite. The next year, he added one at Garden Island, so that 'in point of defence, the settlement at this time wore a respectable appearance.' In 1800-1, King rebuilt Dawes's once more, and constructed a fourth battery at the Heads.[13]

The colony began to play its intended strategic part in the midst of these preparations. While the Administration saw this as solely a role for government, the Governors found that they needed some help from private enterprise to perform it. They ran some risk in using this help, for while they were mindful of the restrictions which the East India Company's charter placed on the colony's trade, the merchants, with their eyes on profit, were a good deal less so. Given the limited amount of shipping available to them, however, the governors had little choice; and the co-operation did work to the benefit of both parties, for it enabled New South Wales to contribute to Britain's general war effort, and it gave the merchants additional cargoes.

As Banks, Matra, Call, and Young had suggested they might, the British now paid some attention to New Zealand. In November 1793, Captain Raven reported that

> there are various kinds of timber in Dusky Bay, but that which is principally fit for shipbuilding is the spruce fir, which may be cut along the shore in any quantity or size for the construction of vessels from a first-rate to a small wherry.

The next September, Bampton acted on this report, when he took the *Fancy* and *Endeavour* there, and loaded some 'two hundred very fine trees, from sixty to one hundred and forty feet in length.' In June 1798, Campbell sent the *Hunter* to New Zealand for a return cargo of spars.[14]

Hunter harvested New South Wales timber, too. In December 1795, he enumerated suitable varieties in the Hawkesbury Valley; and across the next years, he had convicts cut them, and convict shipwrights season them, and use them to repair the *Reliance*, and to build some small boats and a brig to replace the decrepit *Supply*. Simultaneously, local merchants developed a private industry, so as to give themselves the means to pursue the coastal carrying trade and the Bass Strait seal trade. Though they had exported little, by the end of 1801 the colonists had found that a range of local timber was suitable for naval purposes.[15]

Timber was not the only product to which officials and merchants attended. In June 1797, Hunter reported the discovery by survivors making their way from the wreck of the *Sydney Cove*, of large deposits of coal in cliffs south of Sydney. The next January, he reported a similar discovery at the Coal (Hunter) River to the north. The Administration quickly saw that these offered the means of killing two birds with one stone, for New South Wales still needed supplies of food and livestock, and the Cape of Good Hope, which they had now made into a Crown colony, had no forests and therefore lacked fuel and building and naval timbers. The two settlements might co-operate mutually to lessen their dependence on European supplies by exchanging their resources, and thereby increase the nation's capacity in the East.[16]

strategic elements seem an after thought.

The ministers accordingly discussed the situation with King, who was again in England. Portland then requested Hunter to

> dispatch the Buffalo and Porpoise, loaded with coals, to the Cape as soon as possible after the receipt of this letter, directing them to return with as large a supply of live stock for the use of the settlement as they can conveniently stow;

and Dundas asked Macartney, the Governor of the Cape, to discuss with the once more outward-bound King what timber New South Wales might send, and to establish 'a regular intercourse' between the two settlements.[17]

Hunter was not able to meet this request immediately, for, as he explained to Portland in July 1799, he had neither begun mining the coal nor had he ships free to carry it. He soon after made a beginning at exporting strategic materials, though, when he arranged for a ship returning to India to take a cargo of coal. The next year, either at his behest or with his concurrence, the colonial merchants Lord and Davies sent a cargo of New Zealand masts and spars to Bengal.[18]

King furthered his beginnings when he became governor in 1800. First, he set a convict miner to cutting an experimental shaft into a coal deposit on the south-west side of Botany Bay. Then, in January 1801, he cleared the *El Plumier*, a Spanish prize purchased by local merchants, to load a cargo of spars at New Zealand for the Cape. In March, the *Royal Admiral*, which had carried convicts out, went to New Zealand to gather spars for India.[19]

In June, King had Paterson and Grant survey the coal deposits at the mouth of the Hunter River, and when they reported favorably, he established a small settlement there to mine the coal for the Government, and ordered that private persons must henceforth do so only under licence. In July, he exchanged one hundred tons ('the first cargo of coals brought from the Coal River in a Government vessel') with the master of the *Earl Cornwallis* for goods the colony needed; and Simeon Lord sold that master some one hundred and fifty tons of coal and spars. Two months later, King engaged Robert Campbell to take one hundred tons on the *Hunter* to India. In October, he gave Lord and his partners permission to take 'the long-expected cargo of coals from this country to the Cape' on their prize the *Anna Josepha*, and the merchants added some 4,000 feet of spars. King intended to have sent more coal to the Cape of H.M.S. *Porpoise*, but had to give this idea up when she returned from Tahiti needing extensive repairs.[20]

The Administration also thought to use the colony as a staging base in these years. In January 1797, recurring to the scheme which Sandwich, Mulgrave, and Fullarton had evolved in 1780, and using Ewart's more recent description of efficacious routes, Dundas planned secretly to send a force against the Spanish settlements in South America. His idea was to have 1800 men proceed from the Cape of Good Hope to New South Wales, where they would collect reinforcements and then cross the Pacific to raise rebellion against the Spanish rule and occupy territory, so as to obtain 'glory and permanent advantage' for Britain. He soon encountered problems in mounting this force, however, and he gave the idea up when Jervis and Nelson crushed the Spanish fleet off Cape St. Vincent in February.[21]

Though they abandoned this major attempt, the British did some minor damage to the Spanish on the west coast of South America from New South Wales. In 1798, Hunter issued letters of marque to a number of Southern whalers 'animated by the hopes of privateering to advantage,' who then crossed the Pacific and cruised off the coast of Peru, where they took some small prizes. These they sent to Sydney, where, as just described, local merchants bought them, loaded them with coal and spars, and in turn sold them at Bengal and the Cape.[22]

II   *The British consolidate their position in New South Wales*

One cannot say that the New South Wales colony's playing of its strategic part in the years between 1793 and 1802 was more than tentative. Still, the experience showed that the player had some potential, and that the playwright might, therefore, develop the part in time of future need.

European circumstances soon indicated that this time was imminent. The peace which Britain and France concluded in March 1802 was uneasy from the first, for Bonaparte had framed its terms so as to preclude Britain's having a role in Europe, and to obtain a breathing space in which to prepare for further expansion; and as he made these preparations, the British responded with counters. As William James observed,

> the activity which reigned on the ocean . . . [was] much greater than any which had been witnessed during the last two or three years of the war, [and] gave to the treaty the air of a truce, or suspension of arms, in which each of the belligerents, some of whom signed it for no other purpose, was striving to gain an advantageous position, in order, when the tocsin should again sound, to be ready for the recommencement of hostilities. French, Dutch, and Spanish fleets were preparing to put to sea; and English fleets, to follow them and watch their motions: who, then could doubt that, although the wax upon the seals of the treaty concluding the last had scarcely cooled, a new war was on the eve of bursting forth?[1]

So over-reaching was Bonaparte's ambition that he gave the first signs of it even before he signed the peace. One of these bore directly on Australia. In October 1800, he sent Baudin and a party of scientists in the *Géographie* and *Naturaliste* to examine in detail the *south-west, west, north-west* and *north* coasts of *New Holland*, some of which are still entirely unknown, while others are known only imperfectly. By combining the work which will be done on these various parts with that of the English navigators on the *east* coast and of d'Entrecasteaux on *Anthony van Diemen's Land*, we shall come to know the entire coastline of this great south land, which, situated not far from the countries of *Asia* where, for three centuries, Europeans have been forming settlements, has seemed until recently to be condemned to a sort of oblivion.[2]

The alarmed British soon moved to counter the threat to their right to possess other areas of the southern continent implied in Baudin's voyage. Across the first half of 1801, Banks organized an expedition to complete the survey of the entire coastline. At his suggestion, the Admiralty entrusted Matthew Flinders with this task, instructing him to make 'a complete examination and survey,' to note the winds, currents, and weather in different seasons, chart harbours and rivers, and outlying shoals, to record and collect 'the produce of the earth,' and to report results at every opportunity. Banks and the Admiralty gathered skilled persons to assist in these tasks, and the party sailed in the *Investigator* in July.[3]

Ahead of Flinders, Baudin sighted Cape Leeuin at the end of May. After charting the north-west coast and refreshing at Timor, he turned south, and reached Van Diemen's Land in January 1802. In March, he examined Bass Strait, then followed the coast westwards, assiduously giving appropriate names to this 'Terre Napoleon,' until he met Flinders in Encounter Bay (139°E long.) on 8 April. With scurvy ravaging his crew, he turned for Port Jackson. Aware of Baudin's attention to the area, King reported home in May 1802 that the French probably intended to settle the mainland coast of Bass Strait. He accordingly recommended that the Administration establish a convict settlement at Port Phillip, which Murray and Flinders reported as offering 'a very noble and spacious harbour,' and 'beautiful and fertile' country suitable for wheat-growing and which was, of course, well-placed to serve the sealers working the neighbouring islands.[4]

Despite his suspicions, King welcomed Baudin on his arrival at Sydney in June, and extended his hospitality and the colony's resources to the French across the next months. He was most disturbed to learn on 18 November, the day after they sailed again, however, that some of the party had talked loosely about settling Storm Bay (Hobart). King immediately sent Robbins to examine Port Phillip, King Island, and other sites for 'the best situation for settlements, in which you will have a view to the commercial advantages, access for vessels, obtaining fresh water, and its defence.' He gave Robbins a letter to Baudin requesting an explanation of the rumours; and he wrote to the Administration describing his measures to confirm 'His Majesty's Right to [Van Diemen's Land] being within the limits of this Territory.'[5]

Baudin's reply from King Island was not encouraging. Robbins had arrived too late to prevent the French establishing their right to possess there, the explorer wrote, and he pointed out as well that Tasman, a Dutchman, had first discovered Van Diemen's Land.[6] His suspicions confirmed by this reply, in September 1803 King sent ·a party under Bowen to settle Risdon Cove in the Derwent estuary. In England, Hobart acted simultaneously to counter the threat, between November 1802 and the following March appointing David Collins to head a settlement at Port Phillip, and equipping HMS *Calcutta* to carry him and a party of some four hundred and fifty marines and convicts out to begin it.

Collins sailed in April 1803, and reached his destination in October. Disappointed with the site he chose on the Mornington Peninsula, he shifted his party to the Derwent estuary in February 1804, and six months later, those at Risdon came down to join in beginning Hobart Town. In June, King received Hobart's instruction to settle Port Dalrymple (Launceston), and he sent Paterson to do so in October. By the end of 1804, the British had consolidated their claim to the south-eastern coasts of Australia, and secured Bass Strait.[7]

As the British expanded their colonization, they of course continued their efforts to make it self-sufficient, and to develop the area's resources. In February 1803, fulfilling a contract with King, Campbell landed six horses, three hundred and seven cattle, and four asses in good condition, and a year later, another one hundred and thirty-seven cattle. As the government conserved and bred these, private settlers developed their herds, so that the colony soon had more than enough meat for its immediate needs. In May 1803, King reported he had three years' salted supply, and he reserved the wild cattle, then roaming the Cow Pastures in their thousands, as an additional resource against future dearth.[8]

There was similar progress at agriculture, and in March 1804, King was able to report that he had eleven months' supply of wheat and flour in the government store, and a further 11,000 bushels of wheat and 7,000 of maize 'in stacks.'

> Respecting grain, [he observed] our internal resources will be sufficient to preclude the necessity of any being ever sent here again; for let what will happen, those supplies could not arrive before the effects of such unforeseen accidents would be replaced by the next crop of maize or wheat . . . The general cultivation of potatoes, as well as every other vegetable, the settlers and inhabitants at large have within the last two years attended more to than they ever have done before, which has added greatly to their general comfort.[9]

By this time, too, the Governor had consolidated his beginning at cloth manufacture. At the end of 1804, he reported that the production of linen was progressing 'as well as can possibly be expected,' with the factory now having twelve looms, including two for sailcloth. The women made over one hundred yards of cloth each week, and he had bartered some 2,100 yards for settlers' wheat. He had sown some Indian hemp, which had grown luxuriantly, and European hemp, which 'might also be manufactured and sent from hence in cordage,' promised 'a very abundant return on the low lands about the Hawkesbury and Nepean Rivers.'[10]

In this year, King moved to secure to Britain the benefit of these improvements, when he began building Fort Phillip. He located this pentagon on the western hill overlooking the cove, so that it should command 'the town and country round to a very great extent and the approach to the harbour.' To arm it, he imported from Norfolk Island the guns salvaged from the *Sirius*, and as it neared completion, he reported that it should be 'of the greatest consequence in repelling any attack from an enemy who may approach either by sea or land.'[11]

In the spring of 1802, so as to reduce mortality and lessen costs, the Addington Administration decided henceforth to transport convicts to New South Wales in Royal Navy ships. Seeking return cargoes, the Admiralty obtained from Hunter a lengthy description of the colony's prospective exports. The former Governor particularly emphasized the naval potential of the timber, and mentioned as well flax, turpentine, bark for tanning, timber for fuel, coal, iron, wool, indigo, and seal skins. The English dockyards were competently stocked with masts and hemp at this time, but were very short of large timber. Knowing that this shortage required that they procure suitable timber at 'every opportunity,' the Admiralty proposed that the ships 'bring home as much . . . as they can conveniently contain,' and the Navy Board accordingly provided the Colonial Office with 'Drawings of the Frame Timbers of a 98, 74, and 38 Gunship, with proper Dimensions and necessary Information for the purpose of providing [it].'

In August, Hobart sent King a summary of Hunter's paper and the Navy Board's sketches, and instructed him to gather supplies of the timbers, to manufacture iron into bars for export to India and Britain, to encourage returning captains to load coal for India and the Cape, to send home some cakes of indigo for assessment, to continue efforts to manufacture flax, and to encourage the production of wool, especially with a view to 'the future exportation . . . for the market of this country.'[12]

King did not receive these instructions in time to gather a full cargo of timber for HMS *Glatton*, which reached Sydney with a party of convicts in March 1803, but he moved quickly thereafter to realize them. In June, he proclaimed an embargo on private use of the timbers which Hunter had listed, and, employing 'a great proportion of the convicts at public labour' and building a vessel for the purpose, he set to gathering supplies from about the harbour. Early the next year, he was able to load HMS *Calcutta* with as much timber as she could stow. In 1805, he extended this use of local materials for naval purposes, when he made sails for the *Buffalo* from cloth from his female factory.[13]

(margin annotations: defence; poss. exports)

By the end of 1804, then, the British had consolidated their initially-precarious settlement on the south shores of Port Jackson into a permanent occupation of the south-eastern coasts of the continent. At Sydney, a large group had established a substantial port, and fortified it. Behind it, they were transforming the Cumberland Plain into a resemblance of rural England. At Norfolk Island, Hobart, and Port Dalrymple, smaller groups held sites which confirmed the nation's possession of the territory, and gave her means to command the adjacent seas. These colonists were a resource in themselves, from among whom the home government might recruit for particular purposes. Those about Sydney produced more food than they needed, and were therefore able to refresh ships and expeditions proceeding to distant parts. From the coasts north and south, and from New Zealand, they drew naval timbers and coal, strategic materials needed elsewhere in the empire. While it had taken more years than the three Pitt, Dundas, Mulgrave, Grenville, Nepean, and Phillip had first thought it would, the colony was now well able to play the role of strategic outlier. It is one of history's niceties, as it is a tribute both to their percipience and their political longevity, that those who in the mid-1780s created it with this role in mind called it onto the stage of war with the Emperor Napoleon.

III *The Colony's role in the Napoleonic war*

In April 1803, Sir Joseph Banks wrote to his old friend Phillip Gidley King, that

> the political situation of Europe is troublesome and turbulent in the extreme. The French nation wishes to be at rest; the Chief Consul wishes to be at war; and in order to bring about this event he assails us with uninterrupted affronts of the most serious nature. Flesh and blood can scarcely bear it, and I fear this nation will not bear it much longer. We have already had a message from the King to say that the French are arming, and have refused to say for what purpose, which has put the spirit of this nation very much up. How it will end I cannot foresee, but it cannot go on — well as long as the Chief Consul lives.

Events soon showed the accuracy of these presentiments. In May, after each had made demands over Malta that the other could not admit, Britain declared war so as not to give France more time to re-arm.[1]

The Addington Administration's strategy was essentially that of Pitt and Dundas on a reduced scale — to have the Navy patrol the seas and protect the colonies, leaving Bonaparte in control of Europe, but needing to invade England to conclude the struggle. In the first twelve months of the renewed war, the dictator obligingly played out this part, when he gathered forces in northern France, and ordered barges and boats to carry them across the Channel.

The lack of British involvement in Europe, and the time that the French needed to prepare for their invasion, meant that there was no decisive issue to the hostilities before May 1804, when Pitt formed a second administration, with Dundas (now Lord Melville) as First Lord of the Admiralty. Inevitably, the pair renewed the strategy in which they believed, and which they had followed consistently through the previous twenty-five years. With intricate negotiations across 1804 into 1805, Pitt brought Russia and Austria into a Third Coalition with Britain to oppose the now self-proclaimed Emperor Napoleon in Europe and he and Dundas organized British forces to move against the French, and, after the autumn of 1804, the Spanish ones in the West and East Indies and South America.

The war then took the usual course, which neither the retirement from office, nor death of those involved in its early direction much altered. In August 1805, Pitt and Middleton (now Lord Barham and Melville's successor at the Admiralty) sent Popham and a squadron, and Baird and 6,000 men to recapture the Cape of Good Hope, which they did the next January. In October, Nelson re-asserted Britain's control of the seas when his squadron destroyed the French fleet off Trafalgar. In the same month, the French compelled the Austrian army under Mack to surrender, and in early December they defeated a combined Russian-Austrian one at Austerlitz. The Austrians then reached a separate peace with France, the Prussians an understanding on future spoils, and the Third Coalition collapsed.

Worn-out, Pitt died on 23 January 1806, and Grenville took office at the head of a 'Ministry of All the Talents.' After an unsuccessful attempt to force a bridgehead in southern Europe, these fell back to attacking the Spanish about the River Plate. At the same time, Napoleon pressed ahead with his continental strategy, defeating the Russians in June 1807, and then persuading Csar Alexander to close Russia's ports to Britain. Soon afterwards, he forced Denmark and Sweden to do the same. The Portland Ministry (formed March 1807) responded by sending a force against the Danes, which destroyed much of Copenhagen and carried off the fleet and all available naval stores. Soon afterwards, however, the British lost their last prospect of an entry to northern Europe, when Sweden turned against them. Then, in November 1807, they lost their last one in southern France, when Napoleon sent an army into Portugal, and the government fled to Brazil. In April 1808, the Emperor installed his brother as ruler of Spain, and his hold over Europe was complete.

Denying Britain access to the continent, Napoleon brought her near to ruin in these years; and the desperateness of her situation meant that she needed to make all possible use of her colonies. When the politicians thought of New South Wales, they did so along those lines that had underlain its founding and emerged in the previous period of war. When

Pitt listed the enemy's concentrations about the globe in September 1804, for example, against that at 'Valparayso on the Coast of Chili,' he wrote 'Force concentrated by New Levies or otherwise at New South Wales.' The next month, he and Dundas had Popham and Arthur Wellesley draw up schemes for complementary expeditions to South America, in the manner of Sandwich and Mulgrave's of 1780-1. 'With respect to the Pacifick Ocean,' Popham wrote, following Pitt's idea,

> I consider two points of descent as sufficient, one however might suffice but if the other can be accomplished it will have a great effect upon the people to the Southward of Buenos Ayres. I mean in speaking of this which is on the coast of Chili to propose Valpariso, and if the force for that object could either be concentrated at, or taken from New South Wales, by new levies or otherwise, it would make this proposition perfect. The great force however for the Pacifick . . . I will propose to come from India.

The politicians found that the nation lacked the resources to mount these expeditions, but the next year, they made a slighter use of their distant colony, when they sent the China convoy through Bass Strait and round Norfolk Island, so as to avoid the enemy-laden Indian Ocean.[2]

Grenville in his turn also thought to use the colony as a staging-post for an expedition to South America. In what Fortescue terms 'one of the most astonishing plans that ever emanated from the brain even of a British Minister of War,' he and his advisers considered sending a squadron and 4,000 men against the Spanish in Chile. After occupying Valparaiso and establishing control of the country, the expedition would set up a chain of posts across the Andes and link up with the force at Buenos Aires. In a variant of the 1780 scheme, Grenville also proposed attacking the Spanish in Mexico from the East with 9,000 European and Black troops, and from the west with 5,000 European and Indian ones, and those in Peru with a small force from the Cape of Good Hope and New South Wales. Arthur Wellesley again drew up a plan of operations.[3]

The Administration did not proceed with the Mexico scheme, but they did organize an expedition to attack Chile. In the process, Buckingham advised his brother, the Prime Minister, to attend

> very particularly to the advantage of ordering Murray to carry Crawford's force direct from their *rendezvous* through Bass's Straits to refresh at New South Wales — Port Jackson; and to exchange their less active men for the seasoned flank companies of the New South Wales corps; and to take with them 100 convict pioneers, who will be invaluable, as seasoned to work in the sun.

After this force had sailed with orders to this effect, the ministers learned that that at Buenos Aires had surrendered, and they sent new orders to the Cape for it to go directly to the River Plate.[4]

Grenville and his colleagues sought to obtain strategic supplies from New South Wales, too. In July 1806, the Admiralty asked the Navy

Board to 'lose no opportunity . . . of transporting such Timber, as may be cut and is fit for Ship building from [there] to England.' The Portland Administration continued this effort. In December 1807, the newly-returned King gave the Board a detailed account of Australian and New Zealand timber he considered suitable for masts, spars, plank, frame, and gun-carriage; and he again referred to the prospects of growing and manufacturing hemp in the colony. The Board then asked Castlereagh to instruct Bligh to gather a supply of timber 'agreeably to the Drawings' of the frame timbers sent out in 1802, for shipment home at every opportunity.[5]

The colonists had deposed Bligh by the time this instruction reached New South Wales, but Foveaux saw to it, and gathered some £2,000 worth of timber. Paterson, who became acting-governor in January 1809, also attended to it, but, like King before him, he found that he needed some help from private enterprise to effect it. The combination again bore results. In the last years of the decade, there was an active trade in coal and naval timbers, with such colonial merchants as Macarthur, Blaxcell, Lord, Kable, Underwood, Thompson, and Palmer carrying these materials to Sydney, and from there, either on their own behalf or the government's, despatching them to India and the Cape. Illustrative of the general circumstance is the agreement Paterson made with Lord and his partners in the spring of 1809, for them to take a cargo of coal and timber to the Cape. The merchants loaded the *Boyd* accordingly, and sent her via New Zealand to add some spars.[6]

Such engagements inevitably gave rise to dreams of greater enterprize, for, as Young and Call had a generation earlier, the merchants saw that they might make the south Pacific a source of regular supply of strategic materials. 'A most material point would be accomplished,' Lord and his partners told Macquarie in January 1810,

> if the natural advantages of this Climate could be embraced by producing a quantity of Hemp and Flax sufficient for the demands of the Colony itself, and to enable us to send to England a considerable supply for the British Navy in compliance with the wishes and invitations of His Majesty's Ministers.[7]

Accordingly, the merchants wrote to England for hemp-seed, and to India for seed and for 'Workmen accustomed to the Manufacture of the raw Material into Cordage and Canvas.' Knowing that they would require time to bring these moves to fruition, they asked Macquarie's permission to establish a settlement at the Bay of Islands, on the north-west tip of New Zealand, where the Maoris had 'a plant, capable, in proper hands, of being rendered an object of considerable National importance.' Macquarie approved the project, and the melancholy news that the Maoris had massacred the crew of the *Boyd* and burnt her to the waterline, did not deter them from pursuing it. It came to nothing, however, when the parties they sent over made discretion the better part of valour, and quickly returned.[8]

Ironically, as New South Wales developed its ability to act the part of strategic outlier to the Cape, India, and South America, British gains in the East lessened the need of its doing so. After they took office in 1809, the Percival Administration organized a series of expeditions against the French and Dutch bases in the East, which led to the capture, in 1810-11, of Mauritius, Bourbon, Madagascar, the Seychelles, Java, Amboina, and the Banda Islands.

In June 1811, that great empire-builder Raffles wrote to the Governor-General at Calcutta,

> The annexation of Java and the Eastern Isles to our Indian empire, opens to the English nation views of so enlarged a nature, as seem equally to demand and justify a bolder policy, both of a commercial and political kind, than we could have lately contemplated. The countries which must, directly or indirectly, fall under our influence and authority, form a range of possessions which, with intervals of no great importance, extend nearly from the Bay of Bengal to our settlements on the continent of New Holland.[9]

Raffles's perspective was commercial more than strategic, of course, but his description shows how well the British had then concluded the eastern naval strategy which Pitt, Dundas, Mulgrave, and Grenville had developed twenty-five years earlier. Their success gave Britain the naval dominance of the Indian and Pacific Oceans for the next one hundred years, and a second empire.

Envoy

The first considerable influence in William Pitt's imperial outlook was, of course, his family experience. His great-grandfather, Thomas, had founded their fortune during his years as Governor of Madras, and this could not but have led the Pitts instinctively to link colonial activity with wealth and position. This impulse found full public statement in Chatham's policy in the Seven Years War, when Britain built a great navy which brought her mastery of the seas, and dominance of France and Spain in North America and the West Indies, and in the East. Chatham put his essential view concisely when he said of the Peace of Paris (1763),

> France is chiefly, if not solely, to be dreaded by us in the light of a maritime and commercial power . . . by restoring to her all the valuable West-India islands, and by our concessions in the Newfoundland fishery, we had given to her the means of recovering her prodigious losses and of becoming once more formidable to us at sea.

This Pitt family outlook, of course, coincided with the age's. The view prevailing amongst the British, French, and the other Europeans in the mid and later Eighteenth century was that, for supplying cheap raw materials and desirable luxuries to the mother country, forming a market for her manufactures, and constituting a reservoir of manpower (especially seamen), colonies were both valuable and necessary. With these mercantilist views, the European nations maintained colonies where they could obtain them in the fertile parts of the Americas, Africa, and the East, and national companies to conduct their trade with these areas and with the Levant. When at war, they consistently tried to reduce each other's empire and trade. As J. H. Parry summarizes,

> The maritime powers of western Europe in the eighteenth century committed to colonial theatres of war a far greater proportion of their formal armaments—especially, of course, their naval armaments—than they had ever done before, or than they were ever to do subsequently. Few European wars, it is true, originated wholly or even primarily in colonial disputes; but every major eighteenth century war had its colonial aspect; colonial territory and overseas commercial concessions figured prominently in every major treaty of peace.

From time to time, when faced with the expenses of maintaining colonies and waging war about them, and with reverses in these wars, the

European nations' enthusiasm for their colonies certainly ebbed. Few voices questioned the prevailing mercantilist assumptions, however, and general interest in colonies always surged again after the periodic remissions. Immediately after the nations concluded the Peace of Paris, for example, Choiseul, the French Minister of Marine, began a massive programme of naval reconstruction, and encouraged the Spanish to do the same, so as to prepare the way for defeating Britain on the seas and in her colonies, and thereby diminishing her wealth and power.

Britain's consolidating her control of Bengal in the 1770s, and the resultant increase in her trade, inevitably increased French jealousy and desire; and when Britain's losses in the wars of 1776-83 diminished her bargaining position, France insisted on regaining old territories and trading rights in the West and East Indies. The French claims in this settlement signalled their general ambition in the following decades — to reduce Britain's dominance in the East, to increase their own influence and commerce there. This ambition was central to their diplomacy in the mid 1780s — as Harris indicated when he reported that 'Our Wealth and Power in India is their great and constant Object of jealousy; and they never will miss an opportunity of attempting to wrest it out of our hands' — as it was to their war efforts in the 1790s and 1800s — as Delacroix indicated when he told Harris 'Your Indian empire alone has enabled you to subsidize all the Powers of Europe against us, and your monopoly of trade has put you in possession of a fund of inexhaustible wealth.'

His father's policy and counsel, and his knowledge of recent history alike made Pitt aware that these were the imperatives according to which the European nations with extensive interests overseas conducted their affairs; and what he learned when he entered public life in 1781 confirmed this awareness. By 1782/3, he had arrived at the strategic and commercial perceptions which thereafter underlaid his general endeavours, which he revealed when, in speaking against the North Administration's American policies, he described the 'calamities of the empire', and when, in defending Shelburne's peace settlement, he said that the Royal Navy's power and pre-eminence deriving from the victories of his father's time had passed away.

Pitt wove the fabric of his first administration about these perceptions, when he concerted with Dundas, Mulgrave, and Grenville to obtain more benefit for the nation from the East India Company's activities and to increase the nation's naval capacity to prevent the French overthrowing the Company's establishment and trade. Grenville revealed a principal aspect of the group's general outlook when he described the situation when they came to power:

the extent and disasters of the Indian War, aggravated by the general difficulties of the Empire, had absorbed the resources and nearly destroyed the credit of the Company. America was already lost to us; And our fortunes in the East seemed hastening to irrecoverable ruin, the consequence of the same inherent Vices which had before subverted both the Portugueze and the Dutch Dominion.

Pitt revealed another when, at the end of 1796, he defended his determination to retain the Cape and Ceylon in any peace settlement, by saying that, in refusing to return these, he only refused

> to put into the hands of the enemy the means of carrying into effect the deep laid schemes of ambition they have long cherished, and the plan they have conceived of undermining our Indian empire, and destroying our Indian commerce, by ceding out of our own hands, what may be deemed the bulwark of the wealth of this country, and the security of the Indian Empire.

Dundas revealed another when, in 1787, he said that the nation's 'one original great object' was 'to maintain and preserve the Empire which she has acquired, in comparison of which even trade is a subordinate or collateral consideration.' Mulgrave revealed a fourth when he requested the surveys of the Indian Ocean in order to discover 'the places most worthy of attention either for offensive or defensive operations in the extensive possessions of this Country in that part of the World.'

Pitt and his colleagues undertook many separate moves in their pursuit of the general end of ensuring Britain's continuing dominance of India. They sought by diplomatic means to deliver Holland from French influence, and to gain control of the Dutch bases in the East; and when these means failed, they resorted to military and naval ones. Repeatedly, they diminished or destroyed France and Spain's naval capability. They sent British squadrons into the Baltic to retain access to that region's naval materials. They countered, first, France's diplomatic moves in Egypt, and then, her military ones. They surveyed the southwest coast of Africa for a site for a naval base. They surveyed the Indian Ocean, and settled the Andaman Islands. They resolved to build warships in India. They sent the convicts sentenced to transportation to establish a base on the eastern coast of New Holland, so as to preclude the French settling there, so as to have a strategic outlier to India and South America, and a source of naval materials for India.

While Pitt, Dundas, Mulgrave, and Grenville do not seem to have drawn up a plan, no doubt their conversations of the mid-1780s, if recoverable, would give at least a general outline of the strategic policy which they followed in the East in the next twenty and more years. This policy was both unified and consistent. There was, as Parry points out,

> no rush to acquire territorial dominion for its own sake, no vindictive demand to rob the French of all they had possessed; merely a calculated resolve that resources of revenue or essential materials, valuable markets and major trade routes should be protected against any possible recurrence of French or other interference.

The unity and consistency came partly from the cohesion between the four in 1784-6, and their shared outlook then, and partly from their reliance on a small group (Blankett, Thompson, Phillip, Baldwin, Baring, Blair, Popham) for advice and for the effecting of that advice.

In long-term consequence, though not in immediate result, the settlement of New South Wales was the most important of the moves which Pitt and his colleagues took in pursuit of their policy. More limited in initial conception, certainly, than other of the nation's plantings, this was a true colonization nonetheless, for it involved the transference of the nation's laws and customs (if not of her best subjects) to a non-European region. The politicians decided on it quite consciously, on the basis of the best knowledge available to them; and it led, in time, to a vast expansion of the British empire in the East. The historical circumstances simply do not justify the belief that Britain acquired this second empire in 'a fit of absence of mind.'

Pitt and his friends, and the officers whom they employed, had great hopes for the moves which they undertook at a time when they believed that the East was almost the nation's 'last stake,' and when they looked with 'more than ordinary anxiety to the safety and preservation of every part of the British dominions.' The politicians saw that a supply of naval materials from New South Wales would be 'of great consequence to us as a naval power.' Phillip looked to that colony's becoming 'of the greatest consequence to this Country;' and he struggled mightily to make it so during his time there. In the absence of Trincomalee, Dundas thought that the Andamans would be of 'essential consequence' to the nation's endeavour in the East. Blair reported Commodore Cornwallis's 'perfect' satisfaction that Port Cornwallis was 'a place of infinite national importance.' Blankett and Baring saw that 'Whatever tends to give to France the means of obtaining a footing in India is of consequence to us to prevent.' Mulgrave saw that it was 'of the greatest importance' to have surer knowledge of strategic sites in and about the Indian Ocean. The politicians together saw that 'France in possession of Egypt would possess the Master Key of all the trading Nations of the Earth.'

It may seem strange to us now that these men should have expected so much from moves which so lacked decisive issue (always allowing, of course, that the preservation of Britain and her establishment in the East was not a decisive issue). But to interpret according to this perception of strangeness, and therefore to claim that they held their hopes either fraudulently or foolishly, is to impose our reality, based on hindsight, a different technology, and an opposing sense of the morality and efficacy of colonies, on those who guided Britain through the storms and shoals that so often threatened her destruction in the late Eighteenth and early Nineteenth centuries.

Pitt, Dundas, Mulgrave, and Grenville wove their views out of what they saw to be the imperatives of empire in the East, and the naval

N

defence of it; and they were not eccentric in these perceptions. As Phillip began the settlement of New South Wales, for example, the Spanish observer Muñoz de San Clemente wrote that Cook's discovery had given Britain a country almost as vast as North America, with the potential to become 'one of the most flourishing and advantageous on account of its position.' The colonists there, he saw,

> will have a Navy of their own, obtaining from the southern region everything necessary to create it, and when they have it ready formed they will be able to invade our neighbouring possessions with expeditions less costly and surer than from the ports of England, and it will not be difficult to foretell even now, which will be their first conquests.

In December 1788, Flores, the Viceroy of Mexico, pointed out to his Government the danger they faced from the 'probes' which the British, who based all their 'hopes and resources on navigation and commerce', would inevitably make from New South Wales. In 1790, in the midst of the Nootka Sound crisis, the next Viceroy advised that there were 'not enough forces in our South Sea and the Department of San Blas to counteract those which the English have at their Botany Bay.' In 1796, Delacroix told the British that, if they were 'master of the Cape and Trincomalé,' the French would hold all their settlements in the East 'entirely' at British will and pleasure—'they will be ours only so long as you choose we should retain them.' In 1810, Napoleon planned to capture New South Wales, 'which lies to the south of [Mauritius], and which would furnish us with considerable supplies.'

The British occupation of the French and Dutch bases in the East between 1806 and 1811 was the logical fulfilment of the policy that Pitt, Dundas, Mulgrave, and Grenville developed in the mid-1780s, and pursued so consistently in the next twenty years. We would therefore expect Britain to have benefited greatly from it; and from one point of view—that of an Eighteenth century nation with an empire beyond Europe—clearly she did so. In the next decades, extending her influence in and occupation of southern Africa, India, Ceylon, Malaya and the East Indies, Australia, New Zealand, and the Pacific Islands, she built up a second empire which brought her great wealth.

There are good reasons, however, for seeing that the blockades, bombardments, and assaults which led to the British's capturing their rivals' bases in the East also signalled the end of the perceptions and policies which underlay them. In December 1810, the aged George III, under whose general supervision Pitt and his colleagues had governed, relapsed into insanity; and the Prince of Wales ruled as regent until his father's death a decade later. By 1811, Mulgrave, Pitt, and Dundas were dead, and Grenville's effective political career was over. Nepean was shortly to go to Bombay, to enjoy some well-deserved fruits of devoted service as Governor there. Two of the men on whose advice the politicians had built their policy, and whom they had then sent to accomplish it had died, their bodies worn out in arduous service in distant stations. A third, Phillip, was shortly to die in the same condition. And the policy itself had lost its old efficacy. As many historians have pointed out, the destruction of shipping, and the ravaging of colonies and trade might contain, but could not defeat, a power in control of a continent; and, having landed in Portugal with a small army in 1809, Wellesley (Wellington) had by 1811 developed tactics for the new dispensation, which he then made the basis of his triumph over Napoleon at Waterloo. The forebodings of a new naval technology emerged simultaneously, when the Navy Board began experimenting with steel knees, and chain and steel cables. By 1811, too, the New South Wales colony had moved beyond the Pitt Administration's original conception of it. The settlement was by then well-established, with the colonists having built up abundant herds and flocks, and an extensive agriculture. Already with the benefit of Macquarie's more socially-enlightened attitude to reformed convicts, and soon to be released from the strait-jackets of the East India Company's commercial monopoly and the Cumberland Plain, the colony was poised for its striking advance from a strategic spot at the south-eastern extremities of the Indian Ocean, to a vigorous nation possessing a continent on the south-western margin of the Pacific Ocean.

So poised, the colony then promised the realization of the hopes of those who had first proposed its establishment, and who, except for one, were now dead. Matra was the least of these men. Moving among the ripples that the prows of the great created, he yearned to be like them, and aspired always to roles and stations to which he was befitted neither by breadth of intellect nor by emotional capacity. Still, he did sail with Cook, he was an intimate of Banks, he did some good work for his King and his adopted country, and he did conceive that a colony in New South Wales might have 'a very commanding Influence in the policy of Europe.'

Young possessed greater abilities than Matra, and he was deeply conscious of Cook's achievements and the possibilities which they offered. He may have known the explorer in the desperate days at Louisberg and on the St. Lawrence River, he certainly knew him through his published works. 'To what *End* are all the Discoveries of our great Forefathers, and, lately, those of the wonderful Cook?' he asked in the longer version of his proposal:

> Shall so wide, so noble a Field for the Exercise of enterprising Spirits, be relinquished by this Nation to her faithless Neighbours? Shall we rest contented with the Loss of America, and tamely circumscribe ourselves to our present discontented Colonies? And shall we not look forward to other Channels of Trade, when we are assured of a Commercial Correspondence with the greater Part of the South-Eastern and North-Western World. *Surely no*: or a

doubt cannot remain a moment in the Breast of any thinking man, but that the Spirit for Discovery, the Genius for Trade, and Skill in Navigation, for which we have always been, and *still* are famous, will soon be transferred. — Commerce, 'tis well known, has often changed its Course; but was never known to fall asleep; And however *our* Politics may succeed in limiting the Inclinations of our own People, we have no Power over those of Foreigners, much less over the Designs of *Providence*: For certain it is, *Cook's Discoveries* were not given in vain; and a very small Beginning on this Plan, is sufficient to promote the general Good of the human Race.

Whatever the limitations of his character, and of his parliamentary performance, John Call had what was quite rare in his age — a genuine historical imagination. His investigation into the state of the Royal forests required the collection and collation of statistics for the previous one hundred and fifty years. At a time when the belief was widespread that England's population was declining, he inspected parish registers about Cornwall, to conclude in anticipation of Malthus that the population had in fact increased since the middle of the century; and that this increase was probably due to one in the food supply. When he proposed a new water supply for Plymouth, he remarked that

Sir Francis Drake brought Water into Plymouth and his Name will [be] remembered as long as the Stream runs. Whoever shall be fortunate enough to promote and accomplish the bringing a similar Stream to the Dock, (where it is of much more Importance) will confer a Benefit, of which the Value cannot be estimated.

Nowhere did Call show this sense of the historical moment more strongly that in his proposal for a colony in the South Pacific Ocean, when he observed that

the Experience of Ages has shewn that every Invention, Discovery or Enterprize for which Nations are most distinguished was originally suggested, and frequently undertaken and perfected by the Perseverance & Exertions of Individuals; [and that], upon these occasions it has often happened, that the first Projectors or Undertakers have been deemed little better than Madmen — or have acted in a Character bordering on Piracy. Notwithstanding this, it is to such reputed Madmen, Pirates & Projectors, that the European Nations owe the Establishments & Trade of the East and West Indies; North and South America; — and the Western Coast of Africa.

In the preamble to his proposal, Call stressed that he had made himself 'geographically, and descriptively acquainted with the new Discoveries of the late Circum-navigators.' The details show that he did indeed have an intimate knowledge of Cook's voyages; and he concluded his proposal with:

Should other Inducements be wanting to give a serious Consideration to some Enterprize of the Kind pointed out and to derive some immediate or lay the foundation for some future Advantages to be drawn from the Discoveries of

Captain Cook, and other Circum-Navigators, many Objects not undeserving Notice might be enumerated.

Banks was the greatest of these men. Like Call, he had an historical imagination, but he added to it a breadth of vision, and an absence of venal concerns. As a young man, he had made a grand tour of the whole world with Cook. A dozen years later, a more mature President of Europe's most prestigious scientific society, it had been his painful duty to tell the circumnavigator's grieving widow not 'to lament a man whose virtues have exacted a tribute of regret from a large portion of the natives of the earth.' Banks pushed forward the colonization of New South Wales for the benefit of science and of his nation, and for his private satisfaction; and he had, more clearly than all the others involved in the venture, an imperial view. 'I see the future prospect of empires and dominions which now cannot be disappointed,' he told Hunter in March 1797, 'Who knows but that England may revive in New South Wales when it is sunk in Europe.'

In 1807, the Scottish geographer John Pinkerton observed of the colony,

> [It] met with considerable difficulties in regard to subsistence, and the expence was considered as too great for the object. But men of more extensive and philosophical views beheld with complacence the design of transferring the English race and name to such a distant and important region of the globe, which might supply new objects to commerce and science, and in the course of a few centuries present as it were another America, a country of rising knowledge and civilization, in the midst of a benighted and savage region of the globe. Nor were views of ambition and glory undelighted with this new diffusion of the great and surprizing people of a remote European isle, in the most distant extremities of the navigable ocean.

Extensive and philosophical views did underlie Matra, Young, Call, and Banks's proposals for the colonization of the south Pacific islands, which the Pitt Administration then adopted. Loyalist, naval captain, merchant, scientist, they were the true 'fathers' of Australia—they, and he of whose achievements they were so conscious, who made the way for the British migration to the extremity of the navigable ocean—Captain James Cook, R.N., F.R.S., the greatest navigator that Britain or any other nation has ever known.

My search for a less gratuitous beginning for Australia has led me from Sydney's radiant foreshores, to Britain atlantic-grey with winter, to north America profligate with spring. Mostly, I have followed in others' paths; sometimes, a chance deviation here and there has given me *that pleasure which naturally results to a Man from being the first discoverer, even was it nothing more than sands or shoals.* The need to know from whence we came is personal as well as national, of course. As much as for others who may wonder, I have journeyed for myself, who lived in childhood by the great ocean whose limits Cook described.

PART III

Appendix and Notes

Appendix and Notes

The Case Against the Pitt Administration's having had commercial motives for colonizing New South Wales

I have been concerned to set forth the Pitt Administration's strategic motive for colonizing New South Wales, and at the same time, of course, to place this motive in its context of British circumstances in, and aspirations for, the East.

As readers will have seen, these circumstances and aspirations involved desire to preserve a territorial empire and expand a commercial one, and conflict with the French over doing so. Consideration of this general context has led some writers to suggest that Pitt and his advisers may have had commercial motives for settling New South Wales. K. M. Dallas first advanced this view substantially, when in 1952 he pointed to the development of the Nootka Sound fur trade and the extension of the Southern Whale Fishery, and argued that 'the convicts were what they had always been — the servants of mercantilist interests.' Michael Roe, David Mackay, and R. A. Swan subsequently supported this connection. Roe also cited the beginnings of British trade with the Pacific Islands, and concluded that 'the foundation of Australia has an unquestionable place in the history of England's new imperialism.' Barbara Atkins then followed up Roe's statement with the suggestion that the British might have had some idea of promoting trade with the Spanish colonies in South America and the Philippines. More recently, H. T. Fry and Ged Martin have emphasized the decision's relevance to Britain's trade with China, with Fry seeing that

> [it] was taken primarily to safeguard the only route to China that would remain really safe for British ships approaching from the west if the threatened Franco-Dutch *rapprochement* became a reality,

and Martin that

> Sydney was founded . . . [from] the need to safeguard and extend the East India Company's tea trade.[1]

These suggestions of commercial motive are based much more on assumption and implication than on explicit evidence, but, offering a sensible explanation of the decision, they are attractive, and the historical context gives them an initial plausibility. Despite their attractiveness and plausibility, however, they constitute a striking example of how writers who lose sight of historical reality can be enticing and plausible, and yet quite wrong.

The fundamental feature of all British trade in and about the Indian and Pacific Oceans (the 'East' for present purposes) throughout the Eighteenth cen-

185

tury was that it was conducted either by, or under the auspices of, first the East
India Company, and second and to a much lesser degree, the South Sea Company. By the settlement sanctioned by Parliament in 1708,[2] the United Company of Merchants trading into the East Indies held the 'whole, sole, and exclusive Trade in, to, and from the *East Indies*, and all Places between the *Cape of
Good Hope* and the Streights of Magellan,' Successive Administrations reaffirmed
this right, and successive Courts of Directors guarded it zealously, insisting that
any trade which the Company did not itself undertake be conducted by others
only under its licence, and prosecuting transgressors.

By the Charter which Anne granted in 1711, the Merchants of Great Britain
trading to the South Sea held, *forever*, exclusive rights to trade with the Spanish
colonies on the east side of South America from the Orinoco to Tierra del Fuego,
and with those on the west side of the New World from Tierra del Fuego northwards to Alaska (including 'all Countries, Islands, and Places . . . which shall
hereafter be found out or discovered within the said Limits, not exceeding three
hundred Leagues from the Continent.)[3] Again, all trade to these areas which this
Company did not itself undertake could be conducted by others only under its
licence; and while it did not trade after 1736, it did not disband until 1855, so
that its directors continued to insist on licencing trade by others throughout the
Eighteenth century.

It is certainly true that Pitt and his colleagues had the expansion of Britain's
commerce very much at heart, and that, in order to promote this, they sought to
direct the activities of the Chartered Companies. Soon after they came to power,
they defined a distinct separation of government and company spheres of activity. In their view, it was the government's business to administer territory and
provide for its defence, and to deal with resulting political issues: it was the companies' business to pursue trade.

The politicians enunciated this separation in their India Act of 1784, which
had the effect of taking from the East India Company 'the entire management of
the territorial possessions [in], and the political government of [India],'[4] and then
set about enforcing it. Since the South Sea Company's only significant activity at
this time was the administration of government-backed bonds, its directors gave
them no trouble. It was another story with the East India Company, however,
the members of which saw it to threaten their wealth and patronage. Pitt and
Dundas had a number of intense conflicts with the Courts of Directors, and while
they generally made their will prevail, the Company did not become a mere
cipher for their wishes. For almost twenty years, the situation was one of an
uneasy truce, with Pitt and his friends insisting on the Directors concurring with
their views in matters which they saw to touch either their political authority or
the nation's welfare, and the Directors insisting on retaining arrangements which
the Company valued, which almost always turned on the monopoly of trade
with India and China.[5]

There is also no doubt that, in the mid-1780s, Pitt, Dundas, and Grenville
hoped eventually to abolish the Chartered Companies' monopolies, but their
political circumstances in the next years were never such as to allow them to
think that they might succeed in doing so. Indeed, these circumstances
necessitated that they in fact reaffirm and renew the East India Company's
privileges, rather than reduce or remove them. In 1786, for example, they
legislated heavy penalties against

any Person or Persons who shall repair, sail, or go to, or traffick, trade, or adventure in, or be or be found in any Place within the Limits [of the said Company's exclusive Trade], without Licence having been obtained from the said Company, or without having been in the said Company's Service.

They gave Company officials in India, the East Indies, and Canton the power to arrest and imprison suspected offenders, and to seize their 'Ships, Vessels, Goods, or Effects.' And whereas these officials had previously had to return suspected interlopers to Britain for trial (a necessity which had presented grave evidential burdens), now, the Administration gave the British courts in India power to adjudicate questions of guilt, confiscation, and recompense. The next year, meeting as the Board of Control, Pitt and Dundas followed up this un-equivocal legislative statement of support for the Company's entrenched privilege with instructions to eastern officials concerning illegal trading there by British subjects sailing under Danish and Imperialist (Austrian) flags. In 1793, they renewed the Company's Charter without extensive change.[6]

At the same time as they supported the East India Company's Charter, and dealt with the practicalities of its application, Pitt and his colleagues were careful to work within the legal and administrative frameworks which it and the South Sea Company's gave rise to. They therefore followed a standard procedure when presented with a private proposal for a new venture in the East. If Hawkesbury and the other members of the Board of Trade saw promise in it, Pitt, Dundas and Hawkesbury would encourage the proposers, have them apply to the Companies for licences, and, if necessary, press these to issue them. (Since its directors were always eager for the accompanying fees, applications to the South Sea Company were formalities, but those to the East India Company had a much more difficult passage, and led to intricate negotiations between the politicians, the Directors, and the supplicatory merchants.) When the parties had reached agreement, the Administration would legislate the form of the East India Company's licence, as the law required.

We see this procedure in the beginning of the north-west American Fur Trade, and the extension of the Southern Whale Fishery. In 1785, a group of merchants headed by Richard Etches proposed 'an Expedition of Experiment' to develop the trade in sea otter furs which Cook's men had pioneered in 1778/9. The merchants asked the Administration for permission to establish a factory at Nootka Sound, and for a charter granting them a monopoly of the trade, and took pains to stress that they did not intend to impinge upon the East India Company's established commerce. They had no intention, they said,

of trading with the Chinese in any Article whatever except the produce of the said North-West Continent of America — nor to return to Europe with any traffic, the manufactory or produce of China.[7]

The Directors of the East India Company considered this proposal in early May 1785, and reluctantly agreed to licence two ships for one voyage, 'by way of experiment.' They wrote stringent restrictions into the licence and deed of cove-nant which they sent to the Administration. After proceeding round Cape Horn to collect their furs, the traders could take their ships to Japan, and to other places in northern Asia, but they could not go to any country to the south or west of Canton, or to the west of New Holland. If distressed, they could refresh in these areas, but they must not conduct any trade in European goods. If unable to sell their furs in Japan or Kamschatka, they could trade down the Asian coast towards Canton, where they were to present an inventory of their cargoes to Company officials, and to allow these to search their ships. They must remit all monies via Company channels. There would be severe fines for breaches of these conditions.[8]

The Directors of the South Sea Company followed form by telling the ministry that they needed an explicit application before they could agree to grant a licence for Etches's voyage. When this was made, they accepted that it was 'an undertaking and adventure which may probably be attended with Advantage in point of Commerce,' and gave permission for the group 'to fit and lade out two Ships or Vessels . . . for the purpose of trading and trafficing . . . into unto and from the said North West Coast of America' for five years (September 1785-September 1790). Their one condition was that the group give in copies of the commanders and masters' journals immediately on the ships' return.[9]

Paying the requisite licence fees, the merchants then proceeded with their 'voyage of experiment,' to follow it with others in succeeding years. Through various delays, the Administration did not move to formalize the arrangement with the East India Company until 1791, when they drafted the 'Heads of [a] proposed new Bill' to effect this, but then, rather than legislating separately, they provided for the East India Company to licence the trade when they renewed its charter in 1793, after which Dundas and the Directors negotiated new terms for doing so.[10]

The extension of the Southern Whale Fishery shows the same procedure. Pitt had the Board of Trade consider the industry's circumstances in late 1785, and early the next year, Samuel Enderby and others asked for bounties to help generally, and for permission to hunt in the southern oceans beyond Cape Horn and the Cape of Good Hope, where Cook had reported whales abounding. Hawkesbury consulted Pitt, Dundas, and Cook's old mentor, Admiral Sir Hugh Palliser. Palliser thought that

> the Fishery may be much increased and extended by encouraging the most adventurous to extend their searches after Whales. . . . By this means many fresh places of resort for Whales may be discovered and certain distant Seas and Coasts, now very little known, may be explored and be better known.

Accordingly, he recommended that the whalers be allowed to pass the Cape of Good Hope to 15° East, with a northern limit of 26° South; and that they be able to go into the Pacific up to 7° North latitude, with no western limit.

When Dundas gave the East India Company these suggestions, the Directors objected strongly, for they suspected that 'there must be some other object in View'—i.e., illicit trade. They feared that whalers sailing outwards would carry goods for eastern markets to the Cape of Good Hope; and that, conversely, those homeward-bound would collect goods for sale in Europe and North America. Hawkesbury responded that it was

> of great Importance in the present Moment . . . that a proper effort should now be made to secure to this Country, the advantages of a Fishery which was once so lucrative to the Americans.

The Chairmen at first repeated their objections, but then said that while they continued to think that the move would harm their Company, they would agree to it if they were to licence the ships, and if those sailing round the Horn into the Pacific did not go north of the Equator, nor more than one hundred leagues west of the American coast. A week later, they relaxed the western limit to five hundred leagues. The Directors gave their most reluctant approval finally at the end of May 1786, and the Administration formalized the new arrangements with an Act 'for the Encouragement of the Southern Whale Fishery.'[11]

From these dealings, then, we may conclude that three of the following four circumstances would have obtained were New South Wales settled for commercial reasons:

(1) the area offered products that would give rise to an immediate and desirable trade;

(2) the East India Company wished to develop that trade;

or

(3) Private parties wished and had the Administration's encouragement, to do so, and their help in obtaining the Chartered Companies' licences;

(4) the Administration continued to encourage the merchants once they had begun the venture.

We find *none* of these circumstances. Matra, Call, and Young did indeed suggest that a settlement in New South Wales might play a part in the extension of British commerce in the East, but the items which they saw it itself offering were (a) naval materials, and (b) perhaps spices. The Administration were clearly very interested in the naval materials, but, equally clearly, they saw these as strategic materials and therefore legitimately the concern of a government which did not deal in such usual commercial items as tea and silk. And while it is also true that Nepean pointed to the possibility of growing spices, in the second last paragraph of 'Heads of a Plan,' this is the only sign in all the official documents of any Administrative interest in this prospect, and, to judge from the lack of preparation for realizing it in the mounting of the First Fleet, it soon waned.[12]

Otherwise, there is no evidence of Pitt, Dundas, Mulgrave, and Grenville's ever seeing that New South Wales might play any primary role in the expansion of the nation's eastern trade before they decided to colonize it. 'If you were to carry Convicts a Voyage of probably 6 months to a place where no kind of Trade is carried on how much per Man would you contract for?' they had a friendly member of the 1785 Committee of Transportation ask Duncan Campbell. The 'Heads of a Plan' contains no reference to any prospect of extending either the East India Company's established trade, or the Fur Trade, or the Southern Whale Fishery. Nepean did not mention any such prospect when he sought the Company's approval of the venture. And Dundas did not take any account of the new settlement when, in 1790, he considered what steps the Administration should take to extend far eastern commerce.[13]

Second, we find no evidence that the East India Company ever contemplated committing its resources to the actual settlement, or that the Administration ever thought of asking it to do so. From the first moment of discernible official interest in the idea of settling a south Pacific island, when Sydney sought Matra out towards the end of March 1784, it is clear that the politicians thought exclusively in terms of a government venture involving convicts. In September 1786, they sought the Company's agreement on this basis alone; and they did not deviate from it as they developed the colonization. Given the division of powers and responsibilities which Pitt and his colleagues enunciated, all this tells greatly against their having had a commercial motive.

Third, though Matra, Call and Young certainly wanted official permission to establish a private trading settlement, there is only suspect evidence that the politicians encouraged them to hope for it. Rowcroft did say later that Young and his associates supposed they had Pitt's 'approbation,' but if this were so, it must have been tentative and short-lived, for the rest of the evidence is to the contrary. Pitt neither had the Board of Trade assess the adventurers' proposals, nor worked to have the East India Company agree to them, nor did he make any attempt to legislate the licence under which they might have furthered them. Given the freshness of the precedents, these omissions could not have been oversights.

Fourth, not only did the politicians not provide in the slightest way for a private trading settlement, they also gave Phillip the strictest instructions enjoining such trade. There was to be no trade, they told him, between New South Wales and either the Company's settlements in India or China, or the Dutch possessions in the East Indies. In order to preclude this, the colonists were to build no decked boat, and no open boat with a keel of more than twenty feet. They were to render unseaworthy any such vessel driven ashore. They might give emergency aid to ships in distress, but that was all. The only trade which they were to engage in was the officially-conducted and subsistence one in food with adjacent islands not inhabited by Europeans, and to which no other European country laid claim; and this of course, was a trade which could not in any way be seen as impinging on the East India Company's.[14]

The lack of any immediate prospect of private trade from New South Wales, and the Administration's firm commitment to seeing that this remained so, no doubt explain the East India Company's easy acceptance of the scheme (and, despite the hoary saw to the contrary, if we are to judge from the available documentary evidence, this acceptance *was* easy). These things also presumably explain the Company's willingness to co-operate with the Administration by hiring some of the convict transports to carry home cargos of China tea. On the face of it, this arrangement may seem to suggest a commercial motive (and certainly it has misled a number of writers so to argue), but it is important to understand that it was a convenience to which the Administration and Company came for their mutual benefit *after* the Administration had decided to colonize, and that, in itself, it had nothing to do with the decision.

The Navy Board advertised for tenders of transports for the First Fleet on 1 September 1786. Considering how he could best present his bid, the enterprizing William Richards studied his charts, and hit on the idea of the Administration and Company sharing the costs, with the Administration engaging the transports to carry the convicts outwards, and the Company engaging them to carry tea homewards. Richards discussed the idea with John Motteux, the Company's Deputy Chairman, and Sir Charles Middleton. Both saw its merit, and encouraged him to develop it, which he did by giving Pitt details of it, saying that he thought it might save the Administration some £4000, and the Company some £18000.[15]

Predictably attracted by a prospect of reducing public expenditure, the First Lord of the Treasury adopted the suggestion, having Rose tell the Company Chairmen that it has occurred to My Lords Com.ᵗˢ of yᵉ Treasury that yᵉ charge of sending out the Convicts will be much lessened if the Ships which convey them to the said place can have a freight of Tea home from China, and that a considerable saving will also be effected to the East India Company thereby,

and ask them to 'submit this suggestion to the Court of Directors for their consideration.' Simultaneously, Richards asked the Company for freights of tea for his charters, the *Scarborough, Brothers, William & Mary, Britania,* and *Brittania,* which he announced as being 'in the service of the Government,' 'to be discharged from that employ in New Holland.'¹⁶

The Court of Directors considered these requests together on 19 September, and decided 'that the said Letters & Plan be referred to the consideration of a Committee of the whole Court.' The Whole Court duly considered the same on 21 September, and 'Resolved Unanimously' that the Company should licence Richards' ships to carry tea home. The Court of Directors endorsed this decision on 27 September. On 30 October, the minutes of the Directors' deliberations were read and approved by the Board of Control (which consisted that day of Sydney, Pitt, and Grenville).¹⁷

Some difficulties then arose, however. By late September, the Administration intended to despatch the First Fleet by 15 November, and the Company accordingly specified that the transports it was hiring should reach Canton by 15 January 1788. Richards told Pitt that the owners of his ships did not think there would be sufficient time for this, and that they, therefore, wanted the Navy Board to agree to pay for the homeward passage if the ships should miss the China convoy's sailing. He suggested that a way out of the difficulty would be for Pitt to have the Company guarantee to load the ships whenever they arrived at Canton, but Pitt's solution was to have Rose tell the Navy Board and the Admiralty that he wished the Governor and the Captain of the King's escort 'to use their best Endeavours to enable the Ships to leave Botany Bay in time to arrive at China by the 1ˢᵗ day of January 1788.' When the Fleet did not sail in November, Rose and Nepean arranged with the Company to relax the time limit.¹⁸

When the First Fleet did sail, in May 1787, only the *Scarborough* remained of the ships which Richards had initially chartered, with the *Charlotte* and *Lady Penrhyn* replacing the others. The Administration instructed Phillip to make every possible effort upon his arrival at Botany Bay to disembark quickly

the Officers and Men composing the Civil and Military Establishments, together with the Convicts, Stores, Provisions, &c., [so as] . . . to discharge all the said Transports or Victuallers, in order that such of them as may be engaged by the East India Company may proceed to China, and that the rest may return home.

This Phillip duly did; and the *Scarborough, Charlotte,* and *Lady Penrhyn* sailed from Port Jackson in early may 1788 to collect their cargoes at Canton.¹⁹

The Administration and the East India Company renewed this arrangement repeatedly in the next fifteen years. Among the numerous occasions was that in 1789, when the *Lady Juliana, Scarborough,* and *Surprize* carried convicts outwards, and tea home. Another was that in 1790, when Rose asked the Company to engage some of the Third Fleet transports to carry home cargoes of Bombay cotton (or some other such item). The Directors replied that the Company could not ship cotton to England profitably, but that they were willing to issue licences if the owners of the transports wished to try. Rose then asked for names of owners who might be interested; and in time the *Active, Albermarle, Queen,* and *Admiral Barrington* sailed from Port Jackson to Bombay. Nor was it always a case of the Administration asking, and the Company obliging. In 1803, for instance, some owners asked the Company for a cargo of either tea or cotton for their convict transport. The ship did not meet the Company's requirements, however, and the Directors decided to advertise instead for a copper-bottomed convict transport of about 500 tons to carry home tea and other China goods.[20]

While the Directors co-operated with the Pitt Administration in arranging shipping to and from New South Wales, they were always concerned to protect the Company's monopoly, by seeing that any trade arising incidentally from the colonization went forward under its auspices. And there were occasional ripples. Some of these arose from the Company's insistence that the ships it engaged should meet its requirements, which included a dry dock inspection to ascertain soundness. Through not being able to effect this, the Directors declined to give the *Pitt* a homeward cargo in 1793, and they cavilled greatly about giving one to the *Minerva* in 1798.[21] Others came with instances of what the Company most feared. The owners of the Third Fleet transports destined for Bombay loaded them with 'a very considerable quantity of copper, lead, iron, and cordage,' for sale at Goa. Phillip discovered this, but not certain that the masters did not have authority to do so, allowed them to proceed. This leniency earned Dundas's reprimand, and the Administration resolved

> for the future, to transport both the convicts and such articles for the settlement as shall be sent from hence by ships in the service of the East India Company, and I trust that by this means the evils which have hitherto subsisted will be put an end to.

In 1796, when the British capture of the Cape of Good Hope had once more raised the spectre of illicit trade, the Board of Trade confirmed that only the Company's ships, or those sailing under its licence, might go east of the Cape.[22]

Despite these ripples, however, the Administration and the Company remained reasonably happy with the arrangement into the 1800s. Both saved money, and there was relatively little illicit trade. David Scott, then the Deputy Chairman, incidentally explained why this should have been so, when he considered questions concerning eastern commerce in early 1796. Observing that 'the only Ships that could be supposed able to Smuggle Teas, by the Cape becoming a free Port, would be, the Company's own Regular Ships, & the Casual Botany Bay Ships which the Company freight home with Teas,' he continued:

> The Botany Bay Ships have a freight out from Government, but their Home freight does not become due from the Company until they have delivered their Cargoes, & given satisfaction to the Company. The places in their Ship which they are to fill, are also regulated by the Court, & the Freight which becomes due upon their Whole Cargo is so much larger a Sum, than they could reasonably expect by the Gain of Smuggling on a Triffle, that there appears no sufficient Interest to induce them to Smuggle. If Smuggling took place, it must first be at the Cape, & then at Hamburgh, or the landing Port, for the Expence and hazard of Smuggling Tea from a Ship in England is beyond Calculation.[23]

Two commercial developments in the East at the turn of the century generated considerable pressure to change this comfortable situation, however. First, taking advantage of Pitt, Dundas, and Grenville's 1790 decision to supply the New

South Wales colony as much as possible from India, 'country' traders (independent merchants having the East India Company's permission to trade in and about India, but not between there and Europe) began sending speculative cargoes to Sydney, where they found a market for livestock, cloth, food, and rum.

Second, British and colonial adventurers began to fish the South Pacific. The southern whalers who had sailed on the Third Fleet had seen that they might have good hauls, and they thereafter pressed for the relaxation of the restrictions on their doing so. In 1798, the Administration negotiated their entry into the area, and, in 1802/3, their release from the need to obtain licences to fish anywhere in this ocean east of 180°, and permission to return from it via Torres Strait. These relaxations co-incided with the discovery and exploitation of the Bass Strait sealing grounds, and the whalers were soon making the colony a base for lucrative ventures.[24]

The colonial entrepreneurs inevitably wished to share in their ocean's largesse.[25] As much as he saw it to be compatible with the colony's general interest and the East India Company's monopoly, King encouraged them to do so, allowing them to build larger boats that the regulations permitted, and to place sealing parties on the Bass Strait islands. By 1803, the colonists were reaping a rich harvest in oil and skins, for which they, of course, needed markets. Unlike the Southern Whalers, they had no access to England. Neither did they have direct access to China, but they could get their products there by selling either to the 'country' traders, who shipped via India, or to captains of passing Indiamen, or by the subterfuges of selling to American captains, or buying and loading prizes for sale in India.

Despite this restricted access to markets, the colonial sealing industry flourished, and Campbell and Lord soon glutted the Canton one. With hundreds of tons of oil and tens of thousands of skins accumulating in their Sydney warehouses, they became anxious to gain access to the European market, where new processing techniques were creating strong demand for these products. In 1803, with King's help, Campbell sent a trial shipment of oil and skins on the *Glatton* to London, which succeeded better than he could have hoped, for the Navy Board did not charge him freight, the East India Company made no protest, and the goods sold.

This trial inevitably gave rise to grander schemes. In England, John Princep, wealthy shipbroker and 'country' trader, stated to Hobart

the determination of his House to undertake the Establishment of a regular Trade to Port Jackson in New South Wales provided no political objection arises on the part of Government, and that Wood, Oil, Wool, Seal Skins and Hair and such other Articles as they may be able to obtain, may be allowed to be imported from His Majesty's other settlements abroad.[26]

In the colony, Campbell and Lord gathered large quantities of oil and skins.

Both home and colonial officials informally favoured allowing the trade to develop. When he passed on Princep's request to the Board of Trade, Hobart said that the thought that 'the Navigation and revenues of the Empire might be benefited by such a Commercial Intercourse of the Nature alluded to under such regulations as the particular Circumstances of the Settlement may render expedient.' And King, when he reported on the colony's general circumstances at the

o

end of 1804, suggested that the Administration allow the colonists to build three boats of about two hundred tons 'to take the produce from hence to China or England.'[27]

Encouraged by these attitudes, and the success of the trial, Campbell loaded the *Lady Barlow* with 260 tons of sea-elephant oil, 13,700 sealskins, and 3763 feet of she-oak, and, arranging for the *Sydney* to follow with a cargo of some 50,000 skins, 600 tons of oil, and timber for the Navy Board, sailed for London. His arrival in July 1805 caused a furore. The Directors seized the *Lady Barlow* and her cargo for the breach of the East India Company's monopoly, and the southern whalers protested vigorously about the threat to their business. After some months of considerataion and negotiation, the Board of Trade persuaded the Company to release the cargo (though for re-export only) and allow the ship to return to India, and to permit the expected *Sydney* to land her cargo. In the event, the *Sydney* did not arrive (King having chartered her instead to bring food from India), but the *Honduras Packet*, a Spanish prize chartered by Lord and freighted with some 34,000 skins, did.

The merchants accompanied these probes with pleas for change. Campbell's London agent, for example, pointed out that the *Sydney* would 'be freighted with the collective industry of the colony,' and that

> the opposition of the old whaling owners does them no honor. They may redouble their dilligence, but they ought not to complain. They have still the advantage. The colonists receive no bounties. They separate no seamen from the Navy by statute protections, but are actually training seamen, when on some future emergency it may be salutary for His Majesty's officers to be able to mann a ship or strengthen an expedition.[28]

These probes and pleas led the Board of Trade into a thorough reconsideration of the question of trade from New South Wales, in which the fundamental issue was (as Auckland told Grenville) whether it was 'the intention and policy of Government that these establishments shall be considered as colonies, with all the privileges of colonists?'[29] Banks produced a number of lengthy memoranda on the subject, and the Board discussed it intensively with the Company and the Whalers.

The Directors were at first wary, but ended by being accommodating. The Whalers remained opposed. The Administration's decision was for change. As Auckland told the man who twenty years before had helped frame the strategy of which the colonization had been a part,

> You approved of our preparing a Bill to put that 'rising [   ] in a new world' on the footing of a British colony; and a short Bill is proposed accordingly: but the question is connected with many considerations respecting Chinese trade, American intercourse, whale fishery, ship building, East India privileges; and I find neither time nor abilities to bring it to any sudden shape or conclusion.[30]

The use of a statement made so long after the event as evidence of motive would normally be suspect, of course, but in this case the implication is plain — in 1806, the Board of Trade faced the issues Auckland defined for the first time, because no previous Administration had considered the New South Wales settlement in a trading light.

The Bill which Auckland, Banks, and the other Lords of Trade drafted provided for the colony's having essentially the same privileges as those of its North American counterparts. It required the East India and South Sea Companies to issue licences for trade between New South Wales and Britain, and the recipients of these licences to conform to the usual procedures and regulations (e.g., to discharge all cargoes at the East India Company's London docks). In moving to release the colonists from the restrictions with which they had hitherto been encumbered, however, the Lords of Trade took pains to emphasize the continuing reality of the Companies' monopolies. 'Be it further enacted,' they concluded their draft bill with,

> that this Act or any thing herein contained shall not extend or be construed to extend to take away abridge vary or alter any of the Rights and Privileges belonging to or vested in the United Company of Merchants of England trading to the East Indies or the Rights and Privileges of the Company of Merchants of Great Britain trading to the South Sea, but all Persons resident within any of His Majesty's Territories in New South Wales, and all Trade to be carried on from any such Territories shall be subject to all and every the Provisions, Restrictions, Regulations, Licences and Conditions in every respect as any other Trade carried on by any British Subjects is now or hereafter may be liable to by Law; and shall be subject to the like Penalties and Forfeitures and all other Matters and Things which any British Subjects, and the Goods Merchandize and Trade which any British Subject would be subject and liable to by Law for doing any Thing in Violation of the Rights and Privileges of the said United Company of Merchants of England trading to the East Indies or of the Company of Merchants of Great Britain trading to the South Seas except to the Importation of Goods Wares and merchandize into, or the Exportation from the said Territories according to the Directions of this Act and except also that no Goods and Merchandize so imported from New South Wales into this Kingdom shall be subject to the regulations of the said Company of Merchants trading to the East Indies respecting Goods and Merchandize imported from the East Indies.[31]

The Grenville Administration continued to discuss this Bill among themselves and with the East India Company, but it dropped from sight after they left office in March 1807. For the next half dozen years, the New South Wales traders had to follow old arrangements to market their produce, though, ever-enterprizing, Lord developed a new subterfuge when he bought vessels, mortgaged them to British merchants, but used them himself.[32] Only in 1813, when the Liverpool Administration renewed the Company's monopoly only of the China tea trade, were the colonists at last able to trade within the general framework of the Navigation Acts, and even then, they did so at a disadvantage, for both home and colonial governments placed heavy tariffs on their produce.

Though ingenious colonial merchants found minor circumventions, then, the point made by the editor of *The History of New Holland* in 1787 remained true for another twenty-five years — New South Wales had the potential to play an important role in Britain's commercial development, but it could only be a 'passive instrument' so long as the East India Company's charter existed, for it could not have a commerce of its own.[33] This was so because successive Administrations chose to have it so; and in view of Pitt and his colleagues' public and sustained commitment during their time in office to maintaining that Company's monopoly, it seems pointless to argue that they in fact sought to subvert it, and had clandestine commercial motives for colonizing New South Wales. The available evidence simply does not support this conclusion. Rather, it flies in its face, at the same time as it shows that their keenly-felt desire to strengthen the nation's strategic position in the East was their profound motive for the venture.

Key to the location of unpublished manuscripts

Beinecke Library, Yale University	Beinecke
Bodleian Library, Oxford	Bodleian
British Library, London	
Additional Manuscripts	Add. ms
Egerton	Eger.
British Museum (Natural History), London	
Dawson Turner Transcripts	DTC
Brotherton Library, University of Leeds	Brotherton
William L. Clements Library, University of Michigan	Clements
Cleveland Public Library, Cleveland	
Karl Zamboni Purchase	Zamboni
Dawson, Warren R., Collection of	Dawson
Dixson Library, The Library of New South Wales, Sydney	Dixson
Essex County Record Office, Chelmsford	Essex
Houghton Library, Harvard University	Houghton
Huntington Library, San Marino	Huntington
India Office Records, London	
Court Minutes	B
Correspondence Committee	D
Home Correspondence	E
Board of Control	F
Factory Records	G
Home Miscellaneous	H
Europeans in India	I
Political and Secret	L/P & S
Mitchell Library, The Library of New South Wales, Sydney	Mitchell
Bonwick Transcripts, 1st series	Bonwick
National Library of Australia, Canberra	NLA
National Library of Scotland, Edinburgh	NLS
National Maritime Museum, London	NMM
New York Historical Society	NYHS
New York Public Library	NYPL
Perkins Library, Duke University	Perkins
Public Record Office, London	
Admiralty	ADM
Audit Office	AO
Board of Trade	BT
Colonial Office	CO
Foreign Office	FO
Home Office	HO
Privy Council	PC
Chatham Deposit	PRO

State Papers	*SP*
Treasury	*T*
War Office	*WO*
Royal Botanic Gardens Library, Kew	
Banks Papers	*Kew*
Royal Society, London	*Royal Society*
Royal Society of Arts, London	*Royal Society of Arts*
John Rylands Library, Manchester	*Rylands*
Scottish Record Office, Edinburgh	
Melville Papers	*GD*
Suffolk Record Office, Ipswich	*Suffolk*
Sutro Library, San Francisco	*Sutro*

List of printed sources, with abbreviations

Ashborne, Lord. *Pitt: Some Chapters of his Life and* Ashbourne
Times. 2nd ed. London: Longmans, Green, and
Co., 1898.

The Journal and Correspondence of William, Lord Auckland
Auckland. 4 vols. London: Richard Bentley,
1861-2.

The 'Endeavour' Journal of Joseph Banks. Banks
Ed. J. C. Beaglehole. 2nd ed. 2 vols. Sydney:
The Trustees of the Public Library of New
South Wales in association with Angus and
Robertson, 1963

Letters and Papers of Charles, Lord Barham. Barham
Ed. J. K. Laughton. 3 vols. (London):
The Navy Records Society, 1907-11.

Buckingham and Chandos, Duke of. *Memoirs of* Buckingham and Chandos
the Court and Cabinets of George III. 4 vols.
London: Hurst and Blackett, 1853-5.

Colenbrander, H. T. *De Patriottentijd, III,* Colenbrander
Appendix. (n.p.): Martinus Nijhoff, 1899.

The Journals of Captain James Cook. Ed. Cook
J. C. Beaglehole. 4 vols. Cambridge: Published
for the Hakluyt Society at the University Press,
1955-74.

Correspondence of Charles, First Marquis Cornwallis. Cornwallis
Ed. Charles Ross. 3 vols. London: John Murray,
1859.

Dalrymple, Sir John. *Memoirs of Great Britain and* Dalrymple
Ireland: New ed. 3 vols. London: A. Strahan
and T. Cadell, 1790.

Despatches from Paris 1784-90, I. Ed. O. Browning. Despatches
3rd. ser. XVI. London: The Camden Society,
1909.

Report on the Manuscripts on J. B. Fortescue, Esq., Dropmore
Preserved at Dropmore. 10 vols. London: Historical
Manuscripts Commission, 1892-1927.

The Correspondence of George III. Ed. Sir J. George III (Fortescue)
Fortescue. 6 vols. 1927-8. Rept. London: Frank
Cass & Co., 1967.

The Later Correspondence of George III. Ed. George III (Aspinall)
A. Aspinall. 5 vols. Cambridge: At the University
Press, 1966-70.

British Colonial Developments 1774-1834: Select Harlow and Madden
Documents. Ed. V. T. Harlow and F. Madden.
Oxford: At the Clarendon Press, 1953.

Historical Records of Australia.   HRA
    1st ser. 26 vols. (Sydney): The Library Committee
    of the Commonwealth Parliament, 1914-25.

Historical Records of New South Wales   HRNSW
    Ed. A. Britton and F. M. Bladen. 7 vols.
    Sydney: Charles Potter, Government Printer,
    1892-1901.

British Diplomatic Instructions, VII: France,   Instructions
    IV, 1745-1789. Ed. L. G. W. Legg. 3rd ser.
    XLIX. London: The Camden Society, 1934.

The Keith Papers. Ed. W. G. Perrin and   Keith
    Christopher Lloyd. 3 vols. (London):
    The Navy Records Society, 1927-54.

The Political Memoranda of Francis Fifth Duke of Leeds.   Leeds
    Ed. O. Browning. NS. XXXV London: the
    Camden Society, 1884.

Diaries and Correspondence of James Harris, First Earl of   Malmesbury
    Malmesbury. Ed. 3rd Earl of Malmesbury.
    2nd ed. 4 vols. London: Richard Bentley, 1845.

Letters and Papers of Admiral of the Fleet Sir   Martin
    Thos. Byam Martin. Ed. Sir Richard Vesey
    Hamilton. 3 vols. (London): The Navy Records
    Society, 1898-1903.

Report on the Sandwich Papers held by Victor Montagu.   Montagu
    London:Historical Manuscripts Commission,
    1976.

Report on the Palk Manuscripts in the Possession of   Palk
    Mrs Bannatyne. London: Historical Manuscripts
    Commission, 1922.

Cobbett's Parliamentary History of England.   PH
    36 vols. London: R. Bagshaw, et. al., 1806-20.

The Parliamentary Register. 1st ser. 17 vols. 2nd ser.   PR
    45 vols. London: J. Almon, J. Debrett, 1774-80,
    1780-96.

The Speeches of the Right Honorable William Pitt, in   Pitt
    the House of Commons. Ed. W. S. Hathaway.
    2nd ed. 3 vols. London: Longman, Hurst, Rees,
    & Orme, 1808.

Correspondence between the Right Honorable William Pitt   Pitt—Rutland
    and Charles Duke of Rutland Lord Lieutenant of Ireland
    (1781-7). Edinburgh and London: William
    Blackwood and Sons, 1890.

Letters of Admiral of the Fleet the Earl of St. Vincent.   St. Vincent
    Ed. D. B. Smith. 2 vols. (London): The Navy
    Records Society, 1922-7.

The Private Papers of John, Earl of Sandwich (1771-82).   Sandwich
    Ed. G. R. Barnes and J. H. Owen. 4 vols.
    (London): The Navy Records Society, 1932-8.

The Diary and Papers of William Smith, 1784-1793.   Smith
    Ed. L. S. F. Upton. 2 vols. Toronto: Champlain
    Society, 1963-5.

Private Papers of George, Second Earl Spencer (1794-1801). Spencer
    Ed. H. W. Richmond. 4 vols. (London): The
    Navy Records Society, 1913-24.

Earl Stanhope, *Life of the Right Honorable William*   Stanhope
    Pitt. 4 vols. London: John Murray, 1861.

Report on the Manuscripts of Mrs. Stopford-Sackville.   Stopford-Sackville
    2 vols. London: Historical Manuscripts
    Commission, 1904, 1910.

G. Tomline, *Memoirs of the Life of the Right Honorable*   Tomline
    William Pitt. 2 vols. London: John Murray, 1821.

Report on Manuscripts in Various Collections, VI.   *Various*
    London: Historical Manuscripts Commission, 1909.

Notes

CHAPTERS 1-9

Form of the citation of documents
    Writer   Report/to recipient   date   File: page, folio, or item/
                                         Printed source, page

CHAPTER 1   I   *The Lapse of transportation to America*

[1] A. G. L. Shaw has described this background in greater detail in his *Convicts and the Colonies* (London: Faber and Faber, 1966), Ch.1.

[2] *PR*, 3 (1776), 473; 4 (1776), 104-6, 117.

[3] W. W. Grenville, Commentaries on my own Political Life and of Public Transactions connected with it, Perkins, MS bk.2, p.30, bk.6, p.4.

[4] *PR*, 9 (1778), 83.

[5] *HCJ*, 36 (1776-8), 848, 926-32, 952, 963, 970, 987, 997.

[6] *HCJ*, 37 (1778-80), 307-14.

[7] Ibid., 418, 419, 424, 428, 432, 443, 445-6, 450, 458.

[8] Roberts to Gilbert Ross, undated by c. December 1784, HO 42/5:465.

[9] Shelburne, memorandum for Townshend, undated but before 11 July 1782, Brotherton, R 8; Nepean to Africa Company, [2?] October 1782, T 70/145.

[10] Wright to Townshend, 24 August, Robertson to Townshend, 30 November, Townshend to Robertson, 2 December, Robertson to Townshend, 10 December 1782, HO 42/1.

[11] Morse to Pitt, 24 November 1784, PRO 30/8/363:76, to Nepean, 27 January and 1 February 1787, HO 42/11:14, 17.

II   *Lord North at the Home Office, and James Matra*

[1] North to the King, 11 and 18 July, the King to North, 12 and 18 July 1783, George III (Fortescue), VI, 415-9; Shaw, p.45; Eris O'Brien, *The Foundation of Australia*, 2nd ed. (Sydney: Angus and Robertson, 1950), pp.115-6.

[2] Matra to Banks, 28 July 1783, Add. ms 33977:206.

[3] There is a brief sketch for a shipbuilding colony amongst the Banks papers in the Beinecke Library which *may* relate to the first. In Banks's hand, this is undated and unsigned, and does not specify a location. Banks first sets out the likely establishment — consul, lieutenant colonel, major, four captains, five lieutenants, five ensigns, four hundred and ninety privates and non-commissioned officers. He follows this with a list of expenditures; and another of equipment, including 'Boat Rigging & Tools for Boat building / Tools for Cutting Timber'—Beinecke, Osborn Collection d 10 217 / 11:27.

[4] I have gathered the following details from material in the British Library, the Public Record Office, the William L. Clements Library, the New York Public Library, the New York Historical Society, the Perkins Library, and the printed works cited.

[5] Matra to Banks, 7 May 1790, Add. ms 33979:29; Cook, I, 323.

Cook recorded of 23 May 1770:

> Last Night some time in the Middle watch a very extraordinary affair happend to Mr Orton my Clerk, he having been drinking in the Evening, some Malicious person or persons in the Ship took the advantage of his being drunk and cut off all the cloaths from off his back, not being satisfied with this they some time after went into his Cabbin and cut off a part of both his Ears as he lay asleep in his bed. The person whome he suspected to have done this was Mr Magra one of the Midshipmen, but this did not appear to me upon inquirey. However as I know'd Magra had once or twice before this in their drunken frolicks cut of his Cloaths and had been heard to say (as I was told) that if it was not for the Law he would Murder him, these things consider'd induc'd me to think that Magra was not altogether innocent. I therefore, for the present dismiss'd him the quarter deck and susspended him from doing any duty in the Ship. (I, 323).

No more details of this curious incident emerged, however, and Cook restored Matra to duty on 14 June (I, 347).

[6] Cook,I,cclviii.

[7] George III, Royal Licence of 19 February 1776, SP, 44/383.

[8] Elizabeth Magra, Memorial of 31 March 1780, AO 13/56.

[9] Matra to Banks, 28 July 1783, Add. ms 33977:206. The Commissioners heard Mrs Magra's case on 20 May 1783 (AO 12/99).

[10] See the *Private Papers of James Boswell, XVI,* ed. Geoffrey Scott and Frederick A. Pottle (Privately Printed, 1932), pp. 84, 184, 193, 201, 203, 208, 212.

[11] Matra to [North], 23 August 1783, CO 201/1:57-61.

III   *Lord Sydney and the Transportation Act of 1784*

[1] *PH*, 24 (1783-5), 755-7; *HCJ*, 39 (1782-4), 990, 993, 1032, 1034, 1035-6, 1040-6, 1048, 1050.

[2] Matra to Nepean, 6 April 1784, CO 201/1:64.

[3] Daniel Hill, Deposition of 4 July 1788, CO 123/11:319-30; Sydney to Clarke, 5 October 1784, CO 137/84:146-7.

[4] Sydney to Clarke, 5 October 1784, ibid.

[5] [Arden] to Sydney, c.13-18 August 1784, HO 42/6:55; Enclosure, Clements, Sydney 11.

[6] *HCJ*, 40 (1784-5), 384, 395, 407, 446, 450; Nepean to Arden, 21 August 1784, HO 48/1A:681.

[7] John Ehrman, *The Younger Pitt: The Years of Acclaim* (London: Constable, 1969), p.215.

[8] Michaud, Memorandum on Convicts, 19 May 1784, Rylands R 937.

IV   *The Administration considers suggestions for transportation*

[1] I have taken these details from the *DNB*, and from Thompson's diary for 1783-5, Add. ms 46120.

[2] Thompson to Rose, and enclosure, 1 August, to Mahon, 3 and 10 August 1784, NMM, Thompson Letterbook.

[3] Thompson to Sydney, 8 August 1784, ibid.

[4] Matra to Fox, 7 August 1784, Add. ms 47568:240-6; to de Lancey, 31 August 1784, (unrecovered); de Lancey to Matra, 12 October 1784, CO 201/1:68.

[5] I have taken the following details from the *DNB*, from Alan Valentine, *The British Establishment 1760-1784* (Norman: University of Oklahoma Press, 1970), and from letters in the PRO, IOR, and elsewhere.

[6] In 1767, offering parcels of land revenues as security, the Nabob of Arcot borrowed £450,000 from private lenders, among whom were many Company servants (the Consolidated Loan of 1767). He subsequently came to owe the Company some £3,000,000 for defence and administration (the Cavalry Loan of 1777). Then, in order to delay repayment, the Nabob set up a competition for funds between the Company and the individual creditors by further lavish private borrowings (the Consolidated Loan of 1777), and by admitting the validity of all claims (though many of the private ones seem to have been either much inflated, or fraudulent). The Nabob's private creditors appointed Call as their agent in England, and in 1784, he pressed their interest with the newly established Board of Control for India Affairs. Against strong Company objections, he obtained recognition of the validity of all claims.
(See V. T. Harlow, *The Founding of the Second British Empire* [London: Longmans, 1964], II,169-74, and C. H. Philips, *The East India Company* 1784-1834 [Manchester: Manchester University Press, 1961], pp. 36-40.)

[7] Goodlad to Palk, 12 May 1768, 6 February 1770, Palk, pp.78, 122.

[8] Call to Pitt, 17 December 1793, PRO 30/8/119:80, to the Court of Directors, 31 July 1770, H/102:513-35, and views, I/1/17, to Shelburne, 28 April 1782, and enclosures, Clements, Shelburne 136:524-32.

[9] Call to Pitt, 15 June 1788, PRO 30/8/119:62-72.

[10] Call to Hastings, 3 September 1784, Add. ms 29166:27-8, Plan for liquidating the Company's debts, undated, Add. ms 12567:95-6.

[11] Call to Pitt, 17 June 1788, PRO 30/8/119:63, to Dundas, 11 January 1800, NLS 1071:27.

[12] For details of this survey, see variously: Call to Pitt, 19 March 1788, and Report, PRO 30/8/119:33-60; *HCJ*, 47 (1792), 264-374; Call to Banks, 15 May 1800, Royal Society Ms 1:36.

[13] Call to [Pitt?], undated but c. August 1784, HO 42/7:49-57.

[14] I have taken these details from the *DNB*, and from Sir George Young, *Young of Formosa* (Privately printed).

[15] Royal Society, Certificates 1778-84.

[16] See Young to Davidson, 3 February 1793, CO 201/8:148-9.

[17] Young to [Pitt], undated but c. August 1784, PRO 30/8/342, pt.2:283-4.
This is the first of five presently-known versions of Young's proposal for New South Wales. The others are
  (b) 'A Rough Outline,' to Arden, c. January 1785, CO 201/1:52-3;
  (c) 'A Rough Outline,' printed, but undated, CO 201/1:55-6;

(d) A fuller printed version, undated, Young Family papers (I am grateful to Sir Robin Mackworth-Young for a copy of this);

(e) 'A Rough Outline,' 21 April 1785, CO 201/8:152-3.

[18] Matra to Nepean, 1 [November] 1784, CO 201/1:65.

[19] Young to Arden, c. January 1785, CO 201/1:53.

[20] That this was Phillip's idea is a matter of some reconstruction. However, the circumstances make it most unlikely that it came from anyone else — see p. 92.

[21] Thompson to Mahon, 10 August 1784, NMM, Thompson Letterbook; Thompson, Diary entries of 29 September and 1 October 1784, Add. ms 46120; Freire to Nepean, 17 November 1784, HO 42/5:382; Matra to Nepean, 1 [November] 1784, CO 201/1:66; Pitt to Howe, [24 December 1784], (unrecovered); Sydney to Howe, 25 December 1784, (unrecovered).

[22] On the interest in Guiana, see p. 89; Freire to Nepean, 17 November 1784, HO 42/5:382; Howe to Sydney, 26 December 1784, HO 28/4:386; Arden to Sydney, 13 January 1785, CO 201/1:51.

V *Sydney's decision for Africa*

[1] Wallis to Sydney, 29 December 1784, HO 42/5:459; Bastard to Sydney, 4 February, Higgin to Sydney, 9 February, Frankland to [?], 11 March 1785, HO 42/6:76, 84, 155; Fraser to Nepean, 21 November 1784, HO 32/1; Sydney to Spencer, 18 December 1784, HO 42/5:448.

[2] [John Roberts?] to Gilbert Ross, c. December 1784, HO 42/5:465-9; Sydney to Africa Company, 14 and 21 December 1784, HO 43/1:353, 355; Calvert to Treasury Lords, 15 January 1785, T 1/619; Sydney to Treasury Lords, 16 February 1785, T 1/614; Calvert to Nepean, 9 April 1785, HO 42/6:208; Nepean to Rose, 13 April 1785, T 1/619.

One curious consequence of the Africa Company's intransigence was that a Lieutenant Clark suggested the Government disenfranchise them, and establish another company to form a convict colony on the Gold Coast, and trade in the area — Clark to [Pitt?], 11 March 1785, PRO 30/8/363:56-66.

[3] Barnes described the origins of the scheme in his testimony to the Beauchamp Committee, 2 May 1785, HO 7/1.

[4] Bradley to Nepean, c. December 1784, HO 42/4:93; Nepean to Nichol, 29 December 1784, HO 42/5:461.

[5] Barnes to Nepean, 3 January 1785, HO 42/6:9-10.

[6] Barnes to Nepean, 13 January 1785, enclosing Gill Stater to Thomas Rutherford, 7 January 1785, and Robert Heatley to John Barnes, 12 January 1785, HO 42/6:29-32.

[7] 'A Description of the Island Lemain,' HO 35/1.

[8] Sydney to Treasury Lords, 9 February 1785, HO 35/1, 12 February 1785, T 1/614.

[9] Navy Board to Treasury Lords, 28 February 1785, T 1/616.

[10] Nepean to Campbell, 4 March 1785, (unrecovered); Campbell to Nepean, 5 March 1785, Sydney to Treasury Lords, 20 March 1785, T 1/619.

[11] Bradley to Sydney, 9 November 1785, T 1/614.

[12] Bradley to Sydney, 29 November 1785, Nepean to Rose, 3 February 1786, T 1/627; Treasury Board, Minute of 18 August 1786, T 29/58:11.

CHAPTER 2   I   *The Lemane embroglio*

[1] Nepean to Nichol, 29 December 1784, HO 42/5:461.

[2] Thompson, Diary entry of 3 January 1785, Add. ms 46120:45-6.

[3] Thompson, Diary entry of 31 July 1783, ibid.:7.

Why Thompson should have concluded that the Das Voltas Bay region was fertile is puzzling. The Portuguese, who were the first European navigators of this part of the African coast, had found it barren, with Pacheco Pereira reporting:

> This Angra das Voltas runs inland a good league and a half, and a hundred ships can anchor here in ten to twelve fathoms, safe in all weathers. The bay is a league or more across and contains some rocky islets, and there is good fishing here; it was discovered by Bertholameu Diaz at the bidding of the late King John and is located 29° 20′ south of the Equator. The country is bare and unwooded. Item. Twenty leagues beyond Angra das Voltas is the Serra da Pena; this range is fairly high, treeless and covered with rocks. All this country along the coast is deserted.
>
> —Pacheco Pereira, *Esmeraldo de Situ Orbis*, trans. and ed. G. H. T. Kimble (London: Hakluyt Society, 1937), pp.151-2.

Pacheco's description of the navigation to the East was not known in its entirety in Eighteenth century England, but neither was the Das Voltas Bay region much visited after the early Sixteenth century; and [Green], *A New General Collection of Voyages and Travels, I* (London: Thomas Astley, 1745), for example, gave no indication that it was fertile.

[4] Thompson, Diary entries of 18 and 25 February, 7, 9, and 20 March 1785, ibid.: 55, 60, 62.

[5] *HCJ*, 40 (1784-5), 479.

[6] *PH*, 25 (1785-6), 391-2.

[7] Ibid., 430-1.

[8] *PR*, 17 (1785), 838, 870; *HCJ*, 40 (1784-5), 954.

[9] *HCJ*, 40 (1784-5), 870. The membership of the 1785 Committee far exceeded those of the earlier ones. Why it should have been made potentially so large is not clear, though there may have been an idea that a consensus of the House might thereby be obtained.

[10] I have taken these and the following details from the minutes of the Committee's hearings, HO 7/1. For simplicity, however, I have referred to the published version of the testimony in the notes immediately following.

[11] *HCJ*, 40 (1784-5), 954, 955-6.

[12] Ibid., 957-8.

[13] Ibid., 956.

[14] Ibid., 954, 958-9.

[15] Ibid., 958.

[16] Ibid., 959, 957.

[17] Ibid., 956-7, 957, 954-5.

II   *Botany Bay or Das Voltas Bay*

[1] These and all following excerpts of the Committee's minutes are from HO 7/1.

[2] List of questions, undated, HO 42/6:53-4.

³ Nepean, Memorandum on Das Voltas Bay (incomplete), undated, HO 42/1:462.

⁴ *PH*, 25 (1785-6), 906.

⁵ Beauchamp presented the report to Parliament on 28 July, but the manuscript copy in HO 42/7:3-22 is dated 21 June.

⁶ The report appears in *HCJ*, 40 (1784-5), 1161-4.

⁷ Sydney to the Admiralty Lords, 22 August 1785, HO 28/5:118-20; Thompson to Howe, 29 December 1784, to Nepean, 5 January 1785, NMM Thompson Letterbook.

III   *After the decision for Das Voltas Bay*

¹ Nepean to Despard, 15 September 1785, CO 123/11:330-1; Howe to Sydney, 13 October, de Lynden to Sydney, 17 October 1785, HO 28/5:139ff.
For the extensive documentation of the Langston Harbour scheme, see HO 28/5:143-4, HO 31/14, HO 42/7:103-4, T 1/616, ADM 1/4151:108, 112.

² Smith, II, 123-4.

³ Young and Call to Court of Directors, 21 June 1785, E/1/76:213.

⁴ Court of Directors, Minute of 22 June 1785, B/101:149.

⁵ Dalrymple's letter of 13 July 1785 appears over his signature in a work which he published anonymously, *A Serious Admonition to the Public, on the Intended Thief-Colony at Botany Bay* (London, 1786), pp.8-17.

⁶ Call to Hastings, 3 September 1784, Add. ms 29166:27.

⁷ Correspondence Committee, Report of 13 July 1785, D/32:32; Court of Directors, Minute of 13 July 1785, B/101:238; Ramsay to Young and Call, 20 July 1785, E/1/224:282.

⁸ Young to Alexander Davidson, 3 February 1793, CO 201/8:148.

⁹ Thomas Rowcroft (1768?-1824) is a romantic figure. He was educated in France; and when nothing came of Young's Botany Bay scheme, he sailed to the East. When his ship stopped at Mauritius en route, he walked about the island in order to survey its strategic resources, and was arrested. Trading extensively, he had 'been in the three great oceans' before he was twenty-one, seeing Ascension, the Cape, Madagascar, Mauritius, Bourbon, India, and Sumatra.

He did not succeed in business in the East, however. (He claimed to have lost £48,000.) On his return to England in the 1790s, he joined the family business, and advanced himself in the City. He was elected Alderman for Walbrook in December 1802, and held the office until 1808; and during this time, he worked actively for public charities.

Rowcroft's business was based largely on the naval stores trade with Russia, and in 1810 he suffered a great reverse, when the Russian Government impounded British ships and cargoes. He strove unsuccessfully for the next six years to obtain compensation for himself and fellow merchants for this action; and he claimed to have lost some £300,000 as a result.

With his business failed, and disappointed at not having been chosen either Lord Mayor or MP for the City, Rowcroft sought a diplomatic post. He asked the 2nd Earl Liverpool for the Consulship at Constantinople in October 1817, who replied that this was not in his gift; and in February 1819, he offered himself for service in Sierra Leone. In the end, the government sent him as Consul to Peru, where he died on 11 December 1824, after having been shot by a sentry in Bolivar's army, whose challenge he ignored.

Thomas Hubbert (?-1790) appears as a 'sailcloth factor, sail maker, and ship-broker' in the London Directories of the time. He worked partly out of Lloyd's Coffee House, where he doubtless knew Brook Watson.

Like the Ancient Mariner, Rowcroft found it difficult not to tell his story. I have taken these details from: Rowcroft to T. B. Thompson, 4 August 1810, Young Family Papers; to Brogden, 13 January 1816, Essex D/DSe 13; to [Rose?], 15 April 1816, Add. ms 42774b:15; to 2nd Earl Liverpool, 8 April 1819, Add. ms 38276:182. Miss Betty Masters, Deputy Keeper of the Corporation of London Records, has kindly supplied some details.

[10] Young and Call to Sydney, 24 May 1788, CO 201/3:171.
[11] Matra to Nepean, 18 May 1785, HO 42/6.
[12] Matra to Banks, 6 May 1787, Add. ms 33978:119.

CHAPTER 3   I   *European seaborne empires*

[1] For this section, I have drawn principally on: C. R. Boxer, *The Dutch Seaborne Empire 1600-1800* and *The Portuguese Seabourne Empire 1415-1825* (London: Hutchinson, 1965, 9); J. H. Rose, A. P. Newton, and E. A. Benians, ed., *The Cambridge History of the British Empire, I* (Cambridge: At the University Press, 1929); Holden Furber, *Rival Empires of Trade in the Orient, 1600-1800* (Minneapolis: University of Minnesota Press, 1976); C. N. Parkinson, *Trade in the Eastern Seas 1793-1813* (Cambridge: At the University Press, 1937); J. H. Parry, *The Age of Reconnaissance* (Cleveland and New York: The World Publishing Company, 1963), *The Establishment of European Hegemony 1415-1715*, 3rd ed., rev. (New York: Harper Torchbooks, 1966), and *Trade and Dominion: The European Overseas Empires in the Eighteenth Century* (London: Weidenfeld and Nicolson, 1971).

II   *British schemes to attack their neighbours' colonies*

[1] Vernon to Stephens, 25 July, 16 August, and 31 October 1778, ADM 1/165:36-7, 38-9, 40-2; Young and Call, Memorial of 24 May 1788, CO 201/3:171.

[2] Call described his South American scheme in his memorandum on the colonization of New South Wales, c. August 1784, HO 42/5:50.

As with other of his schemes, he was disappointed in not having the Government adopt it. 'Had it been undertaken at the time and in the manner suggested,' he said, 'it must have been attended with great Loss to the Spaniards and probably with future advantages to this Country in its consequences, because the Natives soon after without foreign Assistance attempted to liberate themselves.'

[3] Dalrymple to Germain, 31 July 1779, Clements, Sackville-Germaine 9; Dalrymple, III, 284-91.

[4] Dalrymple, III, 288, 291-4, 294-304; and various papers, Clements, Sackville-Germaine 10. Sandwich's memorandum is undated, but belongs to late 1779, and is reprinted in H. Richmond, *The Navy in India 1763-1783* (London: Ernest Benn, 1931), pp.420-3.

⁵ Fullarton to Germain, 22 January 1780, Clements, Sackville-Germaine 11; Germain to Dalling, 4 January 1780, Dalrymple to Germain, 1 February and 1 March 1780, Stopford-Sackville, II, 282, 153, 158-9; and various papers, Clements, Shelburne 79:41-61.

⁶ Fullarton and Humberson to Amhurst, 3 February 1780, WO 34/123:21-2; Germain to Ordnance Board, 10 April 1780, CO 5/261.

⁷ See the debates in *PH*, 21 (1780-1), 294-6.

⁸ Mulgrave, Memorandum, undated, PRO 30/8/360:87-93. There is internal evidence to the date. Cook described the discovery of the Sandwich (Hawaiian) Islands in a despatch of 20 October 1778, of which he sent two copies via the Russians in Northern Asia, and which the Admiralty received on 10 January and 6 March 1780 (see Cook, III, pt. 2, 1530-3). Since Mulgrave cites these islands, he could not have written before the beginning of 1780. Again, he would hardly have urged that that Trincomalee be a rendezvous if Britain were at war with Holland, so that a date before the end of 1780 is indicated. The reference to the possibility of orders being sent to Madras 'early in June' points to his writing in, say, March or April 1780. On the point of Mulgrave's suggesting the use of the Hawaiian Islands as a place of refreshment, further instructive is Sir John Dalrymple's remark that 'I have sometimes talked of [my] project to Sir Joseph Banks, who observed, that since the discovery of the Sandwich Islands by Captain Cook, in his last voyage, such adventures are become much more easy; because, in these islands, the adventurers will find places of refuge for their ships, provisions for their crews, strong stations in which to lodge their plunder, from whence they may return to get more, and inhabitants in the islands to assist their seamen in sailing either to the east or the west'—Dalrymple, III, 313.

⁹ Fullarton, Memorandum of 3 June 1780, L/P & S/1/6.

¹⁰ Secret Committee (Devaynes and Sulivan), Sketch of an Expedition to the South Seas, 18 July, Cabinet, Minute of 5 August 1780, L/P & S/1/6.

¹¹ Chairman to Hillsborough, 9 and 19 August 1780, H/146:147-9, 131-7.

¹² Cabinet, Minute of 31 August 1780, H/146:155; Hillsborough to Chairmen, 7 September 1780, H/147:257-64; Chairmen to Hillsborough, 8, 12, and 26 September 1780, H/154:119-20, H/147:277-81, 289; Cabinet and Chairmen, Agreement of 30 September 1780, H/147:315-30.

¹³ See G. Rutherford, 'Sidelights on Commodore Johnstone's Expedition to the Cape: Part I,' *Mariner's Mirror*, 28 (1942), 195-8; George III (Fortescue), V, 155-6.

¹⁴ Phillip to Sandwich, 17 January 1781, Montagu, F/26/23.

¹⁵ George III (Fortescue), V, 173-4; Harlow, I, 114-7.

¹⁶ Harlow, I, 116-20. One contemporary report held that 'One thing is certain—the Commodore sailed in ill-humour, saying he had lost £100,000 by a change in his orders' (*Political Magazine*, June 1781).

¹⁷ Chairmen to Hillsborough, 8 September 1781: H/154:119-20.

¹⁸ Same to same, 18 October 1781, ibid.: 227-32.

¹⁹ Same to same, 25 October 1781. ibid., 277-85.

²⁰ Same to same, 7 November 1781, H/155:79-93.

²¹ Cabinet, Minute of 8 November 1781, George III (Fortescue), V, 298; Chairmen to Hillsborough, 15 November 1781, H/155:341-6.

²² Chairmen to Hillsborough, 16 and 28 November, Hillsborough to Chairmen,

24 November and 6 December 1781, H/155:364-5, 409-10, 417-8, 441-2; Court of Directors to Bengal Government, 8 December 1781, H/219:595-6.

III *The naval war about India*

[1] Hughes to Stephens, [5] April 1780, ADM 1/164:187.
[2] Same to same, 20 March 1781, ibid.: 222.
[3] These details are from Hughes's letterbook, ADM 7/733.
[4] Richmond, pp.205-30, passim.
[5] ADM 7/733.
[6] Richmond, pp.235, 253, 260, 265-70.
[7] Richmond, pp.253, 258-9; Hughes to Stephens, 15 July and 12 August 1782, ADM 1/164:328-43, 347-52.
[8] Richmond, pp.309-15. W. W. Grenville later wrote, 'One of the greatest advantages which France had in the late war, and which we should derive from an intimate union with the Dutch East India Company, is the use of their several arsenals, particularly that of Batavia which is considerable' (to Dundas, 26 August 1787, Dropmore, I, 281).
[9] ADM 7/734; Hughes to Bombay Government, 27 January 1784, H/178:917.
[10] Hughes to Stephens, 10 September 1784, HO 28/5:28.
[11] Hughes to Bombay Government, 27 January 1784, H/178:916-7.

IV *The peace settlement*

[1] This section is largely a summary of Harlow, I, Ch.7: 'Shelburne and the Peace Settlement: France, Spain, and Holland.'
[2] Thompson to Rose, and enclosure, 1 August, to Mahon, 3 and 10 August 1784, NMM, Thompson Letterbook. (I am grateful to Dr. Roger Knight for sending me a microfilm of this recently-acquired item.)
[3] News of de Suffren's having captured Trincomalee did not reach Europe until after the nations reached general terms of peace.
[4] Keppel to [Townshend], 25 September 1782, Clements, Sydney 9.
[5] Three captains turned back. Phillip proceeded alone on the mission, and reached Rio de Janeiro on 15 April, where he learned of the peace. He reported to Townshend, 'the situation of the Spanish Settlements are such as I always thought them. Of five Companies of Regulars, · sent out from Cordova only Seven Men returned, the rest were either killed or deserted to the Indians. Only fifteen Leagues from Monte Vedio, of three hundred Men that went out against the Indians, not ten Men returned, the rest were killed. All the Regulars in Buenos Ayres Monte Vedio, and the different Guards in the River of Plate do not amount to five hundred Men—No ship of the Line, and only two frigates in the River. You will Sir, easily suppose how much I must be mortified in being so near & not at liberty to Act'—25 April 1783, H/175:237.
[6] Grantham to Fitzherbert, 18 December 1782, FO 27/2:468-72.
[7] Vergennes to Rayneval, 3 January 1783, Harlow and Madden, pp.8-9.
[8] Shelburne to Fitzherbert, 9 January 1783, Add. ms 42390:270-2.
[9] Grantham to Fitzherbert, 9 January 1783, FO 27/5:127-8.

P

[10] Secret Committee to Grantham, 12 February and 8 March 1783, FO 27/15:89-90, 115.

[11] Cabinet, Minute of 20 August 1783, Add. ms 47559:99.

[12] Cabinet, Minute of 18 September 1783, Add. ms 47559:111; Manchester to Fox, 9 October 1783, Add. ms 47563:134; Court of Directors, Minute of 15 October 1783, FO 37/6.

[13] Hughes to Bombay Government, 27 January 1784, H/178:916.

CHAPTER 4   I   *William Pitt and his colleagues*

[1] I have taken the biographical details mostly from Ehrman.

[2] *PR*, 2nd; ser., 2 (1781), 17.

[3] Ibid., 5 (1782), 49.

[4] Pitt, Notes, undated, Suffolk T 108/33.

[5] Pitt, Speech of 12 May 1785, *PH*, 25 (1785-6), 587.

[6] The characterizations of Gower and Camden are Ehrman's (p.184). The rest are from W. W. Grenville, 'Commentaries on my own Political Life and of Public Transactions connected with it,' Perkins, MS bk.6, pp.3-6.

[7] Quoted in Ehrman, p.303.

[8] Dundas to Lowther, 25 July 1806, quoted in C. Matheson, *The Life of Henry Dundas* (London: Constable, 1933), p.375; Banks, Annotation, NH microfilm (I am grateful to Mr. H. B. Carter for this reference); Secret Committee, Minute of 30 September 1795, L/P & S/5/583.

[9] Cathcart to Secret Committee, 12 August 1786, L/P & S/5/20; Board of Control, Secret minute of 26 August 1786, L/P & S/2/1:14; 'Mr. Pitt and Lord Mulgrave are here . . .'—Dundas to Hawkesbury, 16 September 1786, Add. ms 38192:44; 'I drew the first sketch, but Mr. Pitt and Lord Mulgrave lived with me on the subject for a week at Wimbledon'—Dundas to Eden, 28 September 1786, Add. ms 34466:353-5.

[10] Pitt to Carmarthen, 16 September 1786, Bodleian English Letters d.122; Carmarthen to Pitt, 18 September 1786, Add. ms 28061:306; Pitt to Carmarthen, 18 September 1786, Eger. 3498:165; Carmarthen to Hailes for Eden, 20 September 1786, Add. ms 34466:30.

[11] Board of Control, Secret minute of 20 September 1786, L/P & S/2/1:15; and Draft to Bengal Government, 20 September 1786, L/P & S/5/562:52-62. (The Secret Committee signed this despatch on 22 September—L/P & S/1/9:145.)

[12] Dundas to Hawkesbury, 8, 11 and 16 September 1786, Add. ms 38192:40-1, 42, 44; Dundas to Eden, 28 September 1786, and 26 June 1787, Add. mss 38446:353-5, 34467:47-8; Board of Control, Secret minutes of 19 October 1786 and 29 January 1787, L/P & S/2/1:16, 17; Dundas to Pitt, 7 April 1787, Clements, Pitt 2; Eden to Pitt, 2 September 1787, PRO 30/8/110:131-2; Pitt to Dundas, 8 September 1787, Clements, Pitt 2. There is as well extensive documentation of this negotiation in L/P & S/5/562.

II   *Pitt's outlook and policies*

[1] For detailed discussions, see Ehrman, Chs. X and XI.

[2] Memorandum, undated, Sandwich, IV, 303-4.

[3] Pitt, Speech of 21 February 1783, Pitt, I,28.

[4] Pitt's younger brother entered the Navy; and Ehrman reports that his 'early letters home, from London [are] full of its doings' (p.313). Pitt spoke forcefully during the Commons inquiry into Sandwich's administration of the Admiralty in February 1782, and showed an impressive grasp of detail—see *PR*, 2nd ser. 5 (1782), 405 ff, 6 (1782), 252-3. He also dealt at length with the nation's naval circumstances when he defended Shelburne's peace settlement on 21 February 1782—Pitt, I,26-8.

[5] Martin, III, 381. Middleton's papers to Pitt are in PRO 30/8/111.

[6] Pitt to Rutland, 7 October 1784, Pitt-Rutland, p.43; to Orde, 19 September 1784, Ashbourne, pp.85-6.

[7] Carmarthen, Memorandum of 9 June 1784, Eger, 3498:36-7; Memoranda of 11 and 25 June, Leeds, pp.101, 106-7, 108.

[8] Grenville, Commentaries, Perkins, MS. bk 5, p.36.

[9] Tomline, I, 381; Pitt, Speeches of 12 and 14 January 1784, Pitt, I, 68, 71.

[10] Pitt, Speech of 5 March 1788, *PR*, 2nd ser. 23 (1788), 301.

[11] Sydney to Pitt, 24 September 1784, Stanhope, I,228; Dundas to Cornwallis, 29 July 1787, Cornwallis, I, 321.

[12] Dundas to Cornwallis, 20 July 1786 and 27 July 1787, Cornwallis, I,244-5, 321.

[13] Carmarthen, Memorandum of 9 June 1784, Eger. 3498:36-7; Pitt to Rutland, 8 August 1785, Pitt-Rutland, 111-2.

III   *French outlook and policies*

[1] Bussy, Memorandum on the proposed expedition to India, 1781, in Richmond, pp.389-94.

[2] 'Par l'Égypte nous toucherons à l'Inde, nous rétablirons l'ancienne circulation par Suez at nous ferons déserter la route du cap de Bonne-Espérance'—quoted in Albert Sorel, *L'Europe et la Révolution Française*, 11th ed. (Paris: Librairie Plon, 1908), I, 328-9.

[3] J. H. Rose, *William Pitt and National Revival* (London: G. Bell and Sons, 1912), p.344; Hailes to Carmarthen, 10 August 1786, FO 27/18.

[4] 'Notre Politique et nos Vues sont & doivent être principalement dirigées contre notre Rivale Maritime . . . [The Continental agitations have the end] à la première Occasion d'une Rupture, et de preparer ainsi les Voyes pour des Coups decisifs du Coté des Indes Orientales de concert avec les Provinces Unis'—[   ], Memorandum of 15 May 1785, Add. ms 28060:342.

[5] I have taken these and the details following from Colenbrander, pp.1-34.

CHAPTER 5   I   *Naval questions and diplomatic negotiations*

[1] Madras Government to Court of Directors, 28 July 1784, FO 37/6.

[2] Hughes to Stephens, 10 September 1784, HO 28/5:29.

[3] Court of Directors to Carmarthen, 21 January 1785, FO 37/6; Dundas to Sydney, 28 [January 1785], Clements, Melville 2; Bengal Government to Secret Committee, 16 May 1785, PRO 30/8/358:101.

[4] Thompson, Diary entry of 3 May 1783, Add. ms 46120: Cabinet, Minute of 20 August 1783, Add. ms 47559:99; Thompson to Rose, 1 August, to Mahon, 3

August, to Sydney, 8 August 1784, NMM, Thompson Letterbook; Thompson, Diary entries of 4 and 6 November, and 3 December 1784, Add. ms 46120.

⁵ Bengal Government to Secret Committee, 10 January 1786, L/P & S/5/20:8. In 1773, the French King gave two 64-gun ships *'armés en flûte'* for the China trade, which the French then reconverted to warships when war broke out (−[   ], Memorandum on East India shipping, 12 April 1786, Add. ms 38409:83).

⁶ Carmarthen to Stone, 1 January, to Dorset, 16 February 1784, FO 27/11:1-2, 249-51.

⁷ Carmarthen to Dorset, 26 March 1784, FO 27/11:440; Howe to Carmarthen, 11 April, Pitt to Carmarthen, 10 April 1784, Eger. 3498:178, 30; Hailes to Carmarthen, 28 April 1784, FO 27/11:595-7; Carmarthen to Hailes, 1 June, Hailes to Carmarthen, 10 June 1784, FO 27/12:689-92, 715-7.

⁸ Vergennes to Dorset, 9 and 17 October, Dorset to Carmarthen, 14 and 21 October, Carmarthen to Dorset, 19 October 1784, FO 27/13:1144-8, 1152-4; Pitt to Carmarthen, 30 October 1784, Eger. 3498:64.

⁹ Carmarthen to Dorset, 13 February 1784, FO 27/11:209.

¹⁰ Hailes to Carmarthen, 10 June 1784, FO 27/12:715-7; Dorset to Carmarthen, 8 and 22 July, 19 and 26 August 1784, *Despatches*, pp.13, 15, 18, 19; Carmarthen to Dorset, 27 July 1784, *Instructions*, p.251.

¹¹ Hailes to Carmarthen, 28 April, Dorset to Carmarthen, 22 July 1784, *Despatches*, pp.4, 16.

¹² Dorset to Carmarthen, 8 and 29 July 1784, *Despatches*, pp.13, 17; Carmarthen to Dorset, 9 July 1784, *Instructions*, pp.250-1.

¹³ Hailes to Carmarthen, 2 September, Dorset to Carmarthen, 7 October 1784, *Despatches*, pp.19, 23.

¹⁴ Carmarthen to Dorset, 9 July 1784, *Instructions*, p.251. Dundas told Sydney on 2 November 1784, 'Our force now, and hereafter, must be regulated by the intelligence we have of the force kept up by our European rivals, at the Mauritius, Pondichery, Ceylon, or other places in India. Taking it for granted that India is the quarter to be first attacked, we must never lose sight of keeping such a force there as will be sufficient to baffle all surprize. In that shape, I believe, the attack will first be made'— PRO 30/8/157:7.

¹⁵ Carmarthen, Reasons for a Danish Alliance, undated, Leeds, pp. 108-9; Pitt, Memorandum for Instructions to Mr. Fitzherbert, 12 October, to Carmarthen, 13 October, Carmarthen to Fitzherbert, 15 October 1784, Add. ms 28060:163-71; George III, Instructions to Harris, 26 November 1784, FO 37/5:251. Pitt talked to Harris about his tasks on 16 November, and approved the draft of his instructions on 21 November— Pitt to Carmarthen, 21 November 1784, Eger. 3498:82.

¹⁶ Phillip to Stephens, 14 October 1784, ADM 1/2307; Nepean, Entry of 14 November 1784, Secret Service Ledger, Clements, Nepean.

II   *The British consider their naval position in the east*

¹ For de Suffren's views on Acheen, see George Smith to Dundas, 'Observations relating to Trankamale,' 27 January 1785, H/434:44-54; Carmarthen to Hailes, 23 December 1784, Eger. 3499:75-6.

² Lacam's extensive papers concerning New Harbour, and associated ones, are in E/4/630 and F/3/2.

If one or the other is not identical, Sulivan's letter to Hillsborough of 16 November 1781, and his draft of instructions to the Indian Governments (sent to Hillsborough for approval on 28 November 1781) in H/155:364-5, 421-5, doubtless give the substance of his 'Memoire' on Acheen and the Andaman and Nicobar Islands.

For Matra, Young, and Call's proposals for New South Wales, see above, pp. 13-5, 24-5, 27.

³ Howe to Pitt, 25 December 1784, PRO 30/8/146:209-10; to Sydney, 26 December 1784, HO 28/4:386.

⁴ Hailes to Carmarthen, 13 January 1785, Eger. 3499:85; Harris to Carmarthen, 4 January 1785, FO 37/6.

⁵ Phillip to [Nepean], January 1785, FO 95/4/6:499-500.

⁶ Harris to Carmarthen, 1 February, Grenville to Carmarthen, 25 February 1785, Add. ms 28060:247, 273; Dundas, Heads of Conversation between Mr. Dundas and Mr. Baldwin, February [1785], PRO 30/8/360:287-90; Thompson, Diary entries of 18 and 20 February, and 21 March 1785, Add. ms 46120:55, 62.

⁷ Bussy's Instructions, endorsed 'Sent 23 March 1785,' I/1/13; Phillip to [Nepean], 21 March (received 10 May 1785, FO 95/4/6:501; Hailes to [   ], 12 May 1785, Rylands ms 908:IV, 537; enclosure in Harris to Carmarthen, 15 May 1785, Add. ms 28060:342ff.

⁸ Board of Control, Secret Minute of 9 April 1785, L/P & S/2/1:3; Draft of secret despatch, 9 April 1785, L/P & S/5/583.

⁹ For the proceedings of the House of Commons, Committee on Transportation, see above, pp. 35-44, Board of Control, Secret Minute of 27 June 1785, L/P & S/2/1:6; Draft of secret despatch, 27 June 1785, I/1/13.

¹⁰ Hailes to Carmarthen, 2 June and 21 July 1785, Eger. 3499:116, 128-9, 4 August 1785, FO 27/17:782. See also F. L. Nussbaum, 'The Formation of the New East India Company of Calonne,' *American Historical Review*, 38 (1933), 475-97.

¹¹ See 'Private Instructions . . . ,' 'Plan of the Voyage,' 'Extract from the general instructions,' and 'Memoir drawn up by the Academy of Sciences,' in *A Voyage Round the World*, ed. L. A. Milet-Mureau (London: G. G. & J. Robinson, 1799), I, 11-135.

¹² Dorset to Carmarthen, 5 May and 9 June 1785, FO 27/16:553, 605-6; Lord Dalrymple to Carmarthen, 8 June 1785, Eger. 3501:39.

¹³ Dorset to Carmarthen, 30 June 1785, FO 27/16:672-3.

¹⁴ [Mulgrave?], 'Speculations on the Situation and Resources of Egypt (1773-1785),' Add. ms 38346:236-57.

III *The French prepare to begin war*

¹ Carmarthen to Ainslie, 16 August 1785, I/1/13; Fraser to Rouse, 23 August 1785, FO 27/17:529; and see above, p.61.

Sydney to Admiralty Lords, 22 August, Ibbetson to Nepean, 25 August 1785, HO 28/5:118-21; Admiralty Lords, Secret Instruction to Thompson, Banks, Instructions to Hove, 15 September 1785, ADM 2/1342; and see D. L. Mackay,

'British Interest in the Southern Oceans, 1782-1794,' *New Zealand Journal of History*, 3 (1969), 128-30.

[2] Pemberton to Dundas, undated but c. August 1785, G/9/1:18-25.

[3] Diana Dalrymple to Devaynes, undated but September 1785, PRO 30/8/128:64-5.

[4] Devaynes to Dundas, 17 September and 4 October 1785, GD 51/3/17:205, 209-10: Pitt to Grenville, 2 October 1785, Dropmore, I, 257.

[5] Cornwallis, Heads of what the King of Prussia said to Lord Cornwallis at Sans Souci, the 17th September 1785, Cornwallis, I,201-2.

[6] Harris to Carmarthen, 19 August 1785, FO 37/7:42.

[7] Harris to Carmarthen, 23 September 1785, FO 37/8:60; Pitt to Grenville, 4 October 1785, Dropmore, I,257.

[8] Grimoard to Vergennes, 18 and 30 September 1785, de Castries, Observations Relatives à la Hollande, 8 October 1785, Colenbrander, pp.10-16.

[9] Vergennes to de Castries, 9 October 1785, Colenbrander, p.16; Fraser to Carmarthen, 24 October 1785, Add. ms 28060:463; de Castries, Observations, Colenbrander, p.15.

[10] Harris to Carmarthen, 9 and 16 September 1785, FO 37/8:52, 55, 8 November 1785, FO 37/9.

[11] Pitt to Carmarthen, 13 November 1785, Eger. 3498:141-2; Harris to Carmarthen, 15 and 29 November 1785, Carmarthen to Harris, 17 November 1785, FO 37/9:83, 90, 22; Pitt to Carmarthen, 6 December 1785, Eger. 3498:149; Carmarthen to Harris, 6 December 1785, Malmesbury, II,128; Harris to Carmarthen, 30 December 1783, FO 37/9:103.

CHAPTER 6   I   *The results of French diplomacy*

[1] Harris to Carmarthen, 13 December 1785, FO 37/9:93, 11 January 1786, FO 37/6.

[2] Same to same, 13 January 1786, FO 37/10:3.

[3] Same to same, 13 and 30 January 1786, FO 37/10:3, 7.

[4] Same to same, 27 January 1786, FO 37/10:8.

[5] Ibid.

[6] Same to same, 3 February 1786 (two letters), Add. ms 28061:21, FO 37/10:11.

[7] Same to same, 14 and 21 February 1786, FO 37/10:16, Add. ms 28061:36; Carmarthen to Harris, 24 February 1786, FO 37/10:4.

[8] Harris to Carmarthen, 7 March 1786, Add. ms 28061:59-60; Carmarthen to Harris, 10 March 1786, FO 37/10:11.

[9] Harris to Carmarthen, 21 March and 14 April 1786, FO 37/10:28.

[10] Harris to Carmarthen, 24 February and 31 March 1786, FO 37/10:19, 31.

[11] Dorset to Carmarthen, 2 and 9 February 1786, FO 27/18.

[12] Carmarthen to Dorset, 17 February 1786, FO 27/18, to Harris, 24 February 1786, FO 37/10:4.

[13] Dorset to Carmarthen, 9 March 1786, FO 27/18: Vergennes to Dorset, 1 April, Dorset to Carmarthen, 6 April 1786, FO 27/18; Harris to Carmarthen, 7 and 14 April 1786, FO 37/10.

[14] Keith to Carmarthen, 7 December 1785, FO 7/11:631-2; Harris to Carmarthen, 13 December 1785, FO 37/9:93; Ainslie to Morton, 6 February 1786, E/1/78:34.

[15] Fox, Speech of 24 January 1786, *Gentleman's Magazine*, 56 (1786), 159-60.

II   *Pitt moves to meet the threat*

[1] Cornwallis to Ross, 23 February 1786, to Dundas, 16 February 1787, Cornwallis, I, 208, 245.

[2] Harris to Carmarthen, 5, 9, and 16 May 1786, FO 37/10:41, 42, FO 37/11:43.

[3] Same to same, 26 May 1786 (two letters), FO 37/11:46.

[4] Harris to Carmarthen, 6 June 1786, FO 37/11:50; Carmarthen to the King, 17 June 1786, George III (Aspinall), I,229; Harris to Carmarthen, 7 July 1786, Malmesbury, II, 162 and note, 11 July 1786, FO 37/11:59.

[5] Harris to Carmarthen, 6 and 23 June, and 4 July 1786, Add. ms 28061:134-5, 160-1,176-7, 16 June 1786, FO 37/11.

[6] Mulgrave, Observations upon the Naval Establishment in Peace, PRO 30/8/250.

[7] Mulgrave, Memorandum on the transmission of despatches via Suez, [1786], PRO 30/8/360:338-42.

[8] Board of Control to Carmarthen, and Draft of Instructions for Baldwin, 19 May 1786, F/2/1:74-119.

[9] Nepean's queries and Campbell's answers, undated but January 1786, HO 42/10:426-7; Campbell to Nepean, with estimates, 22 January 1786, HO 42/8:8-8a; Pitt, Speech of 7 February 1786, *Gentleman's Magazine*, 56(1786), 168; Pitt to Rolle, 6 May 1786, PRO 30/8/195:31.

[10] Macaulay and Gregory to Nepean, 10 May, Calvert to Nepean, 1 June, Nepean to Steele, 10 June 1786, T 1/632:35-40; Steele to Navy Board, 10 June 1786, ADM/OT; Navy Board to Steele, 13 June 1786, T 1/632:41.

III   *Crisis in Europe and the East*

[1] Macpherson to Secret Committee, 23 September and 27 October 1785, L/P & S/1/9:140, H/555:289.

[2] Treaty of Versailles, 3 September 1783, FO 93/33/2.

[3] Board of Control to Bengal Government, 19 July 1786, I/1/13.

[4] Dangereux to Bengal Government, 6 December 1785, I/ 1/10:341-2.

[5] Bengal Government, Instructions to Cathcart, 31 January 1786, FO 27/18.

[6] Bengal Government to Secret Committee, 9, 10, 26, and 27 January, and 4 February 1786, L/P & S/5/20:8, 9, 10, L/P & S/1/9:144.

[7] Hailes to Carmarthen, 22 June 1786, FO 27/18.

[8] Carmarthen to Hailes, 5 July, Hailes to Carmarthen, 9 July 1786, FO 27/18.

[9] Board of Control to Bengal Government, 19 July 1786, I/1/13.

[10] Carmarthen to Hailes, 4 August, Hailes to Carmarthen, 10 August 1786, FO 27/18.

[11] T. B. Thompson, Log entries of 8, 10, 16, and 22 April, and 17 May 1786, ADM 51/627.

[12] Harris to Carmarthen, 1, 4, and 8 August 1786, FO 37/11:68, 70, 72.

[13] Sydney to the King, and the King's reply, 16 August 1786, George III (Aspinall), I, 244.

CHAPTER 7   I   *The Administration considers alternatives to Das Voltas Bay*

[1] *Annual Register*, 28 (1786), 233-4.

[2] Sydney to the King, 3 August 1786, George III (Aspinall), I, 241.

[3] See *Annual Register*, ibid.

[4] The King to Hertford, 7 August 1786, George III (Aspinall), I, 242; Sydney to Lansdowne, 12 August 1786, Clements, Sydney 13.

[5] Blankett to Howe, with enclosures, 6 August 1786, NMM, How 3.

[6] Blankett to Nepean, 10 August 1786, HO 42/9: 323; Howe, Draft to Blankett, 14 August 1786, Blankett to Howe, 16 August 1786, NMM, How 3.

II   *The attractions of Botany Bay*

[1] Cook, I, 304, 310-11, and Chart XXII.

[2] Cook, I, 306-11, 397; Banks, II,56-9; Banks, Testimony to the Beauchamp Committee, 10 May 1785, HO 7/1.

[3] Cook, I,399; Matra, testimony to the Beauchamp Committee, 9 May 1785, HO 7/1.

[4] Banks, II,122-3, 128: Banks, Testimony to the Beauchamp Committee, 10 May 1785, HO 7/1.

[5] Matra to Fox, 7 August 1784, Add. ms 47568:245; Matra to [North], 23 August 1783, CO 201/1:58; Young to [Pitt], c. August 1784, PRO 30/8/342, pt.2:283; Coggan, Testimony to the Beauchamp Committee, 12 May 1785, HO 7/1; *London Chronicle*, 12-14 September 1786, and *Birmingham Gazette*, 18 September 1786.

[6] White gave La Pérouse's characterization in a letter to Skill, 17 April 1790, HRNSW, I,ii,333.

[7] Cook, II,565-6, 868-9.

[8] The records of gardening at Kew have not survived. However, Cook told of the first failure in his letter of 22 June to Wilson (Cook IV,505); and W. F. Martyn indicated the second, when he wrote that 'Captain Furneaux brought over a small quantity of the seed of this plant, which was sown in Kew Garden; but though, either from want of care or skill, the whole unfortunately failed, it ought not to deter us from future experiments' (*The Geographical Magazine*, 2nd ed. [London: Harrison, 1785-7], I,578.).
Forster's sample is presumably that to which Anna Seward referred when she wrote that 'In New-Zealand is a flag of which the natives make their nets and cordage. The fibres of this vegetable are longer and stronger than our hemp and flax; and some, manufactured in London, is as white and glossy as fine silk'(— *Elegy on Captain Cook* [London: J. Dodsley, 1780]. p. [12]).
Stephens to Cook, 20 July 1776, Cook, III,ii,1513, 1421.

[9] Matra to [North], 23 August 1783, CO 201/1:57; Rowcroft to T. B. Thompson, 4 August 1810, Young Family Papers. (It seems likely that Rowcroft's relative Thomas Hubbert made these samples.)

10 Watson to Edward Winslow, 6 March 1785, *Winslow Papers*, ed. W. O. Raymond (St. John: New Brunswick Historical Society, 1901), p.274; Watson to Hawkesbury, 8 October 1789, HO 31/14. The Board of Trade considered Watson's letter on 13 October, and recommended that Phillip be instructed to send some seed in the manner Watson described (BT 5/5:382). Fawkener passed this request to Nepean two days later (BT 3/2:109).

11 We can deduce that Banks established the plant at Kew about 1790 from William Aiton's including it in the second edition of his *Hortus Kewensis* ([London, 1810-13], II, 284), but not in the first (1789). I am grateful to Mr. H. B. Carter for this information, who also quotes Banks's opinion of the samples in 'Sir Joseph Banks and the Plant Collection from Kew sent to the Empress Catherine II of Russia 1795,' *Bulletin of the British Museum (Natural History)*, IV,v (1974), 346-7.

12 See, e.g., *Gentleman's Magazine*, 41 (1771), 425 and 46 (1776), 119; John Hawkesworth, *An Account of the Voyages Undertaken by the Order of His Present Majesty for Making Discoveries in the Southern Hemisphere* (London: W. Strahan and T. Cadell, 1773), III, 31-41; Sydney Parkinson, *A Journal of a Voyage to the South Seas* (London: Stanfield Parkinson, 1773), p.211; James Cook, *A Voyage Towards the South Pole* (London: W. Strahan and T. Cadell, 1777), II,133-49; Cook to Banks, 10 July 1776, Cook,III,ii,1511; George Forster, *A Voyage Round the World* (London: B. White, et al., 1777), Bk.III; [John Marra], *Journal of the Resolution's Voyage* (London: F. Newbery, 1775), pp.296-301; J. H. Moore, *A New and Complete Collection of Voyages and Travels* (London: A. Hogg, 1778) I,205, II,1117-56; Martyn, op. cit., I,518.

13 Matra, Testimony to the Beauchamp Committee, 9 May 1785, HO 7/1.

14 Nepean, Questions, and Campbell, Answers, undated but January 1786, HO 42/10:426-7; Campbell to Nepean, 22 January 1786, HO 42/8:8-10.

III   *The decision to colonize New South Wales*

1 T. B. Thompson to Stephens, 15 August 1786, ADM 1/2594.

2 Fawkener to Hawkesbury, 16 and 17 August 1786, Add. ms 38219: 349-51; Board of Trade, Minutes of 18 August 1786, Add. ms 38389:262.

3 [Treasury Secretaries], Estimate of expenses, undated but mid-August 1786, HO 42/10:425.

4 Nepean, Estimate of expenses, undated but mid-August 1786, HO 42/7:23.

5 Nepean, Sketch of staff establishment, and estimate of expenses, undated but mid-August 1786, CO 201/2:15, HO 42/7:24.

6 The earliest copy of the 'Heads,' which is unsigned and undated, seems to be that in CO 201/2:11-13. There are others, similarly unsigned and undated, in HO 35/1, T 1/639:2176, and E/1/79.

7 Heads, CO 201/2:11-13.

8 *The Daily Universal Register*, 21 August 1786, states that Cabinet met on Saturday 19 August.

9 Howe, Draft to Blankett, 19 August 1786, NMM, How 3.

10 Thompson, Diary entry of 1 October 1784, Add. ms 46120:22; J. H. Rose, *William Pitt and the Great War* (London: G. Bell and Sons, 1911), p.459.

11 Nepean, Draft of 21 August 1789, HO 35/7.

[12] Nepean, Draft backdated 18 August 1786, with Heads, List of provisions, Estimate of clothing, Sketch of staff establishment, [Middleton and Steele], List of tools, and Macaulay and Gregory to Nepean, 21 August 1786, CO 201/2:3-23.

The same (i.e., the copies sent to the Treasury Lords), endorsed 'R 21 18 August, Read, the same Day,' T 1/639:2176; and Treasury Board, Minutes of 18 August 1786, T 29/58:22-4.

[13] Nepean, Draft to Admiralty Lords, 31 August 1786, CO 201/2:25-30; Sydney to Admiralty Lords, 31 August 1786, ADM 1/4152:25.

[14] Sydney [Nepean] to Chairmen, 15 September 1786, E/1/79:187.

[15] Howe to Sydney, 3 September 1786, CO 201/2:31.

IV *Naval stores and the First Fleet*

[1] Harris to Carmarthen, 5 September 1786, Add. ms 28061:294; Hailes to Carmarthen, 7 September and 12 October 1786, FO 27/18.

[2] Board of Trade, Minutes of 24 August 1786, BT 5/4:4.

[3] Ibid., 7; Navy Board, Account of prices, 21 March 1787, ADM/BP/7.

[4] Richardson to Hawkesbury, 8 September 1786, Add. ms 38220:11-14.

[5] Hawkesbury to Richardson, 8 September 1786, Add. ms 38309:114; Mitchell to Hawkesbury, 21 September 1786, Add. ms 38220:81-2; unsigned report to Grenville, 4 November 1789, CO 42/66.

[6] No one has yet described adequately the mounting of the First Fleet. The relevant documents in *HRNSW* are only a small portion of those extant. Those in Owen Rutter, *The First Fleet* (London: The Golden Cockerel Press, 1937) are more extensive, but nonetheless still a selection only. A comprehensive description of this mounting would lay the myths that the Pitt Administration were generally indolent in assembling the Fleet, that they equipped the colonizing party poorly, and that these features reflect their callous disregard of the convicts' welfare.

[7] Hunter gives these descriptions in *An Historical Journal* (London: John Stockdale, 1793), p.2; for the cannon, see Nepean to Sydney, 9 November 1786, Mitchell, An 53, and HRNSW I,ii, 33.

[8] Watson to Nepean, 2 November 1786, enclosing Twiss to Watson, 29 October 1786, HO 42/10:393-4. On Morley, see Hunter, p.294. On the occupations of the convicts, see John Cobley, *The Crimes of the First Fleet Convicts* (Sydney: Angus and Robertson, 1970).

[9] Sharrow to Nepean, 24 October 1786, (unrecovered); Nepean to Sharrow 27 October 1786, HO 43/2:175.

[10] Sharrow to Nepean, 30 October and November 1786, HO 42/9:92, HO 42/8:12.

[11] Banks, List of seeds, October/November 1786, T 1/639.

[12] Banks, Draft scheme for the breadfruit voyage, undated but c. March, to Nepean, 9 September 1787, HO 42/11:67, HO 42/12:115; Phillip to Nepean, 1 March, Vaughan to [   ], 9 March 1787, CO 201/2:115, 224.

[13] D. L. Mackay, 'British Interest in the Southern Oceans, 1782-1794,' *New Zealand Journal of History*, 3 (1969), 124-42; and 'A Presiding Genius of Exploration: Banks, Cook, and Empire, 1767-1805', in *Captain James Cook and his Times*,

ed. Robin Fisher and Hugh Johnston (Vancouver: Douglas & McIntyre, 1979), pp.21-39.

[14] *Morning Post*, 20 May 1789.

[15] George III, Instructions to Phillip, 25 April 1787, CO 202/5:28-38.

[16] Phillip to Nepean, 28 October 1786, HO 42/9:84.

CHAPTER 8   I   *British strategic planning and European diplomacy*

[1] Blankett to Nepean, 27 October and [November] 1786, HO 42/9:117, HO 42/10:418, to Howe, 27 October and 6 November 1786, NMM How 3.

[2] Cornwallis to Dundas, 5 March, 14 August, and 18 December 1787, NLS 3385:49, 70, 104; Kyd, report of 1 September 1787, G/34/1:241-63.

[3] Bengal Government to Secret Committee, 27 October 1785, H/555:283-9.

[4] Bombay Government to Secret Committee, undated, H/606:5-15.

[5] Board of Control, Memorandum of 25 May 1787, PRO 30/8/360:108-14.

[6] 'We find our Reports so different from different Quarters relative to the Navigation of the Seas in the Eastern World, we have determined, very much on the suggestion of Lord Mulgrave, to send a Person from our own Board to furnish us with such information as we can have recourse to on every occasion, whether for the Objects of Peace or War' — Dundas to Cornwallis, 20 July 1787, NLS 3387:11.

[7] Nepean, Entries of 23 and 31 July 1787, Secret Service Ledger, Clements, Nepean; Pitt to Cornwallis, 2 August 1787, PRO 30/8/102:87.

[8] Grenville to Dundas, 26 August 1787, Dropmore, I,279-81; Eden to Carmarthen, 13 September, Carmarthen to Eden, 13 September, and Pitt to Eden, 14 September 1787, Auckland, I,193-4, 195, 524-30.

[9] Dundas to Grenville, 2 September 1787, Dropmore, III,419-21.

[10] Dundas, Considerations on the Subject of a Treaty, undated but November 1787, PRO 30/8/360:179-98; Baring, Draft of same, 4 November 1787, GD 51/3/23:412ff.

[11] Mulgrave, Sketch of the Heads of a Treaty, undated, PRO 30/8/360:199-212, and Observations on some Articles in the Projet, undated, I/2/26:57-84; Draft Treaty, (with Dundas's emendations), undated, GD 51/3/23:262-79; Board of Control, Report of 20 December 1787, Add. ms 34467:110-19, and final version of the treaty, 21 December 1787, I/2/26:85ff.

II   *The search for naval security in the East*

[1] Board of Control, Observations on the Account of Materials that may be procured in India for Ships of any Size, 15 January 1788, PRO 30/8/360:116-8.

[2] Mulgrave, S.[r] Richard Kings Opinions upon Negapatnam, 19 March 1788, PRO 30/8/360:120-1.

[3] Board of Control, Minute of October 1788, CO 77/26:35; Dundas to Chatham, 6 January, L/P & S/5/583, to Admiralty Lords, 4 February 1789, ADM 12/54:50/6.

[4] Blair, Report of 9 June 1789, Add. ms 34467:145-63.

[5] Cornwallis to Secret Committee, 1 and 10 August 1789, ibid.:165, 170.

[6] Dundas told Grenville on 1 July 1790 that Penang's future importance 'depends entirely on the report Commodore Cornwallis shall make respecting the Andaman harbours; but, even if that report should prove not so favourable as we expect . . .'—Dropmore, I,591.

[7] Moorsom to W. Cornwallis, 19 September, W. Cornwallis to Stephens, 11 November 1789, ADM 1/167:31, 50-1.

[8] W. Cornwallis to Dundas, 1 November 1789, NLS 1066:56-7, to Stephens, 10 November and 4 December 1789, and 27 February 1790, ADM 1/167:29, 58-9, 69; Cornwallis to Dundas, 5 December 1789, and 1 April 1790, NLS 3385:267-8, 314-5; Robert Blair to Dundas, 6 August 1790, enclosing Archibald Blair to Robert Blair, 26 December 1789, Dropmore, I,604-5.

[9] Board of Control, Minute of 17 June 1789, CO 77/25:127-8; Banks to Nepean, 27 August 1789, HO 28/6:314; Grenville to Admiralty Lords, 3 October 1789, ADM 1/4154:43.

III *Phillip follows instructions in New South Wales*

[1] Phillip to Sydney, 15 May 1788, CO 201/3:6-7; Dundas to Phillip, 10 January 1792, CO 201/5:182-3.

[2] Phillip to Sydney, 15 May, 5 July, and 28 September 1788, CO 201/3:11, 112, Dixson Q 162:5-8.

[3] For the despatch of the *Guardian*, see Nepean/Sydney to Admiralty Lords, 13 April, Banks to Nepean, 27 April, Sydney to Treasury Lords, 29 April, and Grenville to Phillip, 24 August 1789, CO 201/4:75-7, 79, 83-6, 39-42; and Phillip to Grenville, 20 June 1790, CO 201/5:146.

[4] Phillip to Sydney, 6 July and 24 September 1788, Dixson Q 162:9-10, 14, to Nepean, 15 April and 16 June, to Grenville, 17 July 1790, CO 201/5: 118-9, 137, 172-8; Grenville to Cornwallis, 6 September 1790, CO 201/5:298-9; David Collins, *An Account of the English colony in New South Wales* (London: T. Cadell and W. Davies, 1798), I,249.

[5] King, Journal entry for 1 February 1788, Bonwick Box 66, p.54; Phillip, Instructions to King of 12 February 1788, CO 201/3:27.

[6] Collins, I,14; King Journal entries of 15 February, 1, 4, 6, and 7 March 1788, Bonwick Box 66, pp.59-73.

[7] An Officer, *An Authentic Journal of the Expedition under Commodore Phillips to Botany Bay* (London: W. Bailey, 1789), p.33; Phillip to Sydney, 15 May 1788, CO 201/3:10-11.

[8] King, Journal, in Hunter, pp.323-7.

[9] King, Journal entry of 18 August 1788, Bonwick Box 66, p.102, and Journal, Hunter, p.326.

[10] Phillip to Sydney, 28 September 1788, CO 201/3:112.

[11] King, Journal entries of 25 October and 9 December 1788, Bonwick Box 66, pp.120, 130; Phillip to Nepean, 16 November 1788, CO 201/3:155.

[12] Collins, I, 77.

[13] Phillip, Instructions to Ross, 2 March 1790, CO 201/5:101-3.

[14] Nepean to Stephens, 17 July 1789, ADM 1/4154:26; Phillip to Grenville, 17 June 1790, CO 201/5:144; Hume to Phillip, 10 February 1791, CO 201/6:29.

IV   *The Nootka Sound crisis*

[1] I have taken details of the incidents at Nootka Sound, and of subsequent negotiations, from Warren L. Cook, *Flood Tide of Empire: Spain and the Pacific Northwest, 1543-1819* (New Haven and London: Yale University Press, 1973), pp.129-79; and Harlow, II,441-64.

[2] Del Campo to Leeds, 10 February 1790, PRO 30/8/341:64-5; Banks to Nepean, 15 February 1790, HO 42/16:8.

[3] Nepean, Sketch of a Letter to the Admiralty, February 1790, HO 28/7:48-57, Heads of Instructions, February 1790, HO 42/16, Instructions to Roberts, and Instructions to the Captain of the Frigate, March 1790, HO 28/61; Nepean/Grenville to Phillip, March 1790, CO 201/5:49-54 (the emendations are in Mulgrave's hand); Admiralty Lords to W. Cornwallis, 31 March 1790, quoted in Bland Burges, *A Narrative of the Negotiations Occasioned by the Dispute Between England and Spain in the Year 1790* (London, 1791), pp.14-15.

[4] Cabinet, Minute of 30 April 1790, Dropmore, I,579; Board of Control, Draft of Instructions for the China ships, 7 May 1790, L/P & S/1/9:155, Minutes of 8 May 1790, L/P & S/5/563:28, Minutes of 11 May 1790, CO 77/26:267; Dundas to Cornwallis, 11 May 1790, NLS 3387:115; Board of Control, Memorandum and Minutes of 12 May 1790, CO 77/26:271-3, Instructions to Cornwallis, 21 May 1790, L/P & S/5/563:29-31.

[5] Grenville to W. Cornwallis, 5 June 1790, CO 77/26:246; Hood to W. Cornwallis, 6 June 1790, Admiralty Lords to W. Cornwallis, 30 July 1790, *Various*, VI,356, 358.

[6] Blankett to Hawkesbury, 15 February, 1 March, and 8 April 1791, Add. ms 38226:105-16.
When Blankett wrote to Nepean on 29 October 1790 to report his arrival at the Cape, he said that 'Lieut King, who will be with you before this, will have informed you fully of the situation of Your Colony & as this comes by a French frigate, I forbear to speak of that or myself' — CO 201/5:308. Blankett's report on the Seas of Japan, 11 December 1784, is in the Sandwich Papers (Montagu F/5/38).

[7] Nepean to Stephens, 11 January 1791, Grenville to Admiralty Lords, 11 and 23 February 1791, ADM 1/4156:5, 14, 17; Admiralty Lords, Instructions to Vancouver, 8 March 1791, in George Vancouver, *A Voyage of Discovery to the North Pacific Ocean* (London: G. G. and J. Robinson, 1798). I, xvii-xxii.

[8] Dundas to Admiralty Lords, 6 July 1791, Vancouver to Phillip, 15 October 1792, Vancouver, Instructions to Hanson, 29 December 1792, HRNSW, I,ii,499-501, 667-9, 681-3; Collins, I,519-21; King, Journal entries for May 1793, Mitchell A1678:129-35; King to Nepean, 19 November 1793, CO 201/1:119.

CHAPTER 9   I   *British strategy and the New South Wales colony*

[1] Dundas to Richmond, 8 July 1793, quoted in Matheson, p.182; Pitt to Grenville, 5 July 1794, Dropmore, II, 595.

[2] Dundas to Grose, 30 June 1793, HRNSW, II, 52; Dundas to Phillip, 5 July 1791, Vancouver to Phillip, and Instructions to Hanson, 29 December 1792, ibid., I,ii, 497, 680-3; Collins, I,282.

³ Collins, I,270; Margaret Steven, *Merchant Campbell* (Melbourne: Oxford University Press, 1965), p.28.

⁴ Bowen to John King, 20 June and 2 July, Dundas to Grose, 30 June and 15 November 1793, HRNSW,II, 48-52, 53-6, 81-2.

⁵ Hunter to John King, 17 September 1796, to Portland, 25 June and 6 July 1797, HRNSW, III, 136, 236, 238; Collins,I, 417, 436-8.

⁶ Grose to Dundas, 16 February 1793, 29 April, 5 July and 31 August 1794, HRNSW, II, 14-5, 210, 238, 254.

⁷ S. M. Onslow, ed., *Some Early Records of the Macarthurs of Camden* (Adelaide: Rigby, 1973 [1914]), p.45.

⁸ Hunter to Portland, 30 August 1799, HRNSW, III, 716; King to Portland, 28 September 1800, and 'State of His Majesty's Settlements in New South Wales,' 31 December 1801, ibid., IV, 181, 118, 651-70.

⁹ King to Portland, 28 September 1800 and 21 August 1801, ibid., IV, 183, 467: 'State of His Majesty's Settlements . . .,' 31 December 1801, ibid., 666.

¹⁰ For details, see HRNSW, III, 312-33, 363-4, 757-818.

¹¹ Portland to Hunter, 26 February 1800, HRNSW, IV, 57-8.

¹² King, Instructions to Grant, 5 March, to Banks, 10 March, Instructions to Murray, 31 October 1801, HRNSW, IV, 305-9, 311, 602-4.

¹³ Hunter to King, 25 September, King to Portland, 28 September 1800, 10 March and 21 August 1801, HRNSW, IV, 152, 197, 331, 493; and Collins, II, 123, 128, 139, 263-4.

¹⁴ King and other officers continued interested in the possibilities of the *phormium tenax*, but the now sceptical Administration offered them little encouragement — see Raven to King, 2 November 1793, HRNSW, II, 95; King to Nepean, 19 November 1793, CO 201/1:119; and Collins, I, 410.

¹⁵ Hunter, Government, and General Order, 8 December 1795, HRNSW, II, 341; to Nepean, 19 November, and Return of Labour at Sydney, 31 December 1797, to Portland, 10 January 1798, ibid., III, 307-8, 337, 346, 350; D. R. Hainsworth, *Builders and Adventurers* (Melbourne: Cassell, 1968), pp.74-9.

¹⁶ Hunter to Portland, 25 June 1797, and 10 January 1798, HRNSW, III, 237, 347.

¹⁷ Portland to Dundas, 19 December 1798, HO 30/2:7-8; to Hunter, 21 December 1798, HRNSW, III, 519-20; Dundas to Macartney, 20 December 1798, HO 30/2:5; John King to P. G. King, 10 January 1799, CO 324/112:71.

¹⁸ Hunter to Portland, 4 July, Thomson to Schanck, 8 September 1799, HRNSW, III, 688-9, 717; Hainsworth, *The Sydney Traders* (Melbourne: Cassell, 1972), pp.40, 65.

¹⁹ Hainsworth, *The Sydney Traders*, pp.41, 164; Steven, pp. 47-8.

²⁰ There is extensive documentation of King's efforts to obtain coal in HRNSW, IV, 51, 206, 390-1, 404-9, 414-6, 428-31, 439, 448-53, 477, 604-5, 610, 621.

²¹J. Ewart, Memorandums respecting the time required to sail from the Cape of Good Hope, and from India to America; the winds which prevail in the respective tracks; and the most eligible places of attack on the American Coast, undated, PRO 30/8/250:185-8; J. Fortescue, *A History of the British Army* (London: Macmillan and Co., 1906), IV, 527-8; Dundas to the King, and the King's reply, 23 January 1797, George III (Aspinall), III, 537-8.

²² Thomson to Schanck, 8 September 1799, HRNSW, III, 717.

II   *The British consolidate their position in New South Wales*

[1] William James, *The Naval History of Great Britain* (London: Richard Bentley, 1837), III, 162.

[2] (Fleurieu/Forfait), Plan of Itinerary for Citizen Baudin, Undated but c. August 1800, in *The Journal of Post Captain Nicolas Baudin*, trans. Christine Cornell (Adelaide: The Libraries Board of South Australia, 1974), p.1.

[3] Admiralty Lords, Instructions to Flinders, 22 June 1801, in Matthew Flinders, *A Voyage to Terra Australis* (London: G. and W. Nicol, 1814), I, 8-12. There is extensive documentation of this voyage in HRNSW, IV.

[4] King to Portland, 29 March and 21 May, Flinders to Admiralty Lords, 11 May, King to Banks, 5 June 1802, HRNSW, IV, 734, 766, 749, 785.

[5] For documentation, see HRNSW, IV, 908-9, 1006-10; and King to Nepean, 9 May 1803, HRA, IV, 248.

[6] Baudin to King, 23 December 1802, HRNSW, IV, 1008-10.

[7] For Collins's expedition, see HRNSW, IV, 921-4, 927, and V, 4, 16-21, 833-6, and St. Vincent, II, 161-3; for Paterson's, see Hobart to King, 24 June 1803, King to Sullivan, 15 May 1804, HRA, IV, 304, 639.

[8] Steven, p.68; King to Hobart, 9 May 1803, HRA, IV, 122.

[9] King to Hobart, 1 March 1804, HRA, IV, 461, 469, 480.

[10] King to Hobart, 14 August and 20 December, to Banks, December 1804, HRNSW, V, 418-30, 522-30.

[11] King to Hobart, 14 August 1804, to Camden, 30 April 1805, HRNSW, V, 419, 597.

[12] Pelham to Admiralty Lords, 9 March 1802, HRA, III, 570; Hunter, Memorandum on the timber of New South Wales, 22 March 1802, HRNSW, IV, 728-32; Navy Board, Produce of our settlements at New South Wales, which the ships carrying out convicts may return with, (March 1802), Admiralty Lords to Pelham, 6 April 1802, HRA III, 570-2; Navy Board to John King, 11 June 1802, ibid, VI, 719: Hobart to P. G. King, 29 August 1802, HRNSW, IV, 823-30.

[13] There is documentation of these activities in HRNSW, IV, 730-2, 832; V, 221, 229, 247, 337, 527; and in HRA, IV, 83, 252-8, V, 685.

III   *The Colony's role in the Napoleonic War*

[1] Banks to King, 8 April 1803, HRNSW, V, 836.

[2] Pitt, Memorandum of 17 September 1804, PRO 30/8/ 196:88; Popham, Memorandum of 14 October 1804, printed in [Anon.], 'Miranda and the British Admiralty, 1804-1806,' *American Historical Review*, 6 (1900-1), 509-17; Fortescue, V, 312-3.

[3] Fortescue, V, 376-8; Buckingham to Grenville, 15 October 1806, Dropmore, VIII, 386-7.

[4] Buckingham to Grenville, 16 November 1806, Dropmore, VIII, 435-6.

[5] Cooke to Bligh, 11 January 1808, with enclosures, HRA, VI, 205-6; King, Memorandum on Australian Timber, etc., December 1807, *Historical Records of New Zealand*, ed. R. McNab (Wellington: Government Printer, 1908), I, 286-7.

[6] Foveaux to Macquarie, 27 February 1810, HRA, VII, 233; Hainsworth, *The Sydney Traders*, pp. 74-5.

[7] Lord and partners to Macquarie, 27 January 1810, HRA VII, 294-5.
[8] Ibid.
[9] Raffles to Minto, 10 June 1811, Harlow and Madden, p.64.

Notes to Appendix

[1] K. M. Dallas, 'The First Settlements in Australia: considered in relation to Sea-Power in World Politics,' *Tasmanian Historical Research Association: Papers and Proceedings*, 3 (1952), 4-12.

Michael Roe, 'Australia's Place in the "Swing to the East," 1788-1810.' *Historical Studies*, 8 (1957-9), 202-13.

David Mackay, 'British Interest in the Southern Oceans, 1782-1794,' *The New Zealand Journal of History*, 3 (1969), 124-42.

R. A. Swan, *To Botany Bay* (Canberra: Roebuck Society, 1973).

Barbara Atkins, 'Australia's Place in the "Swing to the East," 1788-1810: Addendum,' *Historical Studies*, 8 (1957-9), 315-8.

H. T. Fry, ' "Cathay and the way thither:" the background to Botany Bay,' *Historical Studies*, 14 (1971), 497-510.

Ged Martin, 'A London Newspaper on the Founding of Botany Bay, August 1786-May 1787,' *Journal of the Royal Australian Historical Society*, 61 (1975), 73-90.

————, 'Economic Motives behind the Founding of Botany Bay,' *Australian Economic History Review*, 16 (1976), 128-43.

[2] 6 Anne c.17.

[3] 9 Anne c.21.

[4] Pitt, Speech of 5 March 1788, PR, 2nd ser., 23 (1788), 301.

[5] Two of the politicians' most notable defeats came from their attempts in 1784 and 1787 to replace the Company's regiments in India with Royal ones (see Ehrman, 451-6). Interestingly, for five weeks at the height of the first dispute (13 September-19 October 1784), Nepean had spies at India House report *daily* on the Directors' deliberations (Nepean, Entry for 19 October 1784, Secret Service Ledger, Clements).

[6] 26 Geo III c.57; Board of Control, Instructions of 26 March 1787, L/P & S/5/562:116-35; 33 Geo III c.52.

[7] George Taswell to Sydney, 23 March 1785, H/190:617; Harlow and Madden, pp.21-7.

[8] Committee of Correspondence, Minutes of 6 May 1785, H/494:367-82.

[9] Directors of the South Sea Company to Rose, 28 July 1785, Add. ms 25561:119; Minute of (SS) Committee of Treasury, 4 August 1785, Add. ms 25578:134-40.

[10] Harlow, II, 321-6, 425; 33 Geo III c.52, sect.Lxxviii.

[11] I have taken these details variously from Add. ms 38218:344-5, BT 5/3, 6/93, PRO 30/8/353, E/1/78, D/1, *HCJ* 14, and Harlow, II, 300-6; 26 Geo III c. 50.

[12] There were good political reasons for the British not proceeding with the idea of growing spices in New South Wales. Pitt, Dundas, Mulgrave, and Grenville saw that the maintenance of strong political and commercial ties with Holland was the best method of protecting Britain's establishment in the East. Their Dutch friends made it clear that a central point in any *rapprochement* between the estranged nations would be Britain's renouncing the right she had obtained in 1783 to a free navigation amongst the Eastern archipelago, which the Dutch saw to threaten their monopoly of the spice trade. Dundas believed very firmly that it was in Britain's interest to allow the Dutch to retain this monopoly, and by mid 1786, he and the others were willing to entertain the idea of giving up the right to

navigate. There would have been little point in their making this gesture, however, if they were simultaneously undermining the monopoly by growing spices elsewhere.

[13] Beauchamp Committee, Minutes of 12 May 1785, HO 7/1; [Nepean], Heads of a Plan, undated, CO 201/2:11-13: Nepean/Sydney to Court of Directors, 15 September 1785, E/1/79; Dundas to Grenville, 30 May and 1 July 1790, Dropmore, I, 588, 590.

[14] George III, Instructions to Phillip, 25 April 1787, CO 201/1:29-40.

[15] Richards to Pitt, 9 September 1786, PRO 30/8/171:32-3.

[16] Rose to Court of Directors, 15 September, Richards to Court of Directors, 19 September 1786, E/1/79:184, 193.

[17] Court of Directors, Minutes of 19 and 27 September 1786, B/103:570; Whole Court, Minutes of 21 September 1786, D/1; Board of Control, Minutes of 30 October 1786, F/1/1:157.

[18] Richards to Pitt, 28 September and 6 October 1786, PRO 30/8/171:18-9, 34-5; Rose to Navy Board, 20 October 1786, ADM/OT; Rose to Stephens, 21 October 1786, ADM 1/4289; Stephens to Nepean, 18 January 1787, CO 201/2:203; Court of Directors, Minutes of 9 February and 4 April 1787, CO 201/2:324.

[19] George III, Instructions to Phillip, 25 April 1787, CO 201/1:32. Captain Sever took the *Lady Penrhyn* via Tahiti, and reached Macau on 19 October. Captain Marshall, who sailed the *Scarborough* more directly, arrived on 8 September.

[20] Rose to Chairmen, 28 September, Chairmen to Rose, 30 September, Rose to Chairmen, 12 October 1790, E/1/85:141, 155; Court of Directors, Minutes of 2 February 1803, B/136:1146, 1166-7.

[21] Committee of Shipping, Report to Court of Directors, 18 July 1798, HO 30/2:126-7.

[22] Phillip to Grenville, 8 November 1791, Dundas to Phillip, 15 May 1792, HRNSW, I,ii, 547, 623; Lushington to (Dundas?), 12 April 1796, NLS 1070:34-6.

[23] David Scott to Board of Trade, 3 January 1796, NLS 1070:44-5.

[24] Harlow, II, 326; and J. M. Ward, *British Policy in the South Pacific 1786-1893* (Sydney: Australasian Publishing Co., 1948), pp. 19-20.

[25] Margaret Steven and D. R. Hainsworth have described the development of the sealing industry at length in (respectively) *Merchant Campbell 1769-1846* (Melbourne: Oxford University Press, 1965), 105-36, and *The Sydney Traders* (Melbourne: Cassell Australia, 1972), pp.128-147.

[26] Sullivan to Cottrell, 7 November 1803, CO 324/117:79-81.

[27] Ibid. and King to Hobart, 20 December 1804, HRNSW, V, 525-6.

[28] William Wilson to Banks, 27 June 1806, HRNSW, VI, 100-2.

[29] Auckland to Grenville, 31 May 1806, Dropmore, VIII, 165.

[30] Auckland to Grenville, 16 August 1806, ibid., 284.

[31] I have taken these extracts from a copy of the bill in H/494:461-500.

[32] Hainsworth, *The Sydney Traders*, pp.125-6.

[33] (Anon.), *The History of New Holland* (London: John Stockdale, 1787), viii.

Bibliography

I   The Historiography of the Decision to Colonize New South Wales

[Anon.]. *An Historical Narrative of the Discovery of New Holland and New South Wales.* London: John Fielding, 1786.

[Anon.]. *A Description of Botany Bay, on the East side of New Holland, in the Indian Seas.* Lancaster: H. Walmsley, 1787.

[Anon.]. *The History of New Holland.* London: John Stockdale, 1787.

[Anon.]. *The Voyage of Governor Phillip to Botany Bay.* London: John Stockdale, 1789.

Officer, An. *An Authentic and Interesting Narrative of the Late Expedition to Botany Bay.* London: W. Bailey, 1789.

Tench, Watkin. *A Narrative of the Expedition to Botany Bay.* London: J. Debrett, 1789.

White, John. *Journal of a Voyage to New South Wales.* London: J. Debrett, 1790.

Hunter, John. *An Historical Journal of the Transactions at Port Jackson and Norfolk Island.* London: John Stockdale, 1793.

Tench, Watkin. *A Complete Account of the Settlement at Port Jackson, in New South Wales.* London: G. Nicol and J. Sewell, 1793.

Collins, David. *An Account of the English Colony in New South Wales.* 2 vols. London: T. Cadell and W. Davies, 1798, 1802.

Barrington, George. *The History of New South Wales.* London: M. Jones, 1802.

Lang, J. D. *An Historical and Statistical Account of New South Wales.* London: Cochrane and M'Crone, 1834.

Braim, T. H. *A History of New South Wales from its Settlement to the close of the year 1844.* 2 vols. London: Richard Bentley, 1846.

Flanagan, Roderick. *The History of New South Wales.* 2 vols. London: Sampson Low, Son, & Co., 1862.

Bennett, Samuel. *The History of Australian Discovery and Colonisation.* Sydney: Hansom & Bennett, 1865.

Woods, J. E. *A History of the Discovery and Exploration of Australia.* 2 vols. London: Sampson Low, Son, and Marston, 1865.

Sutherland, A. and G. *The History of Australia from 1606 to 1876.* Melbourne, Sydney, and Adelaide: George Robertson, 1877.

Baird, David. *The History of Australasia.* Glasgow, Melbourne, & Dunedin: McCready, Thomson, & Niven, 1878.

Rusden, G. W. *History of Australia.* 3 vols. Melbourne and Sydney: George Robertson, 1883.

Barton, G. B., and Alexander Britton. *History of New South Wales from the Records.* 2 vols. Sydney: Charles Potter, Government Printer, 1889-94.

Jose, A. W. *A Short History of Australasia.* Sydney: Angus and Robertson, 1899.

Scott, Ernest. *A Short History of Australia.* London: Oxford University Press, 1916.

Wood, G. A. 'The Plan of a Colony in New South Wales.' *Journal of the Royal Australian Historical Society,* 6 (1920), 36-68.

Hancock, Keith. *Australia.* London: E. Benn, 1930.

Melbourne, A. C. V. *Early Constitutional Development in Australia.* London: Oxford University Press, 1934.

O'Brien, Eris. *The Foundation of Australia.* London: Sheed and Ward, 1937. (2nd ed. Sydney: Angus and Robertson, 1950).

Rutter, Owen, *The First Fleet.* London: The Golden Cockerel Press, 1937.

Ward, J. M. *British Policy in the South Pacific 1786-1893.* Sydney: Australasian Publishing Company, 1948.

Crawford, R. M. *Australasia.* London: Hutchinson, 1952.

Dallas, K. M. 'The First Settlements in Australia: Considered in relation to Sea-Power in World Politics.' *Tasmanian Historical Research Association,* 3 (1952), 4-12.

Reynolds, John, and M. D. McRae, D. A. Davie, N. J. Holland, and K. M. Dallas. 'The Reasons for Australian Settlement.' *THRA,* 4 (1952), 5-16.

Crowley, F. K. 'The Foundation Years, 1788-1821.' In *Australia: A Social and Political History,* ed. G. Greenwood. Sydney: Angus and Robertson, 1955.

Roe, Michael. 'Australia's Place in the "Swing to the East," 1788-1810.' *Historical Studies,* 8 (1958), 202-13.

Atkins, Barbara. 'Australia's Place in the "Swing to the East," 1788-1810: Addendum.' Ibid., 315-8.

Clark, C. M. H. 'The Choice of Botany Bay.' *Historical Studies,* 9 (1960), 221-32. (Subsequently Ch. 4 of Clark's *A History of Australia, I.* Carlton: Melbourne University Press, 1963.)

Reese, T. R. 'The Origins of Colonial America and New South Wales: An essay on British imperial policy in the eighteenth century.' *The Australian Journal of Politics and History,* 7 (1961), 186-97.

Shaw, A. G. L. *Convicts and the Colonies.* London: Faber and Faber, 1966.

Blainey, Geoffrey. *The Tyranny of Distance.* Melbourne: Sun Books, 1966.

Shaw, A. G. L. 'New Explanations in Australian History.' *Meanjin Quarterly,* 26 (1967), 216-21.

————. 'The Hollow Conqueror and the Tyranny of Distance.' *Historical Studies,* 13 (1968), 195-203.

Blainey, Geoffrey. 'A Reply: "I came, I Shaw . . ."' Ibid., 204-6.

Bolton, G. C. 'The Hollow Conqueror: Flax and the Foundation of Australia.' *Australian Economic History Review,* 9 (1968), 3-16.

Blainey, Geoffrey. 'Botany Bay or Gotham City?' Ibid., 154-63.

Bolton, G. C. 'Broken Reeds and Smoking Flax.' Ibid., 9 (1969) 64-70.

Dallas, K. M. *Trading Posts or Penal Colonies.* Hobart: Fullers Bookshop, 1969.

Nairn, Bede. 'The Selection of Botany Bay.' In *Economic Growth of Australia 1788-1821.* Carlton: Melbourne University Press, 1969.

Fry, H. T. ' "Cathay and the way thither:" the background to Botany Bay.' *Historical Studies,* 14 (April 1971), 497-510.

Remenyi, J. 'Botany Bay Revisited.' *Melbourne Historical Journal,* 10 (1971). 10-14.

Swan, R. A. *To Botany Bay.* Canberra: The Roebuck Society, 1973.

Mackay, D. L. 'Direction and Purpose in British Imperial Policy, 1783-1801.' *The Historical Journal,* 17 (1974), 487-501.

Frost, Alan. 'The Choice of Botany Bay: The scheme to supply the East Indies with naval stores.' AEHR, 15 (1975). 1-20.

————. 'The East India Company and the Choice of Botany Bay.' *Historical Studies*, 16 (1975), 606-12.

Martin, Ged. 'The Alternatives to Botany Bay.' *University of Newcastle Historical Journal*, 3 (1975), 11-16.

————. 'A London Newspaper on the Founding of Botany Bay, August 1786-May 1787.' JRAHS, 61 (1975), 73-90.

————. 'The Founding of Botany Bay, 1778-1790.' In *Reappraisals in British Imperial History*. Ed. R. Hyam and G. Martin. London: The Macmillan Company, 1975.

Atkinson, Alan. 'Whigs and Tories and Botany Bay.' JRAHS, 61 (1976), 289-310.

Martin, Ged. 'Economic Motives behind the Founding of Botany Bay.' AEHR, 16 (1976), 128-43.

Frost, Alan. 'Botany Bay: A Further Comment.' AEHR, 17 (1977), 64-77.

Atkinson, Alan. 'Botany Bay: A Counter-Riposte.' Ibid., 78-82.

Martin, G., ed. *The Founding of Australia: The Argument about Australia's Origins*. Sydney: Hale & Iremonger, 1978.

Ritchie, John. 'Flax and Convicts: More Light on Botany Bay.' *Labour History*, 36 (1979), 106-8.

Frost, Alan. 'Thomas Rowcroft's Testimony and the 'Botany Bay' Debate.' *Labour History*, 37 (1979), 101-7.

II: Select Secondary Works

Albion, R. G. *Forests and Sea Power: The Timber Problem of the Royal Navy 1652-1862*. Cambridge, Mass.: Harvard University Press, 1926.

Anderson, M. S. *Britain's Discovery of Russia 1553-1815*. London: Macmillan & Co., 1958.

Auchmuty, J. J. *John Hunter*. Melbourne: Oxford University Press, 1968.

Bamford, P. W. *Forests and French Sea Power 1660-1789*. (Toronto): University of Toronto Press, 1956.

Bolton, G. C. and B. E. Kennedy, 'William Eden and the Treaty of Mauritius 1786-7.' *The Historical Journal*, 16 (1973), 681-96.

Burden, J. A., ed. *Archives of British Honduras, I*. London: Sifton Praed & Co., 1931.

The Cambridge History of the British Empire, I, II. Ed. J. H. Rose, A. P. Newton, and E. A. Benians. 1929, 1940. Rpt. Cambridge: At the University Press, 1960, 1.

The Cambridge History of British Foreign Policy, I (1783-1815). Ed. A. W. Ward and G. P. Gooch. 1922. Rpt. New York: Octagon Books, 1970.

Christie, I. R. *Crisis of Empire: Great Britain and the American Colonies 1754-1783*. London: Edward Arnold, 1966.

————., and B. W. Labaree. *Empire or Independence 1760-1776*. New York: W. W. Norton & Company, 1977.

————. *The End of North's Ministry 1780-1782*. London: Macmillan & Co., 1958.

————. *Myth and Reality in Late-Eighteenth-Century Politics*. Berkeley and Los Angeles: University of California Press, 1970.

Cobban, A., 'British Secret Service in France, 1784-1792.' *English Historical Review*, 69 (1954), 234-7.

————. *Ambassadors and Secret Agents: The Diplomacy of the First Earl of Malmesbury at the Hague*. London: Jonathan Cape, 1954.

Cobley, John. *The Crimes of the First Fleet Convicts*. Sydney: Angus and Robertson, 1970.

Coupland, R. *The American Revolution and the British Empire*. London: Longmans, Green and Co., 1930.

(Dalrymple, Alexander). *A Serious Admonition to the Publick, on the Intended Thief-Colony at Botany Bay*. London: John Sewell, 1786.

Ehrman, John. *The British Government and Commercial Negotiations with Europe 1783-1793*. Cambridge: At the University Press, 1962.

————. *The Younger Pitt: The Years of Acclaim*. London: Constable, 1969.

Fortescue, Sir John. *A History of the British Army, IV, V*. London: Macmillan and Co., 1906, 1910.

Ford, F. L. *Europe 1780-1830*. (London): Longmans, (1970).

Fry, H. T. *Alexander Dalrymple (1737-1808) and the Expansion of British Trade*. London: Published for the Royal Commonwealth Society by Frank Cass & Co., 1970.

Furber, Holden. *Henry Dundas (1742-1811)*. London: Oxford University Press & Humphrey Milford, 1931.

————. *John Company at Work*. 1948. Rpt. New York: Octagon Books, 1970.

————. *Rival Empires of Trade in the Orient, 1600-1800*. Minneapolis: University of Minnesota Press, 1966.

Giordano, A. *A Dream of the Southern Seas*. Adelaide: The Author, 1973.

Graham, Gerald S. *British Policy and Canada 1774-1791: A Study in Eighteenth Century Trade Practice*. London: Longmans, Green and Co., 1930.

————. *Great Britain in the Indian Ocean: A Study of Maritime Enterprise 1810-1850*. Oxford: At the Clarendon Press, 1967.

————. *Sea Power and British North America 1783-1820*. Cambridge, Mass.: Harvard University Press, 1941.

Hallward, N. L. *William Bolts: A Dutch Adventurer under John Company*. Cambridge: At the University Press, 1920.

Harlow, V. T. *The Founding of the Second British Empire, 1763-1793*. 2 vols. London: Longmans, Green & Co., 1952, 1964.

Hawkins, C. W. 'To New Zealand for Kauri.' *The Mariner's Mirror*, 52 (1966), 315-28.

Hoskins, H. L. *British Routes to India*. 1928. Rpt. London: Frank Cass & Co., 1966.

Jarrett, Derek. *Pitt the Younger*. London: Weidenfeld and Nicolson, 1974,

Madariaga, I. de. *Britain, Russia, and the Armed Neutrality of 1780*. New Haven: Yale University Press, 1962.

Mahan, A. T. *The Influence of Sea Power upon History 1660-1783*. 10th ed. Boston: Little, Brown, and Company, 1895.

Manning, H. T. *British Colonial Government after the American Revolution*. 1933, Rpt. Hamden, Conn.: Archon Books, 1966.

Matheson, C. *The Life of Henry Dundas*. London: Constable, 1933.

Middleton, C. R. *The Administration of British Foreign Policy 1782-1846*. Durham, N. C.: Duke University Press, 1977.

Mouat, F. J. *Adventures and Researches among the Andaman Islanders*. London: Hurst and Blackett, 1863.

Oldham, Wilfrid. The Administration of the System of Transportation of British Convicts 1763-1793. Unpublished PHD dissertation, University of London. 1933.

Pares, Richard. *King George III and the Politicians*. Oxford: At the Clarendon Press, 1953.

Parkinson, C. N. *Trade in the Eastern Seas 1793-1813*. Cambridge: At the University Press, 1937.

—————. *War in the Eastern Seas 1793-1815*. London: George Allen & Unwin, 1954.

Parry, J. H. *The Age of Reconnaissance*. Cleveland and New York: The World Publishing Company, 1963.

—————. *The Establishment of the European Hegemony 1514-1715*. 3rd ed., rev. New York: Harper & Row, 1966.

—————. *Trade and Dominion: The European Overseas Empires in the Eighteenth Century*. London: Weidenfeld and Nicolson, 1971.

Philips, C. H. *The East India Company, 1784-1834*. (Manchester): Manchester University Press, 1961.

Portugaliae Monumenta Cartographica. Ed. Armando Cortesao and Avelino Teixeira da Mota. 6 vols.

Richmond, Sir H. W. *The Navy in India 1763-1783*. London: Ernest Benn, 1931.

Robson, L. L. *The Convict Settlers of Australia*. (Carlton): Melbourne University Press, 1965.

Rodger, A. B. *The War of the Second Coalition (1798 to 1801): A Strategic Commentary*. Oxford: At the Clarendon Press, 1964.

Rose, J. H. *Pitt and Napoleon: Essays and Letters*. London: G. Bell and Sons, 1912.

—————. *William Pitt and National Revival*. London. G. Bell and Sons, 1912.

—————. *William Pitt and the Great War*. London: G. Bell and Sons, 1911.

Rutherford, G. 'Sidelights on Commodore Johnstone's Expedition to the Cape.' *The Mariner's Mirror*, 28 (1942), 189-212, 290-308.

Sainty, J. C. *Home Office Officials 1782-1870*. London: The Athlone Press, 1975.

Scott, H. M. 'The Importance of Bourbon Naval Reconstruction to the Strategy of Choiseul after the Seven Years' War.' *The International History Review*, 1 (1979), 17-35.

Spear, Percival. 'The Rise of the British Dominion, 1740-1818.' *The Oxford History of India*. Ed. Percival Spear. Oxford: At the Clarendon Press, 1958.

Sutherland, Lucy S. *The East India Company in Eighteenth Century Politics*. Oxford: At the Clarendon Press, 1952.

Tarling, N. *Anglo-Dutch Rivalry in the Malay World 1780-1824*. St. Lucia: University of Queensland Press, 1962.

Turner, L. C. F. 'The Cape of Good Hope and Anglo-French Rivalry 1778-1796.' *Historical Sutdies*, 12 (1966), 166-85.

Ward, J. M. *Colonial Self-Government: The British Experience 1759-1856*. London: The Macmillan Press, 1976.

Watson, J. Steven. *The Reign of George III 1760-1815*. Oxford: At the Clarendon Press, 1960.

Williams, J. B. *British Commercial Policy and Trade Expansion 1750-1850*. Oxford: At the Clarendon Press, 1972.

Young, Sir George (3rd Br.) *Young of Formosa*. (Reading: Poynder and Son, The Holybrook Press. N.P.)

Index

Names of persons are given in the form by which their owners were generally known in the period of this volume. References from other forms have been made only in cases where these forms were also in current use.